THE BLUEPRINT FOR
FRANCHISING A BUSINESS

THE BLUEPRINT FOR
FRANCHISING A BUSINESS

STEVEN S. RAAB
with
GREGORY MATUSKY

JOHN WILEY & SONS

New York · Chichester · Brisbane · Toronto · Singapore

Library of Congress Cataloging-in-Publication Data:

Raab, Steven S., 1949-
    The blueprint for franchising a business.

    Bibliography: p.
    Includes index.
    1. Franchises (Retail trade)—United States.
    2. Franchises (Retail trade)—Law and legislation—
United States. I. Matusky, Gregory. II. Title.

HF5429.235.U5R32   1987   658.8'7   87-15932
ISBN 0-471-85617-7

Printed in the United States of America

10 9 8 7 6 5 4 3 2 1

To Susan and Judy, whose unending support made this project possible. And also to Nathan, Jonas, and Sarah, who sacrificed time with their father so this book could be completed.

ACKNOWLEDGMENTS

One of the more rewarding experiences in franchising is learning from skilled and knowledgeable professionals. Writing this book offered such an opportunity. Although it would be impossible to thank everybody who contributed, we would like to acknowledge: John Amico, Neil Balter, Joan Barnes, Becky Bishop, Stanley Bresler, Burt Brodo, Bernard Browning, Doug Bugie, Leslie Charm, William Cherkasky, Jerry Cusack, Fred De-Luca, Richard Dingfelder, John Edwards, Donna Feinhandler, Tom Fleisher, Mark Forseth, George Gardner, Gary Goranson, Terry Green-hut, Bud Hadfeild, Dan Herron, Barbara Kaban, Arthur Karp, Jan Kinney, Andrew Kostecka, William LeVine, Anthony Martino, James McGlinchey, Paul Modzelewski, Robert Morgan, Neil O'Shea, Steve Pataky, Gregory Petras, Hamer Phillips, John Sasser, Jon Seitz, Peter Shea, Robert Snelling, Carla Steiger-Meister, Leonard Swartz, Dr. Donald Synder, Brian Thomas, D'Arcy Williams, Virginia Wise, and Kathryn White.

FRANCHISING NUGGETS

CONTENTS

**THE BLUEPRINT FOR
FRANCHISING A BUSINESS**

CHAPTER 1

FRANCHISING IN TODAY'S ECONOMY

If there were a Hall of Fame for American entrepreneurs, some recent inductees might include:

Fred DeLuca, who at age 17 approached a family friend for money to finance his college education and came away with $1000 and the idea to open a sandwich shop that would pay his tuition. Today, some 20 years later, that small investment has mushroomed into Subway Sandwiches & Salads, a major fast-food franchise with estimated sales of $150 million in 1986.

And Joan Barnes. Once a recreation counselor at a Jewish community center in Southern California, Barnes began offering fitness classes for young children and their mothers in 1976. Today her infant-exercise company, Gymboree, has 200 franchised units nationwide and expects to expand into France, Japan, and Australia.

And Arthur Karp and Michael Coles, who after stumbling upon a busy chocolate chip cookie store in California, decided in 1977 to start a similar operation back home in Atlanta. Karp and Coles are now America's leading cookie moguls, and their company, The Original Great American Choco-

1

late Chip Cookie Company, claims some 400 stores with expected sales of $150 million in 1987.

They all did it! These entrepreneurs attained the Great American Dream of owning a business and watching it grow to national and even international proportions. They're proof that big opportunity is still alive and well and often comes to those who expect it the least. "My initial goal was to become a doctor," DeLuca now says. "It wasn't until Subway started growing that I abandoned that dream and became a full-time businessman." It's a similar story for Karp and Coles. "We started the business for our wives to run," Karp confides. "But it became so successful that Michael and I came aboard to manage it." And did Barnes foresee the possibilities? "In a word, no!" she now laughs. Yet success came to them, and it could come to you, as a franchisor.

WHY FRANCHISE?

Franchising allows companies to expand rapidly and to finance a portion of the growth by using other people's money. Like no other marketing system, it supplies you, the business owner, with the necessary resources to expand your business at a pace that otherwise would be impossible. By concentrating on independent ownership of units, franchising sidesteps the costs of opening new units and provides an additional source of hard-to-come-by capital. It gives you the money and labor to tap distant, out-of-reach markets. Franchising offers small entrepreneurs with limited capital the chance to succeed on a national basis. It can turn small, local companies into regional forces. It moves midsized businesses into national arenas. For large enterprises, franchising helps develop overlooked and international markets. Franchising is a ticket to the fast lane, a Maserati on the road to growth and expansion.

To illustrate the point, think for a moment: How many company-owned units could your business open next year? One, two, three, maybe four? Don't feel bad. Few companies can capitalize the labor, construction, rent, and inventory costs associated with rapid expansion.

Now imagine that a partner offers to pay all these expenses and gives you an additional $10,000 to $50,000 per unit. How many new units could you then open?

The answer boggles the mind. Yet franchising provides this opportunity. And for those who capitalize on it, the results are often staggering. For example, in 1983 Peter Shea took over Stained Glass Overlay, a decorative window franchise based in Southern California, and within the first three years opened 200 units. AAMCO, the nation's leading transmission service franchise, sold 100 franchises during its first full year of operation. In 1975, Gary Goranson started Tidy Car in the rented bay of a corner service station, and three years later the company had more than 2000 franchisees working part-time out of the trunks of their cars.

Are these exceptions? Certainly. Not everyone can attain this degree of success. Then again, not everybody needs to be so big to succeed. Many entrepreneurs set more modest goals, and here, too, franchising can help. For instance, in 1982, Barbara Kaban and Sharon Trauring formed Dental Insurance Services, Inc. to provide dentists with insurance information concerning their patients. The idea worked, and the pair quickly expanded into major Northeast markets near their Massachusetts homes. In order to grow even further, the pair invested $8,000 to $10,000 in legal work and started to franchise. "It was a good strategy for expanding quickly and penetrating markets we could not get into ourselves," says Kaban. Since then, the company has sold franchises in South Carolina, Chicago, New Jersey, and Pennsylvania. "The initial investment was high for our small company, but we raised three to four times that amount of money in franchise fees. Franchising gave our company capital when we needed it most desperately."

And then there is D'Arcy Williams, president and owner of Speedy Transmission Centers, an 18-unit automotive service franchise based in Deerfield Beach, Florida. Williams used franchising to broaden the company's presence on a regional level, increasing sales and profits for both himself and his franchisees. "Franchising made us a major force in the southern Florida market and gave us more than a fighting chance against large, national chains on the local level," Williams says. "The initial costs of franchising were negligible for our company. I did most of the selling and early legwork," he explains. "But the benefits have been a hefty increase in sales; greater exposure through radio, television, and newspaper advertising; and increased credibility with both our customers and local consumer affairs groups." Speedy is now undertaking a national expansion program that includes plans to open two new units a month, with an ultimate goal of 500 centers nationwide.

The moral to these and other stories is that franchising is a dynamic marketing system applicable to a wide variety of companies in various stages of growth and development, from startup to near-total maturity. It has helped others expand and develop their businesses. Can it help you?

THE WORK AHEAD

Clearly, franchising is not for everyone. To succeed requires a serious commitment on your part. Venturing in half-heartedly is like going to war in a paper tank—you're bound to get clobbered! First, you must understand the size of the undertaking, and then you must prepare to invest the time and energy commensurate with the task. In other words, get ready to work hard! Franchising demands great effort and perseverance. Regardless of whether your organization is fully staffed, many of the early responsibilities will fall on your shoulders. If you can't handle those responsibilities, find another method to market your goods and services, because franchising simply is not for you. After 10 years of franchise experience, I am convinced that the biggest factor in franchise success is plain old-fashioned hard work and determination. If you can outperform your competition, you can often succeed in franchising.

THE RISKS

As with any business undertaking, franchising holds its share of risks and chances. But there are ways to manage risk and raise your chances for success. You're doing that right now, by reading books and learning as much as possible. It's common sense: The more you know now, the fewer mistakes you will make later. You owe it to yourself and your company to be fully informed before making such a critical decision. So do your homework! Invest the time, and learn what costly errors can be avoided.

Another dimension to risk is what you stand to lose by waiting. By staying at your present size, you limit your company to fighting local skirmishes over nominal spoils. Franchising widens the battle and guarantees that hard-fought victories reap just rewards. By growing on your own without franchising, you could waste years while competitors expand, perhaps by using the very marketing system you avoid.

THE SACRIFICES

They are many and great. Expanding your business will require long hours, many of which will take you away from family and friends. Your business will no longer be locally centralized. You may have to travel to Tulsa or Tacoma, Butte or Boise, or any of a hundred other locations where your company has franchisees. While friends golf, you will be at the office, training new people or preparing advertising. When the family gets together, you'll be working late hours, writing sales presentations, or evaluating new marketing strategies. "One of the largest sacrifices I had to make in building the business was losing time with my children while they were growing up," says William LeVine, chairman of Postal Instant Press, one of the country's largest instant print franchises. "The demands of the company often left me no more than a half-dozen hours each week to spend with the kids. As a businessperson, you have to make the family understand that if there is going to be an easy life ahead, you have to build a foundation today, and that takes time and work. You have to sacrifice up front, and the sacrifice often comes from the family."

THE QUALITIES YOU ALREADY POSSESS

Hard work, risk, and sacrifice are all part of the franchise formula. Chances are, however, you already have experienced these challenges in building your current business. You know what it is like to work long hours, defeat tough odds, and trade leisure time for positive business results. You might apply that experience to franchising by using your business knowledge and gutsy determination to achieve new and exciting goals. And along the way, you can help some very deserving people.

Franchising lets a lot of people do good things with their lives. It gives people what they often want more than anything else—their own business and an opportunity to prove themselves; not by their boss's standards but through hard work and talent.

"I get an enormous charge out of seeing a franchisee whom I helped succeed," says Bud Hadfield, founder and chairman of Kwik Kopy Printing, based in Houston. "I am with these people from the beginning. I watch their initial struggle and experience their eventual triumphs. It's an incredibly rewarding experience. I see the houses they build, the cars they buy, the airplanes they fly, and the estates some have amassed. It's gratifying to know that my company played a major role in their accomplishments. I would like to feel I made a difference in some people's lives."

A SYSTEM THAT WORKS!

Bud Hadfield has played a role in enriching the lives of some 1000 franchisees. That's a tremendously rewarding experience. But he's not unique. Franchising has an enviable record of success that outshines independent business. This week, 12,000 new businesses are being launched in the United States, an awe-inspiring testimony to the Great American Dream. Check back two or three years from now, however, and half will have disappeared. In five years, only 3600 will still be in operation: That's a 70 percent failure rate—bad odds for the independent entrepreneur. Figure 1 illustrates the failure rates among U.S. businesses. Amazingly, though, franchising reverses this sad saga. According to the U.S. Department of Commerce, only four percent of franchises are discontinued each year, and discontinuance includes such benign causes as retirement, reorganization, and a myriad of other reasons unrelated to failure.

How many franchisees actually throw in the towel? Jiffy Lube, the quick oil-change franchise based in Baltimore, has never closed a shop it has built. Neither has The Hair Performers, a hair styling franchise with more than 250 stores and projected sales of $100 million in 1987. An industrywide survey by the International Franchise Association found that among its members, business failures accounted for less than one percent of all discontinuances.

The evidence is abundant. Franchising provides ample opportunity for

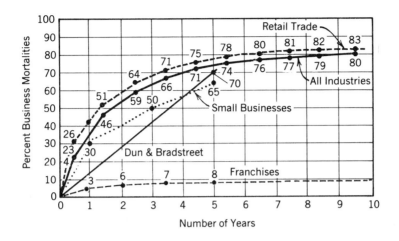

Legend and Sources
— •— — —•— Retail Trade (U.S. Department of Commerce)
————— All Industries (U.S. Department of Commerce)
· · · · · · · · · · · · · Small Businesses (Small Business Administration)
—•———————•— All Businesses (Dun & Bradstreet)
— •— — — •— — Franchises (International Franchise Association)

Figure 1. Failure rates among U.S. businesses

people with ambition and desire. As a franchisor, you would be the purveyor of the Great American Dream!

FRANCHISING IN THE ECONOMY:
A FORMIDABLE FORCE

In 1986, more than 2000 American franchisors with about 500,000 franchised outlets accounted for $550 billion worth of sales, or one-third of all retail sales, according to the Department of Commerce. That represents a 40 percent increase over 1980 franchised sales levels. In terms of Gross National Product (GNP), franchising generated 13 percent of the nation's economic wealth, with a sales figure three times greater than U.S. automobile

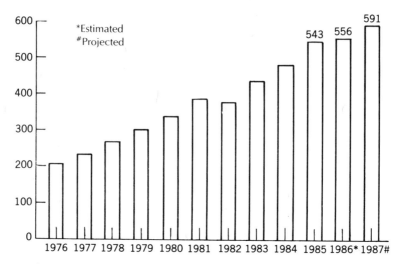

Figure 2. Sales by U.S. franchises. Source: U.S. Department of Commerce

sales in 1986. As an employer, franchising provided 6.3 million jobs in 1986, many for unskilled workers who might not have found employment elsewhere. See Figure 2 for a graphic representation of U.S. franchise sales.

INTERNATIONALLY

As American franchises move abroad to tap burgeoning overseas markets, more and more of the world's economies are adopting franchising. Experts at the Department of Commerce report that in 1971, 156 U.S. companies were present overseas, with 3365 units. Fourteen years later that figure doubled to 342 companies, with nearly nine times the number of units: 30,188. Who's where? Gymboree is in Australia, Canada, and France. Subway Sandwiches & Salads has units in England, Canada, and Puerto Rico; and sells an imitation ham submarine sandwich, in the Middle East country of Bahrain, where pork is taboo. Jiffy Lube has signed a master franchise agreement with Elf Aquitaine, the French oil giant, to bring fast oil changes and lube jobs to the French countryside. And indigenous franchise varieties are springing up outside the United States: Tidy Car of Canada, Home Tune

Ltd. of Great Britain, and Duskin Company of Japan compete with America's biggest and best, overseas and in this country.

FRANCHISING'S FUTURE

Tomorrow looks bright for franchising. According to the Department of Commerce, sales of products and services by franchised companies have grown at an annual rate of 10 percent during the past 12 years. This trend is forecasted to continue through the year 2000, when one-half of all retail sales will be made by franchised companies. "Franchising is the wave of the future," says Andrew Kostecka of the Department of Commerce. Kostecka, who tracks franchising trends for the federal government, believes that long-term prospects for franchising are extremely bright and that growing numbers of smaller companies operating in local or regional markets will turn to franchising for new ways to distribute their goods and services. "These small franchising companies will seek out new services and merchandising alternatives in order to broaden store appeal and attract greater patronage," he says.

Kostecka's assessment is right on target. An increasing number and variety of businesses are looking for alternative marketing systems, and franchising is often first on their list. Many of these firms are service businesses seeking to capitalize on changing consumer demographics.

CHANGING DEMOGRAPHICS

More than half the women in this country now make their living outside the home, and according to the U.S. Bureau of Labor Statistics, the proportion will increase through the remainder of the 1980s and into the 1990s. This trend offers an opportunity for a wide range of franchised businesses willing to perform the services of traditional stay-at-home mothers. Day care, baby-sitting, cooking, dry cleaning, and laundry services are just a sampling of the services two-career families now need and can afford, thanks to higher family income. Likewise, the proliferation of specialty food franchises—particularly cookie, muffin, pop corn, and sweet shops—is largely a result of mothers leaving the kitchen and entering the workplace.

An increase in female workers also provides markets for innovative franchises designed to appeal to women as franchisees. One such chain is Jazzercise, an aerobic and rhythmic dance company based in Carlsbad, California. Although formally founded in 1972, its concept dates back to the late 1960s when Judy Sheppard Missett, a professional jazz dancer and instructor, noticed that students were often intimidated by the rigors of traditional dance. "I realized these people were coming to enjoy the movement and get into shape. They weren't going on to Broadway, and they didn't want to hear me say how bad they looked." So Missett turned the class away from the dance studio mirrors and began teaching a more informal program designed to improve the participants' overall physical conditioning. It was an immediate success. When a friend suggested she recruit others to lead classes, Missett hesitantly obliged. "I never thought it would work, but I trained 10 instructors anyway, to lighten my load," she says.

Today, Missett sits atop a franchised fitness empire. Jazzercise claims nearly 3000 instructors and 350,000 students in 16 countries, including Canada, Australia, Japan, and Italy. "Rarely does Jazzercise provide the sole income of the instructor," says Jan Kinney, the company's vice president for promotions and communications. "The vast majority of our franchisees are women interested in supplementing their own or their husband's income with a second job."

THE IMPORTANCE OF CONVENIENCE

Convenience also provides new franchise possibilities. Strapped for time, tomorrow's busy consumers will demand faster, more efficient service. Quick oil change and engine tune-up franchises will gain more of the automotive service industry. Lawn care franchises that free parents' hectic weekends can expect to grow. Gourmet takeout restaurant franchises that supply tasty and nutritious meals for working mothers should also do well.

These are not the only opportunities. A recent study commissioned by the International Franchise Association and conducted by futurist John Naisbitt found that, despite fears of fast-food saturation, franchised restaurants offering ethnic fare should prosper. Experts predict that in 15 years, one out of every three Americans will be a minority. Franchises catering to diverse Mexican and Asian tastes can expect to increase future market share. Similarly, the trend toward healthier, lighter eating will create new consumer needs and wants. "We think of our menu as the fresh food alternative," says Fred DeLuca, whose Subway Sandwiches & Salads franchise also offers salads. "I think that has helped distinguish us from the competition." Kostecka of the Department of Commerce is monitoring the growth of popcorn, yogurt, and ice-cream franchises; continued expansion is expected in the near future.

BUSINESS SERVICES

"The business services industry is projected to add the most jobs and sustain one of the fastest growth rates through 1995," says Valerie A. Personick, an economist with the U.S. Bureau of Labor Statistics. "The computer and other technological advances have led to new demand for a whole range of consulting and management services. Likewise, requirements for temporary help have expanded beyond clerical jobs to include technical and professional occupations." Franchisors that provide printing, employment, consulting, market research, fund-raising, advertising, and other business-related services should expect future growth and prosperity.

"Many businesses have found it more efficient to contract out services rather than rely on in-house staff, because outside contractors (including franchises) can maintain a large, specialized staff and can enjoy economies of scale not possible for individual firms," Personick says. For permanent operations, such as security and janitorial services, overhead and management expenses are reduced by outside contracts. For one-time services, it is often quicker and cheaper to hire outside expertise than to develop it in-house," Personick adds.

OTHER AREAS OF GROWTH

Sales from nonfood retailers declined during the 1970s, but rebounded through the first half of the 1980s and are expected to sustain a 12.3 percent growth rate over the balance of the decade, according to the International Franchise Association. "Because of improved buying and selling techniques, nonfood retailing is now a highly competitive industry, causing retailers to turn to franchising to enhance distribution and improve employee training," says Kostecka of the Department of Commerce. In his annual review, *Franchising In The Economy*, Kostecka also targets the automotive products and services industries; leisure and travel businesses; personnel and educational services; and construction, home improvement, and cleaning services for future growth and expansion.

A TIME FOR ACTION

You have seen the facts and read the statistics. Franchising has dramatically restructured the way Americans shop and how business distributes goods and services. The opportunities are there for bright, ambitious businesspeople to expand and develop their companies. It's a long road, one pockmarked with many obstacles and pitfalls. But if you want to grow and expand, and are willing to assume the work, risk, and sacrifice, then franchising may be just right for you!

CHAPTER 2

THE RISE OF A MARKETING SYSTEM

Franchising is nothing new. The I.M. Singer Company franchised the right to sell its sewing machines in the 1850s. Oil and automobile companies have claimed franchised dealers since the turn of the century. But franchising didn't gain popular appeal and recognition until the 1950s, when restaurants and hotels started cloning themselves nationwide.

I was still a young boy at that time but remember vividly how franchising affected my life. Back then, my father would close his New Jersey shoe store for a few weeks each winter and the family would travel to Miami. It was a long and tortuous drive. The interstate highway system had yet to be built, so our route was the main streets and back roads of every city, town, county, and hamlet along the eastern seaboard.

Compounding matters was the problem of finding clean and comfortable accommodations and good, nutritious food. Some hotels and diners were acceptable, but the vast majority were third-rate places, waiting to trap hungry or tired tourists. Consequently, breakfast was often powdered eggs followed by antacid. Evenings brought fleabag hotels with cockroaches the size of most houseguests.

Then, in about 1957, a change occurred that took much of the guesswork out of travel. Howard Johnson's, the restaurant chain, aggressively began franchising hotels along the Atlantic coast.

My family would drive for hours, craning our necks around the road's bends to find the next bright orange roof. What made HoJo's so special? Simply stated, the company offered a quality product on a consistent basis to a mobile public. We knew the bathrooms would be clean, and the accommodations would be comfortable. We could depend on the 31 flavors of ice cream and good hot food. Howard Johnson's won us on the initial visit and kept us coming back wherever we roamed.

MCDONALD'S: A NEW ERA IN FRANCHISING

In building McDonald's, Ray Kroc borrowed and expanded Howard Johnson's concept of consistent quality. Kroc, a life-long salesman, became interested in fast food in 1954 after witnessing the bang-up business the McDonald brothers did at a small desert restaurant outside San Bernardino, California.

He later met with the McDonald brothers, Maurice and Richard, and worked out a franchising agreement whereby Kroc would sell the business to independent operators, and the brothers would share in the profits. "Visions of McDonald's restaurants dotting the crossroads of the country paraded through my brain," Kroc later wrote in his autobiography, *Grinding It Out*.

How that vision came to pass! Today, McDonald's is the undisputed leader in fast food and franchising with about 7000 units worldwide and sales of $12.4 billion in 1986. The company still opens one new restaurant every 12 hours.

McDonald's success depended upon its near-fanatical devotion to consistency and quality control. Whereas Howard Johnson's and other early franchises simply replicated the general gist of their businesses, McDonald's duplicated every aspect of its operation. There was no deviation from a predetermined standard. McDonald's developed the method, or format, of the business, and independent owners followed each rigid specification. Hamburgers, for example, weighed precisely 1.6 ounces and contained no more than 19 percent fat. Employees wore crisp white shirts and performed only one job. The griddle person flipped hamburgers. Another worker dunked french fries in scalding oil. Highly systematized, assembly-line techniques were applied to food preparation. This orderliness improved efficiency and reduced waste. McDonald's uniformity catered to a new breed of highly mobile customers. A Texan vacationing in San Francisco would know exactly what to expect from the Golden Arches next to the Golden Gate Bridge; a New Yorker on business in Minnesota could find his favorite thick shake anywhere in the Twin Cities. Other businesspeople saw the trend and joined in.

FRANCHISING AND THE AUTOMOBILE: THE AAMCO STORY

As Ray Kroc was building his empire, Tony Martino was *rebuilding*—automatic transmissions. A street-smart mechanic from Philadelphia's Italian neighborhood, Martino learned his craft while working at his uncle's garage in the 1950s. Automatic transmissions were just coming into vogue and their complexity confounded many good mechanics. Not Martino. He quickly learned to repair the complex mechanisms, and by 1959 owned and operated his own shop—AAMCO (Anthony A. Martino Company). It repaired only transmissions and business boomed. As Martino tells it: "The whole nature of business was changing back then. Specialization was coming into its own. In a lot of ways, AAMCO was in the right place at the right time."

But there was more to the story. Martino was a clever businessman who by the early 1960s owned three highly successful transmission shops and had an enviable talent for spotting profitable ideas. That skill helped in 1963, when a telephone call yielded an unlikely proposition. "How would you like to make a lot of money?" a deep voice asked. "Keep on talking," Martino replied.

The caller was Robert Morgan, a smooth-talking, ambitious businessman who had once owned and operated a chain of dance studios modeled after Arthur Murray's postwar franchise success. Morgan was then founder and president of Safeway Brakes, a Philadelphia-based franchise. The chain was struggling, and Morgan noticed that one of his brake shops had failed on the same street corner a transmission shop later succeeded. He analyzed the problem and decided brakes were not complicated enough to warrant specialized service. "Every corner service station was replacing worn brake pads," he recalls. "A mechanic didn't need any special knowledge or equipment to enter the business."

So Morgan called Martino and the two met. It was an odd pairing. Morgan, articulate and poised, was a gifted chess player who appreciated dance and art. Before opening Safeway Brakes, he had popularized children's mobiles by manufacturing and mass marketing the delicately balanced art to major department stores. Martino, on the other hand, was straight from the shop. He knew the automobile industry from the nuts-and-bolts perspective of worn transmission linkage and blown pan gaskets.

Yet they shared a mutual interest in making money and soon became partners. While Martino worked the shops, systematizing procedures and training new franchisees in the intricacies of transmission repair, Morgan set about designing the franchise package, writing brochures, and selling franchises.

The collaboration proved profitable. During 1963, its first year, AAMCO sold 100 franchises; in 1964, it sold 200. By 1967, the company had 500 franchised units and sales of $14 million—one of the most successful start-ups in franchise history.

Martino left AAMCO that same year and Morgan took full control of the company. "We grew extremely fast in the early stages because we believed in the concept. We knew the automotive market needed transmission specialists," Morgan says. Today, AAMCO is the undisputed leader in transmission repair with 1000 franchised units throughout the country—seven times the number of its closest competitor.

Tony Martino found similar franchising success. In 1972 he established MAACO, an auto-painting franchise, and followed that in 1982 by opening SPARKS Tune-Up. Today, MAACO is an industry leader with about 400 units nationwide. With more than 100 units in 1986, SPARKS is a major player in the fast tune-up market. Martino can rightfully claim to be one of the few franchisors to have developed three major franchises.

THE CHANGING FACE OF FRANCHISING

Howard Johnson's, McDonald's, and AAMCO are important to franchise history because the fast-food and automobile-service industries were the traditional cradling ground for successful franchises. But over the past 30 years, franchising has moved well beyond transmissions and hamburgers to encompass every product and service imaginable. In its *Franchise Opportunity Handbook*, the Department of Commerce lists companies from more than 40 industries that are currently franchising. Duds 'N Suds, for example, is a chain of laundromat/entertainment centers that gives new meaning to the term "good clean fun" by mixing washing machines with pool tables and refreshments. ProTech Restoration, in Santa Barbara, California, provides disaster restoration services to insurance companies. Dahlberg, Inc., franchises hearing aid centers and has 97 stores in 42 states. These are unique companies in uncommon industries, yet they are part of a large and growing portion of the economy—the service sector.

THE SERVICE ECONOMY AND FRANCHISING

"Today, nearly three-fourths of the American work force is employed by service-producing industries," notes Valerie A. Personick. Personick points out that the service sector generated 14 million jobs over the past 25 years, while manufacturing and agriculture's combined employment figures stagnated. Much of franchising's success is linked to this fundamental change. In a recent study by the International Franchise Association, a franchise expert is quoted as saying, "America is moving away from her smokestack industries and toward services, and franchising is spearheading the flow."

Why does franchising fit in so well with the new economy? For two reasons: minimal training and limited inventory requirements. Unlike manufacturing or skilled trades, the management of service businesses can often be taught in a matter of days or weeks. Merry Maids, a domestic cleaning franchise located in Omaha, Nebraska, trains its franchisees with one week of classroom work and supplemental videotapes. MAACO's training course lasts four weeks: three in class and one at a mock shop, learning basic body

NUGGET #1

Samples of Service Sector Franchises

In the past 20 years, the U.S. economy has undergone fundamental changes, and franchising has led the way in many service industries. To give you some idea of franchising impact and diversity, here's a sample of franchises in service industries:

BUSINESS AIDS AND SERVICES

Name	Product or Service
Debit One Mobile Accounting	Mobile Bookkeeping Service
International Merger and Acquisitions	Mergers, Financing, Acquisitions, and Consulting
Corporate Investment Business Brokers	Business Brokers
Communications World	Office Communication Equipment
Dunhill Personnel System	Personnel and Temporary Services
Management Recruiters	Personnel Placement, Search, and Recruiting Services
Pilot Air Freight	Air Freight Forwarding
Mifax-Yourtown	Medical Office Billing Service
Medical Personnel Pool	Nursing and Home Health Care Personnel
Recognition Express	Employee Recognition Products
Foliage Design Systems	Interior Foliage Plants and Maintenance
Barter Exchange	Computerized Commercial Bartering
Clentech Acoustic Clean	Acoustic Ceiling Cleaning
Jani-King	Janitorial Services
Uniclean Systems	Building Maintenance/ Janitorial Services

NUGGET #1 *(Continued)*

DOMESTIC SERVICES

Name	Product or Service
Duraclean International	Carpet and Drapery Cleaning and Damage Restoration
College Pro Painters	Residential Painting
Spring-Green Lawn Care	Lawn and Tree Care Services
Dip 'N Strip	Furniture Stripping
Perma Ceram	Resurfacing Bathroom Tubs, Sinks, and Wall Tile
Merry Maids	Professional Home Cleaning
Roto Rooter	Sewer and Drain Cleaning Services
Pets Are Inn	Pet Boarding Service
H&R Block	Income Tax Preparation
Duds 'N Suds	Laundry and Entertainment Centers
Gymboree	Parent-Child Development Play Centers
Natural Birthing Centers of America	Birth Centers

repair and painting. I Can't Believe It's Yogurt, a Dallas-based franchise, requires only six days to educate its new owners. The brief training periods keep franchisors' costs low and help franchisees make money more quickly.

Limited inventory requirements also attract franchisors to service industries. Low inventories keep a franchisee's initial investment reasonable, thereby helping the franchisor market franchises. For example, Sara Care Services, a temporary service franchise based in El Paso, Texas, requires no investment in costly inventory before a franchisee can start doing business. Similarly, stock for Neal's Cookies of Houston, Texas, costs only $5000, a modest sum compared to the inventory requirements of a manufacturer or wholesaler.

But what exactly is franchising? How is the marketing system defined in both the legal and business senses?

WHAT IS FRANCHISING?

First and foremost, franchising is a marketing system, a method for distributing goods or services to the consumer. In simplest terms, franchising involves two levels of businesspeople: the franchisor, who developed the system and lends its name or trademark to it; and the franchisee, who buys the right to operate the business under the franchisor's name or trademark.

Theoretically, almost any business could use franchising to market its products or services. For example, imagine a genetic engineer who develops a secret method for breeding dairy cows that give three times the normal amount of milk but eat only a quarter of the feed. The market for such a creature would be fantastic. Every dairy farmer in the nation would have to own the cows or risk losing business to more efficient neighbors.

How could the engineer get the product to the farmer? He or she could build company-owned farms throughout the country to distribute the cows. Or he or she could supply the animals directly, by advertising on cable TV and then shipping the cows to farmers who place orders. Finally, the engineer could become a distributor, selling the cows to livestock brokers who in turn would market them to farmers.

But there are big problems with all three methods. Company-owned farms would cost a tremendous sum of money; land alone would run into millions of dollars. Selling direct or to distributors would greatly increase transportation costs. Cows are difficult to move; thus, freight charges would raise the farmer's prices. In the latter two cases, the engineer would relinquish control over quality: As a supplier, he or she would risk having the cows injured during shipping; and as a distributor, would have no control over the care the broker provided for the animals.

Another alternative is franchising. Here, for a price, an engineer teaches (licenses) individuals across the country to administer the series of injections that produces the wonder cows. These franchisees then develop their own herds and sell them to dairy farmers in their regions. The franchisees also use the engineer's company name, by which the cows are known.

PRODUCT OR TRADEMARK FRANCHISING

The genetic engineer is engaged in a very old form of franchising. Called product or trademark franchising, it was first used in the 1800s and is still in use today by automobile dealers, service stations, the soft drink-bottling industry, and others. Under product franchising, the name of the business and the product are identical, and the consumer perceives them as such. For instance, Coca-Cola sells licenses to regional franchisees who mix sugar concentrate with soda water for bottling and distribution in specific areas. The name of the end product refers to both the drink and the business.

According to the Department of Commerce, product or trademark franchising accounted for a significant percent of nationwide franchise sales in 1986. Yet its importance is declining. Since the early 1970s, the number of product franchises fell by 40 percent, led by a net loss of almost 160,000 gasoline service stations between 1972 and 1983. According to a recent study commissioned by the International Franchise Association, future expansion of this franchising sector is expected to slow to an annual growth rate of five percent in 1990.

BUSINESS FORMAT FRANCHISING

The more commonly-recognized form of franchising is business format franchising. Here, a company develops a business system or method for providing products or services, and the trademark identifies all parts of that system or method.

For example, the name Wendy's does not identify one particular item on the restaurant's menu. There is no Wendy's burger or french fries. Rather, the name represents the format by which Wendy's provides fast food. Likewise, the name Midas does not signify a specific automobile muffler; people don't normally ask for a Midas as they would a Pepsi or Oldsmobile. Rather, it refers to the method Midas uses to supply its complete auto service package to the consumer.

Three basic elements determine whether a business is a franchise: Use of a trademark or trade name, payment of fees and royalties, and provision of services.

Use of a Trademark or Trade Name

To be a franchise, a group of restaurants, dentists, or health spas needs to operate jointly under one distinctive name. This name is rented by the franchisee from the franchisor for a specified time period. For instance, a podiatrist who opens Neat Feet service centers is not a franchise. But if he lends the name to other podiatrists, he could meet this requirement.

Why would someone pay to use the Neat Feet name? Perhaps the trade name is well known by consumers in a particular market area, or perhaps other podiatrists believe it lends an appropriate image to their stores. Trademarks and trade names will be discussed at length later in the book; all you need to remember now is that trademarks and trade names are the principal asset of franchise companies and are basic to the definition of a franchise.

Payment of Fees and Royalties

The second element that defines a business format franchise is the payment of a fee for the right to sell the product or service. This charge can be an initial entry fee, ongoing royalty fee, advertising payment, training cost, minimum product purchase requirement, or any number of other required payments. Returning to the Neat Feet example, to be a franchisor, the podiatrist must charge the franchisee for the right to use the center's name. Lending Neat Feet's name for free may make him a nice guy or a poor businessman; it would not, however, qualify him as a franchisor.

Nor would distributing products at wholesale prices. For instance, if the podiatrist simply supplied other podiatrists with customized Neat Feet arch supports at bona fide wholesale prices, he would not be a franchisor. But if he required retailers to pay for the right to carry his exclusive foot pads, or charged them more than wholesale prices, he could be a franchisor.

Provision of Services

The third element of a franchise is defined differently by the Federal Trade Commission and the various states that regulate franchising.

The Federal Trade Commission considers a business to be a franchise if it meets the other two elements and also exerts control or provides significant assistance or services. How do you determine whether assistance or services are significant? Providing advertising support, training new store owners, or granting exclusive market areas are certainly significant, according to the Federal Trade Commission. Giving informal guidance and advice, however, would probably fall outside the Commission's definition.

In most states that regulate franchising, the establishment of a business format is the third element of a franchise. Returning to the example of the podiatrist, if he marketed his business as a total program for podiatric success, complete with trade names, business systems, and royalty responsibilities, he would be considered a franchise under the Federal Trade Commission's significant assistance test and, by definition, would be a franchise in the states that presently regulate franchising.

Therefore, business format franchising is the establishment of a chain of businesses operating under a shared trade name or trademark, which pays the franchisor for the right to do business under that name, operates under a specified, controlled business method or format, and/or receives significant assistance or services from the franchisor.

CONVERSION FRANCHISES

An offshoot of business format franchising is conversion franchising. These businesses often seem identical to business format companies, yet differ in one important way: They target independent businesses already in operation. Century 21 is the most obvious example. The real estate chain, based in Irvine, California, started adding brokers (franchisees) soon after it was formed in 1971. Founders Art Bartlett and Marsh Fischer reasoned that small, local real estate brokers would pay good money to compete effectively with their larger, more successful competitors. The two devised a subfranchise system that divided the country into some 30 regions and had local entrepreneurs sell the franchise to established real estate companies. Franchisees paid a one-time licensing fee and ongoing royalties. They gained national advertising and name recognition, high-quality management, and a national referral system, but little else was changed, except the sign and the color of the agents' sports coats—to Century 21's distinctive gold hue.

Many other franchises also look to conversion to increase market share. For example, The Hair Performers and Jiffy Lube accept independent businesses into their system. Unlike Century 21, however, these companies demand rigid conformity to their respective business systems. "Each year, we choose five independent salons to join our franchise," says John Amico, founder and president of The Hair Performers. "But there is a strict understanding that they must accept our total program. We don't want them to mix their style with ours. We want the salon to be The Hair Performers, period."

SEVEN THINGS FRANCHISING IS NOT

Now that you know what a franchise is, let's examine what it is not.

1. A franchise is not a multilevel distribution system. In other words, it is not Amway Products, which pays people according to sales achieved by those below them. Neither is it a pyramid organization, where commissions are based solely upon the number of other people recruited into the organization. In contrast, a franchisee's compensation is determined by the gross sales of his or her business, minus operating costs and royalties paid to the franchisor.

2. A franchise is not an agency where area businesspeople represent large distant companies on a local level. In a franchise, local franchisees represent themselves. They own the show, make the decisions, and take the losses or enjoy the gains.

3. A franchise is not a distributorship or dealership. Distributors are middlemen. They buy products wholesale from manufacturers to resell to retail stores. Dealers work much the same way, except that they usually sell di-

rectly to the public. In both arrangements, the dealer and distributor have the right to buy and sell products from and to anyone. They are not bound to quality or variety restrictions, nor do they follow a business system prescribed by a parent company. They pay only for the products they sell or think they can sell, and spend nothing on ongoing royalties for the right to use a particular trade name.

4. A franchise is not a security or investment instrument. Investors are passive bystanders who rely on corporate efforts for dividends or income—just as a stockholder might rely on Du Pont or Exxon. Rather, the franchisee is an active player in the business. He or she balances the books, hires and fires employees, helps with operations, opens the door each morning, and closes shop each evening. The franchisees' fortunes rest more on personal initiative than on the franchisor's performance. In fact, business history is replete with franchisees who have out-performed the franchisor. Many franchisees of Pizza Time Theatre restaurants, which combined video games, singing robots, and pizza, are still operating today, even though the parent company, founded by Atari mastermind Nolan Bushnell, collapsed.

5. A franchise is not a fiduciary relationship. In a fiduciary relationship, one person becomes legally obligated to act in the best interests of another. In franchising, the services a franchise company provides are set by contract, and the company has no other obligation to the franchisee. However, this may be more a legal fiction than a real-world fact. Successful franchisors indicated that for moral and business reasons they are obliged to provide many more services than the franchise agreement specifies. "We know our responsibilities go far past those spelled out on paper," one franchisor says. "But for legal reasons, we put clear, definable limits on how far our accountability extends."

6. A franchise is not a partnership or joint venture between the franchisor and the franchisee. There is no common ownership of the business and neither party is responsible for the other's debts or liabilities. The franchisor provides the specifications, business system, and trademarks or trade names; the franchisee owns and operates the business.

7. Finally, a franchise is not an employment relationship. Franchisors pay no salaries and have no direct responsibility over the franchisee. In fact,

most franchisors believe that franchisees who can manage and operate independently, with a minimal amount of assistance, stand better chances of finding success. "We look for self-confidence and ability in a franchisee. These are people who want, almost need, to go into business on their own," says Fred DeLuca.

ON TO THE MAIN COURSE

The preliminaries are complete! The concepts are explained and some history given. You know some past franchise greats and understand the economic forces that gave rise to this marketing system. So let's tackle the key question. Can you franchise your business?

CHAPTER 3

EVALUATING YOURSELF
AS A FRANCHISOR

Grow big fast! Sounds exciting, to be sure. But franchising brings with it a whole new set of responsibilities that some businesspeople simply have no interest in or are incapable of assuming. As a franchisor, you will have to provide a wide variety of management services aimed at increasing a franchisee's chances of success. You will be responsible for training new owners, developing methods and procedures, researching new products or services, providing advice, and lending franchisees a sympathetic ear (even when a sympathetic ear isn't warranted). For many businesspeople, the experience is exhilarating and rewarding. "The fun of franchising is putting people into business, offering them an opportunity they otherwise would not have," says Les Charm, president of Docktor Pet Centers, a 240-store specialty retail chain based in Wilmington, Massachusetts. For other people, providing these services is a tedious and irritating process that they could better do without.

That's why it's critical to evaluate yourself as objectively as possible. You must determine whether you possess the personal and professional characteristics necessary to franchise your business. This is an important first step in a longer, more involved planning process necessary to give focus and direction to your franchised business. "Planning serves to back up the gut instinct of an entrepreneur, forcing the person to think through the validity of the concept," says Bernie Tannenbaum, associate director of The Entrepreneurial Center at The University of Pennsylvania's Wharton School of Business. Plans also are useful in persuading others to become part of your venture, according to Tannenbaum. "Business plans are a reality check. They let the entrepreneur play out his idea to qualified listeners to see whether others think it has potential."

THE INVESTIGATION

Your planning can start here. By determining whether franchising is for you and your business, you will have taken a giant step forward on the road to growth and development. Chapter 1 gave you a taste of the personal challenges that lay ahead. But now it's time to look more closely at your talents to see whether to franchise.

EIGHT QUESTIONS TO ASK YOURSELF

Take stock of yourself. Consider these eight questions, and you will gain valuable insight into whether you have the right stuff for franchise success.

   1. *Do you work well with others?* One of the greatest skills you will need to succeed in franchising is the ability to work effectively with other people. Can you cooperate with people? Can you listen to their suggestions and problems? Are you team-oriented? You may think you do all these things now in running your business. But do you really? Being the boss often means autocratic rule; many businesspeople don't practice or subscribe to participatory management.
   Beware! Authoritarian leadership simply does not work in franchising. What was once accomplished with a simple command now will demand great diplomacy and tact. "You lose a certain degree of control over your organization once you decide to franchise," says John Edwards, president of Pilot Air Freight. "Franchisees are not employees, they don't respond to

your every command." And neither should they. Franchisees are independent businesspeople, capable of making autonomous decisions about day-to-day business operations. That's why you sold them a franchise in the first place! You have to respect their business savvy and commitment to common goals. "If I could have done one thing differently, I would have given more credit to my franchisees' capabilities," says Subway Sandwiches & Salads' Fred DeLuca, looking back over his 12 years of franchise experience. "These are bright, ambitious people whose ideas often result in greater efficiency and higher profits."

Franchisor/franchisee relationships are difficult alliances, complicated by opposing incentives and motivations. As a franchisor, you will walk a fine line between good-intentioned parent and meddling in-law. Offer too much advice and you will be accused of draconian rule. Extend a free rein and you risk losing control of your franchise system.

It all boils down to a question of leadership and your ability to inspire. If you can communicate rather than castigate, and energize rather than chastise, your chances of success increase tremendously. Accepting franchisees as the key to your operation and treating them accordingly are critical components in the franchise formula.

2. *Can you accept and manage risk?* You don't have to be a riverboat gambler to franchise your business. You do, however, have to be willing to roll the dice and take a chance. Like any business undertaking, franchising is a calculated risk. You will invest time and money in an endeavor with an uncertain outcome. Are you prepared to handle this risk? Can you approach the unknown in a professional and effective manner?

Seventy percent of the businesspeople I see who should franchise their businesses, don't. Why? It's not because the risk is too great. It's because they don't know how to manage risk. They see a chance of failure and quit immediately. It's a completely self-defeating strategy. A more practical approach is to determine whether you can mitigate the risks, thereby increasing the odds for success.

Your biggest risk in franchising is losing money. Expanding your business can cost a lot of money. Advertising, marketing, legal, and consultant fees can easily add up to $100,000, $200,000, or more! And even then you are not assured of receiving quality advice and counsel. One major service franchise that wishes to remain anonymous reported that even after investing $125,000 in consulting fees, the recommendations it received were unworkable and unnecessarily complicated. "We learned the hard way that no one knows this business better than we do," says the franchise's top official. "We paid for marketing and feasibility studies that could have been prepared in-house. We gave people money for information we knew all along."

The corollary? Consultants have their place, but they shouldn't take *your* place in the planning and development of the franchise. Only you know what is right for your business. By relying on yourself, you can circumvent many of the early expenses of franchising, reducing the risks of huge up-front investment. For example, by starting now to detail your business and break it into its essential components, you will also be preparing an operating manual that future franchisees can follow for their businesses. Similarly, you can sidestep some advertising costs in the early stages of your franchise program by working with experienced free-lance copywriters instead of full-blown ad agencies. The same holds true for creating innovative and descriptive sales brochures.

Yet some expenses are unavoidable. Franchising is a tightly regulated marketing system. Even the most competent businessperson will need a franchise attorney to write a franchise agreement and disclosure statement. It makes sense from both a legal and business standpoint. "Our first mistake in establishing our franchise was going to a general practice attorney who claimed to know about franchising," says Arthur Karp of the Original Great American Chocolate Chip Cookie Company. "In reality, the lawyer had only a smattering of contract experience, and the resulting franchise agreement was so confused that it was abominable." Luckily, an attorney reviewing the papers for a prospective franchisee knew franchising, and offered to oversee the fledgling venture. "I can't stress how important it is to find a competent franchising attorney early in the game," Karp adds. "It saved us thousands of dollars in lost time and mistakes."

Finding the right franchise attorney is priority number one for reducing the risks of franchising. Franchise law and regulation is a complex web of disclosures, contracts, and compliances. Don't get stuck! Ask your attorney what previous experience he or she has had with franchising. Then contact former clients to check credentials. You will be paying the attorney good money to keep you out of trouble. Get the most from the investment by using a lawyer who knows the intricacies of franchise laws and regulations and isn't learning at your expense. An experienced and knowledgeable franchise lawyer can also counsel you on the franchise programs and services your business is developing. The lawyer should be able to recognize common mistakes and keep you on the right business and legal tracks.

3. *Are you single-minded?* "My friends call me strong-willed, my enemies call me bullheaded," says Kwik Kopy's Hadfield. Whatever you call it, the ability to stay the course and commit to the long-term is a tremendous advantage in business and particularly franchising, which is a long and involved process. All too often, I meet businesspeople caught in a fatal game of second-guessing decisions that have yet to prove good or bad. They weave in and out of marketing systems and operating programs in an attempt to find immediate success. This isn't flexibility; it's confusion and indecision, and it's lethal! Let me tell you two brief stories to illustrate that point. The first concerns a business, which, after some deliberation, developed a franchise program and then sold and opened a few stores. For various reasons, however, continued growth didn't come immediately. Instead of staying on the franchise course and working to refine the system, the company began to scramble. One month, it considered acquiring other companies. When that proved impossible, it began distributing its product to local convenience stores in areas it still hoped to franchise! In trying to be all things, the company undercut its ability to succeed in any one area. Working on acquisitions diverted its energies from franchising. Distributing its product to established stores destroyed the exclusivity franchisees look for to succeed.

The second story involves a more committed franchisor. After months of careful preparation, Dynamic Air Freight, an air-cargo-delivery company based in Dallas, began an ambitious franchise program in March 1985, but didn't sell its first franchise for seven full months. "We found it a bit demoralizing. The company had just invested a lot of money and received a less than overwhelming response. I started second-guessing the decision to franchise," says Dan Herron, executive vice-president and chief operating officer of the company. But the company stayed on course and went on to sell three franchises in four months—a respectable start, considering Dynamic's entire North American market is only 70 franchises. Today, Dynamic is well on its way to becoming a national force in the air-cargo industry.

I think the moral is clear. Franchise sales and growth take time and patience. Success requires discipline, focus, and a degree of determination that separates good businesspeople from great entrepreneurs. "Franchising is not a get-rich-quick business," says Peter Shea of Stained Glass Overlay. "Many of the people I see get into trouble as franchisors because they expect too much too soon. They aren't committed to the long term."

So set your sights on franchising. Then commit to that goal with a single-minded force.

4. *Do you have a strong ego?* The word *ego* conjures up a bad image in most people's minds. But a strong ego, as it relates to a confident and charismatic personality, can be a real asset in franchising. That's because franchisees don't buy businesses. They buy life-styles, the opportunity to start fresh in a venture of their own. "Prospective franchisees are looking for their own business first and to make money second," says Les Charm of Docktor Pet Centers. "They say things like 'I am looking for an opportunity to prove myself' or 'I need focus to my life.' Sure, making money is a big consideration, but it's secondary to psychological factors."

This is where the power of your ego or personality can be a great asset, because selling a franchise is selling a piece of yourself. Talk to a Subway Sandwiches & Salads franchisee and Fred DeLuca's name is bound to pop up. The same is true at Carvel Ice Cream, where franchisees inevitably mention the founder, Tom Carvel, by his first name. The egos and personalities of these and other successful franchisors run through their companies. They built the business. Their names are indelibly etched upon it. It takes tremendous belief in yourself and your company to sell dreams in the form of your business. "We are looking for people to buy into the dream, who have an attitude of quality and an unwillingness to compromise standards," says The Hair Performer's John Amico. If you don't believe in your dream, if you lack a forceful, confident personality, it is difficult to build enthusiasm and interest in others.

Similarly, a strong ego helps absorb the limelight that often comes with franchising. It's a high-profile undertaking. There are inquiries from prospective franchisees, investors, and the press. You will be the front man, the spokesperson, and the ultimate representative of your company—an exciting proposition to some people, a stressful situation for others.

5. *Are you a good salesperson?* Salesmanship is critical to franchise success. Growth depends on finding prospects and then selling them your business. It's tough work that takes persistence, time, and effort. It calls for knocking on doors, fleshing out leads, and following up on prospects—tedious stuff that can often be disheartening. The Athlete's Foot, a footwear franchise based in Atlanta, closes one deal for every 200 inquiries it receives, which means that for every yes salespeople hear, they must listen to many more nos. And their record is quite good! Some franchises go through far more leads before a deal is made. To be successful, you need to harden yourself to rebuff and be prepared to handle rejection.

But there is more to sales than just pitching your program. A good salesperson has to be a good judge of people. In sales, you will encounter many people who will seriously consider the opportunity you are offering, but you also will spend time with people who have no intention of buying your franchise or are simply not qualified to take advantage of the opportunity. Good salespeople need to identify real prospects quickly and focus their energies accordingly.

Similarly, salespeople need a degree of sincerity and empathy. "Franchise sales takes a person who can put himself in the other person's shoes and understand the emotional involvement in purchasing a business," says Steve Berkman, director of franchise sales at Pearle Vision Center in Dallas. Berkman believes that franchise salespeople have to understand the client's perspective and ultimately build a relationship of trust and confidence that establishes the validity of the opportunity. "It is imperative that salespeople relate the fact that your company's success depends on the franchisees' fortunes."

Finally, salespeople must be able to close deals. It's not enough to just interest prospects in your opportunity. You also have to motivate people to sign on the dotted line. Some people call it pushiness. But if you can't move people toward a decision, you won't sell franchises.

6. *Are you a good communicator?* So much of franchising involves communication that a system that doesn't facilitate the free exchange of information is doomed to failure. "Most important to franchising success is the ability to communicate with your franchisees and to realize these people are in business for the same reasons you are," says John Edwards of Pilot Air

Freight. While selling, you have to convey the legitimacy of the opportunity and the sincerity of your organization. In training, you have to explain to novice businesspeople how to operate your program and make money.

To a large degree, franchising is teaching, and teaching is the effective dissemination of information. As a franchisor, it's your responsibility to communicate as much knowledge as franchisees need to succeed. Your telephone will be their hotline. When franchisees have a problem, they will look to the home office for advice and guidance. Deciphering the subtle signals of trouble will be a major challenge. Alleviating those problems in clear, understandable language will be equally critical.

How do franchisors communicate with franchisees? Through newsletters, memos, video and audio tapes, manuals, bulletins, and conferences. But there is much more. Personal interaction and a commitment to the people in your organization are the keys to staying informed. "Tony Martino has an innate ability to penetrate words and get to the bottom of a franchisee's problem," says George Gardner, director of franchise sales for MAACO, explaining Martino's success as a franchisor. "He doesn't bring in attorneys to settle problems. He does it personally, over the telephone." This type of ongoing communication between you and your franchisees is imperative. Listening, probing, and learning will be the primary weapons in a continuing campaign for understanding and mutual success.

7. *Are you an entrepreneur?* Every businessperson I have ever met thinks he or she is an entrepreneur. Yet most simply are not! Yes, they have taken some risks. And yes, they know how to manage their businesses. But entrepreneurship also involves a mode of problem solving that few businesspeople possess. In simplest terms, an entrepreneur sees potential where others see problems, and opportunity where only obstacles appear to exist. Entrepreneurs identify real needs in the market and commit the necessary effort to fill those openings.

Take for example Gary Goranson of Tidy Car. He began his car-care company in response to market conditions that placed greater value on cleaning and maintaining used cars. "Up until the early 1970s, many North American consumers looked at a car as a disposable asset," he says. But that changed as rampant inflation and oil shortages forced car owners to keep older models for longer periods of time. Goranson painfully realized that

NUGGET #2

How to Communicate with Franchisees

Communication is a primary ingredient in a successful franchisor/franchisee relationship. All too often, however, franchisors don't realize the importance of effective communication and weaken the power of the written and spoken word by relying upon assumptions. What are the keys to understanding and being understood? In franchising, the following rules hold true:

1. Define and clarify your ideas before communicating. Too often, franchisors start talking or writing before they fully comprehend the concepts they are trying to convey to franchisees. Think before you speak.

2. Appreciate the franchisee's situation. Don't merely shout orders or commands. Instead, analyze the franchisee's psyche and try an appeal that speaks to his or her state of mind.

3. Cut the interference. Your franchisees receive so many messages everyday—from vendors, customers, employees—that yours may be overlooked if it's not clear, concise, and compact. Say the most in the least amount of time and words.

4. Watch for hidden messages. Nonverbal and unwritten communications are often the most telling. Body language and voice tone can often convey secondary or unintended meanings. Be aware of *all* channels of communication.

5. Listen as well as speak. Conveying a message to franchisees is only half the battle. You also must make them receive it. So listen to their questions, and be prepared to adapt your presentation to facilitate understanding.

6. Obtain feedback. Don't just talk and then walk away. Provide a means for franchisees to respond to your message. And evaluate their responses according to how well they understood the message.

7. Don't kill communication. Statements such as: "We tried that once; it didn't work"; "It would cost too much"; "I haven't time for your idea"; quickly stifle communications. Replace these responses with expressions such as: "That sounds interesting; let's explore it"; "Talk to other franchisees and see if they think the idea sounds good"; "Try to formalize it on paper so we can take a closer look."

8. Let your franchisees know the value of communications. If a franchisee develops a good idea, recognize him or her in front of others. If you're facing a problem, call your franchisees and ask for their input. It's the little things that breed big and profitable ideas.

fact when he tried to sell a five-year-old car. "Because I never expected to own a car for so long, I had not taken proper care of it," he says. The result? Peeling paint, a rusted body, and a model valued at $1500 selling for $250. Then came an idea: Why not start a door-to-door, car-care service that cleaned cars in the owner's driveway, thereby providing a convenient way to maintain a vehicle's appearance?

Goranson's immediate problem was raising cash for equipment and supplies. Unemployed, he could borrow only $5000 to finance the startup. "I think the banker felt bad for me more than anything else," he remembers. So Goranson raised capital by hiring employees who left a $55 deposit on their buffers and polishers. It wasn't much, but it paid early bills.

Goranson then thought others might want the right to own a piece of his business. "It was an extremely easy enterprise to learn, and because I had no trouble recruiting people, I figured others also would not," he says. Goranson started to advertise for franchisees and sent out packets of information regarding the business. To convince prospective franchisees of the opportunity, he asked each to run $15 advertisement in their local newspapers. It read, "Dial-a-wash, $15 and up; you dial, we come." Many paid to run the ad and were quickly inundated with telephone requests for mobile car washes. The validity of the concept was clear, and a small army of franchisees sent Tidy Car their licensing fees. By 1980, the company had more than 2000 franchisees in 13 countries working on a part-time basis out of the trunks of their cars.

In true entrepreneurial style, Goranson recognized a new need and worked to meet it. He saw an opportunity in his own misfortune and applied some clever problem-solving techniques to the situation. Goranson could have conceded defeat when funds were low, and he could have walked away from the challenge of recruiting franchisees. Instead, he found solutions where none seemed to exist, a useful talent for any franchisor.

8. *Are you hard-working?* Getting a franchised operation off the ground is a significant undertaking. You will have to market and sell your franchise, deal with prospective franchisees, develop advertising programs, prepare specifications and details on your business, assist at openings, establish newsletters, help with site selection, oversee management decisions, and perform a hundred other functions, all critical to success. Can you delegate many of these responsibilities? Certainly. But most successful franchises

have at their helm an individual who holds tight rein over the business, at least in its formative years. These people take a personal interest in every aspect of their business, from recruiting franchisees to developing novel marketing programs. For them, franchising is a challenge that calls for the consistent application of talents and abilities. What many lack in capital is made up in hard work and dedication. It's called sweat equity and it works! For example, AAMCO was started with only $3000 in cash. The Original Great American Chocolate Chip Cookie Company began with $8000 in cash from the owners and a $25,000 bank loan. Kwik Kopy was so underfinanced at first that Bud Hadfield sold his printing presses to pay early bills. And National Video, the nation's leading videocassette rental franchise, was launched with only $1000. It now has more than 550 franchised stores.

How was so much done on so little? Hard work. Franchisors who can't afford to hire operations personnel have to service franchisees themselves. If you can't employ salespeople in the beginning, you will have to generate leads and make your own sales presentations. It all takes time and effort, which translates into work.

YOUR EVALUATION

How did you fare in the self-analysis? Chances are you possess many of the personal attributes important in franchising. Those you lack present an entrepreneurial challenge, a chance to creatively solve a difficult problem. For instance, if you work poorly with subordinates, consider taking a Dale Carnegie course in personal development. If you dislike sales, bring someone on board who can sell. If communication is difficult, study people who speak and write effectively, and mimic the things they do correctly. Learning to deal with these first few problems can be valuable training for your later life as a franchisor.

THE NEXT STEP

Now that you have examined yourself, let's turn to your business to see whether it holds the basic characteristics necessary for franchising.

NUGGET #3

Personal Characteristics for Franchisor Success: Ten Franchising Experts Give Their Views.

John F. Amico, founder and president of The Hair Performers: Leadership and optimism. A franchisor must be able to create a win/win situation for both the parent company and its franchisees. He then must be able to infect the company with this enthusiasm and excitement.

Stanley Bresler, president of Bresler's 33 Flavors: Tenacity. A franchisor is someone who can pick up the ball and run with it through hell or high water. Luck and timing also play a critical role.

William Cherkasky, president, The International Franchise Association: The successful franchisor is someone with guts, a risk-taker who has a willingness to put it all on the line. But he is also a pretty cagey businessperson—someone who knows that there is a need in the market for his product. And franchisors are focused thinkers. Their one great interest is their business and how to make it better.

John Edwards, president of Pilot Air Freight: Most important is the ability to communicate with your franchisees and to realize that these people are in business for the same reasons you are. You can't place yourself on a pedestal.

Gary Goranson, president and founder of Tidy Car: Caring that the franchisee succeeds. Displaying the fact that you give a damn about the franchisee's situation.

Bud Hadfield, founder and chairman of Kwik Kopy Printing: You have to love your business. You have to feel in the marrow of your bones that what you're doing is important, and then commit to it one hundred percent. Anything less gives varying degrees of success.

William LeVine, founder and chairman of Postal Instant Press: A personal interest in the franchisee's success. It's your job to interact with franchisees on a one-to-one basis, discover the services they need, and then supply those services. You have to make franchisees succeed and treat them as you would like to be treated. It takes a great amount of drive, desire, and concern, along with a strong belief in your product or service.

NUGGET #3 (*Continued*)

Tony Martino, president and founder of MAACO: I think it takes different things at different times. To begin, you need to be venturesome and willing to take a risk; and have the ability to climb over all the negatives. Then, it takes someone who can make midcourse adjustments, in the understanding that plans are never right and have to be constantly changed.

Robert Morgan, chairman and co-founder of AAMCO: Charisma and a dynamic personality. Aggressive leadership and a strong ego. Great belief in themselves and their ability. Above average communication skills.

Peter Shea, president of Stained Glass Overlay: To succeed as a franchisor you need business sense and honesty. In franchising, more than anything else I can think of, you have to be honest or you will lose your shirt.

CHAPTER 4

IS YOUR BUSINESS FRANCHISABLE?

I frequently meet people with the personal attributes necessary to successfully franchise a business. They are bright, hard-working individuals who want desperately to put others in business using a particular operating system or method. They know the road is long and hard, but they don't shrink from the challenges or problems, and they aren't put off by obstacles and passing dilemmas. No, these people attack difficulties head-on, with a sense of urgency and commitment. They are entrepreneurs in the truest sense of the word, individuals who can inspire and motivate simply through the positive power of their personalities. It's an exciting scene! These are courageous and daring people, and franchising is often their chosen vehicle for achieving super-success.

Still, the above attributes are not enough. You can possess all the right personal characteristics and still lack the essential ingredient in franchising—the right business. More than any other factor, your business will be the final determinant of whether you can become a franchisor. Is it franchisable? Does your business lend itself to this unique marketing system? The Department of Commerce lists more than 2000 companies that are currently franchising. Could your business be one of them? Does it have the basic requirements necessary for franchise success?

These aren't easy questions. They require careful thought and honest responses. Your approach must be critical and your assessment objective. Franchising is a dynamic and intriguing marketing alternative. Yet you cannot allow its glitter and glamour to interfere with sound business judgment. Can your business be franchised? There are five basic factors to answer the question.

WILL THE MARKET ACCEPT YOUR PRODUCT?

Every company's success is based on an ability to profitably identify and satisfy the needs and wants of a particular market. Sometimes this comes in the form of new products. For example, ComputerLand, the nation's largest computer store chain, grew by being one of the first retailers to market home computers. AdventureLand Video, based in Salt Lake City, did the same in the videocassette rental market. On a more modest scale, AcrySyl International Corporation, a sealant manufacturer located in Reading, Pennsylvania, won market acceptance in the roofing industry by developing a compound that substantially reduces maintenance and replacement costs. The sealant, which can be applied over existing roofing, eliminates the need to lift weathered shingles before application. In addition, the compound's white color reflects sunlight, thereby reducing a building's air-conditioning requirements. "AcrySyl's many advantages make it a major advance in the roofing industry," says Dr. Donald Snyder, president of the company, which is using franchising to market the product. "We chose franchising because it provides quick entry into the market."

Yet you don't have to offer a new product to be a successful marketer. Providing a better version of an old standard also can win loyal customers. Wendy's, the hamburger chain, proves that point. Founder David Thomas unveiled plans to build a national franchised chain of hamburger restaurants in 1972, well after McDonald's, Gino's, Hardee's, Burger King, and a half dozen other fast-food restaurants had perfected the art of flipping beef patties. Yet Thomas believed his competitors' offerings were undersized and unappetizing. He developed a colossal burger that cost 55 cents—three times the going McDonald's price—and weighed a full quarter of a pound. The patty overlapped its bun and stuck out between slices of tomato and lettuce.

Today, Wendy's is the third largest hamburger franchise in the world with some 2,300 franchised units. Thomas succeeded by identifying a new need or niche in the market. His larger, more expensive hamburgers appealed to young adults, not the families McDonald's had targeted. The more affluent burger eater expected more and was willing to pay for it. Thomas filled those expectations and proved the frequently quoted Ray Kroc saying, "Saturation is for sponges."

But developing innovative products and discovering new market niches are common marketing strategies used by a wide variety of companies. Franchising, however, gives companies additional means of capturing market share. By offering new formats for the sale of established products and services, franchised companies provide uniformity to disorganized industries, winning widespread brand loyalty among customers. Returning to Ray Kroc's McDonald's, there was nothing new in frying hamburgers when Kroc started the business in 1954. Roadside diners had been grilling and serving beef patties for decades. Kroc discovered neither a new market nor a new product. Yet he did develop a new and exciting business method that captured the hearts and imagination (and dollars) of the American public. Kroc grabbed market share by providing a single, uniform product that consumers would readily identify and patronize.

Similarly, franchising allows companies to win major markets through maximizing advertising possibilities. Century 21, the real estate firm, burst onto the franchise scene by providing small, independent real estate brokers with a common identity through joint advertising. By pooling funds from franchisees, the company financed a large national advertising campaign that gave a single cohesive image to the chain and won a customer following nationwide.

Can you find a market? If your product is new or improved, if your business system is different or innovative, if your advertising provides a cohesive image for a disorganized industry, the chances of your product filling a niche and finding a market increase substantially.

THERE MUST BE A SUCCESSFUL PROTOTYPE

Most successful franchises start with a prototype, or a model store upon which subsequent units are based. Often these prototypes are the franchisor's original business. For example, Joan Barnes' eight company-owned Gymboree infant-exercise centers served as the model for her franchised units. Similarly, Bud Hadfield's single quick-print shop was the basis for his Kwik Kopy franchises.

Prototypes are valuable in convincing outsiders of your business' legitimacy and profitability. Prospective franchisees rarely invest in untried ideas. They want tangible evidence that your business works and makes money. Prototypes provide that proof by showing franchisees what the business is about and how it works in a real-world setting.

Prototypes also provide critical training ground for would-be franchisors, allowing them to make mistakes and refine an operating system before venturing into the franchising world. Remember, franchising is a massive photocopying machine that copies problems as well as triumphs. If you franchise a faulty system, those mistakes will be duplicated at all your franchised units. Unless your goal is to become a full-time troubleshooter, it is wise to first develop an efficient and effective operating system. A prototype provides this opportunity.

How profitable must your prototype be to franchise? It depends. Your business has to generate enough money to attract a desirable franchisee. How much is that in dollars? It's impossible to say. For a part-time commitment that involves a low initial investment, a few thousand dollars in profit may be all your business needs to enchant your target franchisees. If, however, your business demands a 50-to-60-hour-a-week commitment, there should be enough profit to compensate that degree of effort. As a barometer, consider Tony Martino's experience with MAACO. After leaving AAMCO in 1967, he looked for a business to franchise and even advertised in *The Wall Street Journal*. "I was looking for full-time businesses that had sales of $250,000 and profits of about $50,000," he says. Martino believes those numbers would translate into sales of about $500,000 today, while the profits could remain relatively constant. "I have to offer a thirty to fifty percent return-on-investment to attract the type of individual best suited to become a MAACO franchisee," he says. "MAACO's total package runs about $150,000, so if the typical franchisee can earn $50,000, and many do much better, the economics work out."

How profitable your prototype business must be is a function of the type of franchisee you wish to attract, as well as the investment in both time and money the opportunity requires. The best way to determine this is to apply the reasonable person test. Ask yourself: Would a reasonable person be happy earning the income a single store in my company generates? Is the sum high enough to compensate the work, risk, and sacrifice involved?

A related question on prototypes is: How long should they be in business before franchising? It may sound redundant, but, again—it depends. Arthur Karp and Michael Coles of the Original Great American Chocolate Chip Cookie Company began thinking about franchising within three months of their initial store's opening. But they are exceptions. I usually advise being in business at least one year before seriously considering franchising. Three years is the optimal period in which to work the kinks from your business system and perhaps test the concept at additional locations.

However, just as critical as length of operation is the typicality and replicability of your prototype business. Typicality refers to how well your prototype reflects the true operating circumstances franchisees will face. A souvenir shop next to the Grand Canyon, for instance, is an atypical prototype because its success is derived from the tourist trade in this special location. Likewise, a fresh seafood restaurant on the New England coast has an advantage in product supply that similar franchised units in Kansas or Wyoming would not enjoy. To be effective, your prototype must give a valid indication of what franchisees can expect in a broad range of locations.

Replicability refers to how well your prototype can be duplicated, both from a practical and an economic standpoint. Enterprises that involve great complexity in setup, design, and execution are inherently more difficult to duplicate. Airports, for example, with their idiosyncratic design and intricate scheduling procedures, would be nearly impossible to clone from a single prototype. The huge costs of such an undertaking also would restrict a franchisor's ability to duplicate the original prototype on a national basis.

Can you franchise without a prototype? Yes. It's called idea franchising, and it's extremely problematic. Yet inventive entrepreneurs have gone this route and succeeded. The most notable example is Colonel Harlan Sanders, who franchised his idea for Kentucky Fried Chicken by traveling throughout the country, selling his secret recipe to restaurant owners in return for a five-cent royalty on each bird sold. The Colonel, however, is an exception. Most franchisors need the foundation of a well-established, reliable business to attract prospective franchisees and develop a workable operating system.

However, there is a way to enter franchising without spending years to develop a full-blown business. It is called startup franchising, and is based on a prototype store or unit that has yet to prove successful. The test business is either new or has been established with the express intent of franchising. Although startup franchising is more difficult than franchising a business with a lengthy track record, it is certainly feasible if the concept is sound and the prototype is typical and replicable.

CAN YOUR BUSINESS BE DETAILED?

Uniformity is critical to franchise success. Standardized operation increases efficiency and builds a single, easily identifiable image with which consumers can relate. How do franchises standardize their businesses? Mainly through comprehensive operating manuals that leave little to the imagination but detail every aspect or business fundamental a franchisee needs to run an efficient and effective business. For example, in addition to the setup and operation of the shop, Jiffy Lube's operating manual tells managers how to answer the telephone and what refreshments to offer customers while they wait for their cars to be serviced. The Hair Performers operating manual supplies hairstylists with guidelines for how to look, act, and talk while in the salon. "Customers look to hairstylists for fashion tips and advice," says Mary Spidale, director of franchise and management training for the company. "It's imperative that employees project a stylish and attractive image, and we spell that out in the manual."

How do you determine whether your business can be detailed in this way? If you can identify the jobs that need to be performed, if you can precisely specify the procedures and methods involved, if you can define the management skills and techniques that need to be employed, then you can detail your business.

But take heed. Simply because you can detail your business doesn't mean new franchisees will be able to follow your business blueprint. Operating manuals need to be written in clear, understandable language, free from technical jargon. If your business is too complicated for simple description, if it is too sophisticated to be portrayed in concise words and phrases, then maybe it's too difficult for novice businesspeople to learn to operate effectively.

YOU MUST BE ABLE TO TRAIN FRANCHISEES IN A SHORT PERIOD OF TIME

Complexity also increases training time, which is a very expensive proposition. Education is both time- and labor-intensive. To be successful, you need to train franchisees properly and get them into the field as quickly as is prudently possible. Franchisors keep the training period short by teaching franchisees only the management skills necessary to run the business, and hiring technically trained employees. "We don't instruct our franchisees in transmission repair," says D'Arcy Williams of Speedy Transmission Centers. "Instead, we teach them how to find qualified transmission mechanics and then manage these people for optimal results." That's an important point, because transmission repair is a complex skill that requires the knowledge of some 400 working automobile parts. Teaching the trade could take months, even years. The same is true for many personnel-service and health-care franchises. "We don't teach dentistry," says Diane Custati, who has helped open franchised Dental Works centers in southeast Pennsylvania. "We work with managers to teach them to use the Dental Works system of business to the best of its capabilities," she explains. As a franchisor, you must teach effective *management* of your business. This obviously includes product knowledge, but it might also include the actual selling, production, or service of the product.

What's the optimal training period? Franchisee education is an ongoing process that often can be continued through home-study courses. However, to indoctrinate new franchisees into the system, initial training should be comprehensive enough to provide a thorough overview of the franchise business. The length of time this takes varies with the complexity of the business. But operations that require more than six weeks to learn may be too complicated to franchise. Conversely, those offering less than one week of training may be too simple to make the opportunity worthwhile.

YOU MUST BE ABLE TO SERVICE YOUR FRANCHISEES

There is a maturation process in franchising that requires different services at different times. In the early stages, franchisees need training, guidance,

NUGGET #4

Typical Training Periods of Major Franchises

Name	Product or Service	Duration
Athlete's Foot, The	Athletic Clothing and Footwear	5 days
Midas	Brakes, Mufflers, and Shocks	4 weeks
MAACO	Detailing, Rustproofing, Painting, and Body Work	4 weeks
Jiffy Lube	Tune-Up, Lube and Oil Changes	2 weeks and ongoing
Diet Centers	Diet and Weight Control Centers	1 week
Jazzercise	Fitness Centers	4 days
Fantastic Sam's	Hair Care	1 week
California Closet	Closet Organizers	1–2 weeks
General Business Services	Accounting, Consulting and Tax Services	9–14 days
Communications World	Communications Products and Services	5 days
Snelling and Snelling	Employment Agencies	2 weeks
ComputerLand	Computer Hardware and Software	2 weeks
Sylvan Learning Centers	Education-Related Services	2 weeks
Kentucky Fried Chicken	Chicken	4 weeks
Baskin and Robbins	Ice Cream	16.5 days

and advice. New franchisees are business novices. They have little idea of what owning and operating the business entails. You will be their lifeline, serving them with timely suggestions and counsel.

But once the newness wears off and the franchisee gains confidence, other services gain importance. Advertising, growth, and exposure will become the buzzwords as franchisees look to increase sales, market share, and brand recognition. You will have to promote your business and broaden its presence on a regional, perhaps national, basis. "There comes a point where you owe it to your franchisees to grow and expand," says Speedy Transmission Centers' D'Arcy Williams. "Your franchisees want the value of the business to increase, and that only happens through advertising and greater exposure from more units."

It's a self-fulfilling prophecy. Franchisees purchase franchises to belong to a network of businesses, thereby reducing the risk of independent ownership. Once satisfied the system works, franchisees will want you to perpetuate the success through continued expansion and development. As a franchisor, it's your responsibility to provide this opportunity, primarily through increased marketing and advertising services.

Finally, the last phase of the service process takes hold. Here the franchisor has taught franchisees all he or she knows and has exploited the market to its fullest. Yet, knowledgeable franchisees begin to resent paying monthly royalties while their need for many franchise services decreases. "It's at this point a franchisor must concentrate on expansion from within the company," says John Edwards of Pilot Air Freight. "You have to start developing new products and techniques that help franchisees expand their markets." Product research and development is critical to maintaining peace with mature franchisees. MAACO, for instance, is working on auto body repair systems for today's polymer car bodies. "It adds another product our franchisees can offer to their present market," says Martino. Postal Instant Press is exploring instant-communication technology and its implications. "Overnight mail, facsimile transmission, and word-processing services all fit well with our company's concept and give franchisees access to new markets," states William LeVine. Market research showed Subway Sandwiches & Salads the importance of freshness in their consumer's purchasing decision. "We installed ovens so fresh bread could be made daily on the premises," says Fred DeLuca.

Franchisors must provide a variety of services. Consider your organization. Can it give the early assistance needed for success? Will you be willing to assume more responsibilities as your franchise grows and franchisee needs change?

TALLY YOUR SCORE

How does your business rate? Does it meet the franchise criteria? If not, don't despair. These are only indications of whether your business can be franchised. They don't all need to be present. Creative entrepreneurs have succeeded without them. However, if you are serious about franchising and lack some of these requirements, it is wise to work toward acquiring them. For example, if you don't have a prototype, set up a business and prove your concept. If your business cannot be taught in a relatively short time period, try streamlining your operation or recruiting franchisees who have previous experience in your business, thus avoiding an involved training course. For each obstacle, there is an option. If franchising is your goal, solutions to many of these problems can be found.

ALTERNATIVES TO FRANCHISING

But what if the problems are too great? What if you have read the first half of this chapter and decided that your business simply cannot be franchised? What then? Does this leave you out in the cold? Are you doomed to stagnate in a sea of business doldrums? Certainly not! You can still grow. Expansion may not come as fast or take you as far as franchising, but there are a wide variety of alternatives you can employ to help your business grow and develop.

GROWTH THROUGH COMPANY-OWNED UNITS

If your goal is to add a few local stores to your present operation, don't franchise! There is no need to. You can handle that pace of growth on your own. Over the course of a year or two, you can plan your next store's opening and spend time to raise capital from banks or investors. You can select a site, finance the real estate, hire employees, buy inventory, get your building constructed, do some advertising, and then open the business. But remember, the money for each step comes out of your pocket. Company-owned expansion is a slow, plodding strategy. It proves that a business at rest tends to stay at rest unless acted upon forcefully.

Franchising, however, illustrates the opposite effect. "A franchise's growth is geometric in design," says Bill Cherkasky of the International Franchise Association. "Once it reaches a critical mass, it keeps growing, feeding off its own energy." If rapid growth is not your goal, stick to company-owned expansion. Franchising just adds headaches and hard work to your more modest and manageable goals.

GROWTH THROUGH GENERAL DISTRIBUTION

Many businesspeople don't realize that franchising can actually limit the distribution of products. They look at the rapid expansion of many franchises and conclude that with growth comes vast distribution. What they don't realize is that by franchising you often restrict distribution to only those stores or centers within your system. Let me give you an example. A furniture manufacturer would have little to gain in franchising its product. There are thousands of stores throughout the country that sell furniture. This represents an immediate, tremendous market that franchising could never rival. The manufacturer would do better to distribute through these established channels and abandon the dream of building an exclusive marketing system.

But let's change the ground rules. Suppose the furniture manufacturer developed a product that demanded specific design, installation, or follow-up service. I faced this situation a few years ago when a furniture manufacturer knocked on my door looking for advice. The company had developed a curious furniture system that could be shaped into different forms. One month its interchangeable parts made up a coffee table. The next month, a knowledgeable draftsman could convert the pieces into a bed frame or stereo cabinet. It was a highly imaginative product, requiring knowledgeable salespeople and continued support and customer relations. Here, franchising made sense, because it provided control over sales and service, insuring the customer full satisfaction.

Yet if your product has no such extenuating circumstances, franchising may offer little that general distribution could not achieve more easily and effectively with less cost.

SELL TRAINING

As a business owner, one of the most valuable assets you possess is knowledge. Your cumulative business experience is invaluable to making future decisions quickly and effectively. That's why corporations pay seasoned veterans more than new hires! Knowledge is precious, and others will pay good money to learn your secrets.

Franchisors know this and make it their primary selling point. "For a fee, I will teach you everything I know about making money," is the unspoken deal franchisors make with franchisees. Other businesspeople can strike similar bargains by selling training outside the franchise context. And it doesn't have to be cheap. The average 4-year college education costs nearly $40,000, and I know many college graduates who can't find jobs! If you can provide someone with a legitimate opportunity to earn a living and make money, don't shy away from setting your price commensurate with the opportunity.

But there is one problem with teaching others your business. You risk turning students into competitors, particularly if you're a good teacher. Train someone in your hometown how to earn $40,000 a year washing windows, and the two of you may only make $20,000 apiece next year. Franchising eliminates many of the risks through exclusive territories that restrict competition and by continuing royalties that guarantee paybacks for training jobs well done.

BUSINESS OPPORTUNITY VENTURES

A cousin of franchising is business opportunity ventures. Under this arrangement, companies promise to put licensees in business with no royalties, support, or trademark. More specifically, these companies sell or lease products, services, equipment, or supplies to enable the purchaser to start or maintain a business. In general, to be a business opportunity, the seller must claim to provide the purchaser with any or all of the following: a guaranteed profit, a money-back guarantee on the business, locations for the business or its inventory, a buyer for goods produced, repurchase of the goods or services produced, a market for the goods and services being sold or produced, or a sales or marketing program that allows the purchaser to make an income. Moreover, the Federal Trade Commission and many states regulate such business opportunities.

Traditionally, this business system has been marred by extravagant claims that don't hold up to careful scrutiny. A government regulator once told me that in his opinion all business opportunity ventures were scams, promising to put people into highly profitable businesses without offering the continuing support services that novice businesspeople need to succeed. However, the system itself can work and need not be abused.

MOVING AHEAD

You're making progress! By now, you should have decided whether you have the personal qualities required for franchising and whether your business lends itself to franchising. So read on, because Chapter 5 spells out a formula for franchise success!

THE FIVE FACTORS FOR FRANCHISE SUCCESS

Success is the child of audacity . . .
Benjamin Disraeli

Ever since cave men first traded buffalo hides for stone knives, people have searched for the formula to business success. It's only human nature to look for clear, definite answers to complicated issues, and prospective franchisors are no different. They often ask me for a quick, reliable equation to calculate their chances of succeeding in the franchise arena. Unfortunately, there isn't one. Franchising is a complex marketing system that in itself doesn't guarantee success. Just because you decide to franchise doesn't mean you'll become the next Ray Kroc or Colonel Sanders or that your company will grow into a McDonald's or Kentucky Fried Chicken. No, franchising—and business in general—is not so simple.

Franchising success depends on a number of related factors; some fall within your control and others don't. Product development, personnel training, and executive decision-making are but a few fundamentals of business that competent managers can refine and develop. However, other variables such as regulation and consumer demand are less open to management manipulation.

There is no foolproof formula. Franchising is a risk, as is any business endeavor. But after 10 years of experience dealing with companies both large and small, I have noticed certain factors that are often present in businesses that succeed in franchising. And although no company should expect to have all these indicators, the more you possess, the greater your chances of success. Can your business succeed in franchising? These five criteria can help you answer that question.

A DISORGANIZED INDUSTRY, DOMINATED BY "MOM-AND-POP" SHOPS

In determining whether a business should be franchised, there is nothing I like to see more than an industry untouched by centralized decision-making. In this scenario, the businesses are disorganized, dominated by small mom-and-pop operators. There are no franchised companies or company-owned chains controlling large shares of the market. The McDonald's, AAMCOs, Hertzes, Kwik Kopys, Jazzercises, Kentucky Fried Chickens, ComputerLands, and other major franchises have yet to win customer loyalty. Similarly, the corporate giants—the Bloomingdale's, K-marts, Sears', Walmarts, and J.C. Penneys—are conspicuously absent. Instead, these industries are populated with an infinite number of unaffiliated companies that do not share an identity or the use of a common name. There is no specification or standardization within the industry. Quality control in production or sales has yet to be implemented on a widescale basis. Each business unit acts in its own best interest, satisfying consumer needs and wants as it sees fit.

These industries are the hamburger stands and transmission repair shops of the 1950s. They are the pizza parlors and corner grocery stores of the 1960s and 1970s. Large, disorganized industries have launched the truly great franchises of the last 30 years and still offer ample opportunity to the franchise entrepreneur today.

Why are these industries so attractive? Because they are established, so consumer demand obviously exists. The presence of thousands of small, independent operators proves that customers accept the particular product or service as valuable and needed, which avoids guesswork on customer acceptance. Established industries also allow introductory advertising to focus on winning consumers rather than educating them to the use, purpose, or necessity of the product.

"Our biggest initial problem was educating people to quick printing technology," says William LeVine of Postal Instant Press. Instant printing was an unknown process when LeVine opened his first franchise in January 1968. "People thought our product was only mimeograph or ditto quality. So we had to convince the public that we produced a high-quality product at a reasonable price in a matter of minutes."

Disorganized industries also offer a competitive advantage. The absence of large, concentrated companies means new entrants aren't forced to battle highly capitalized and skillfully managed competitors. Firmly entrenched businesses pose formidable challenges to small startup enterprises that are still learning and making mistakes. Established franchisors know this and use it to their full advantage. "We have such a head start in the transmission service industry that small chains have a tough time competing with us even in their own neighborhoods," says Robert Morgan of AAMCO. Morgan believes that the national advertising campaigns of an immense rival can make "copy-catting" an extremely difficult franchise strategy.

How can you tell whether an industry is disorganized? One unscientific yet valid method is the *Yellow Pages* test, which entails flipping open the telephone book and searching for industries with very few easily recognizable names. Try it on your own, and I think you will be amazed at the number of industries that fit the bill. For example, I ran the test recently in the Philadelphia *Yellow Pages* and discovered a startling list of industries dominated by unaffiliated businesses; such as hospitals, office furniture retailers, podiatrists, chiropractors, painting contractors, magic stores, fur coat retailers, funeral homes, fresh seafood stores, karate instructors, kennels, fire protection products, engine overhaulers, tailors, shoe repair outlets, dentists, collection agencies, health food stores, coin dealers, chimney repair outfits, and catering services.

All of these industries are dominated by independent mom-and-pop operators who have no common affiliation except for their industry. Each business is a single island in an ocean of opportunity, the conquest belonging to the franchisors who bring order, efficiency, and standardization to these profitable yet chaotic industries.

SIMPLICITY OF CONCEPT

Complexity undermines the prospects of franchising success. The simpler your business or idea, the greater the chances of having profitable franchisees. It only makes sense. Franchising teaches novice businesspeople how to effectively apply and operate a particular business system. The easier that system is to learn and implement, the better the odds for both franchisor and franchisee success.

Two factors influence simplicity. The first is the retail concept. For example, automotive repair is a basic retail concept. An automotive repair center's goal is to fix the car to the customer's satisfaction. There are no hidden psychological components in the service or purchasing process. People come in with cars that don't work. They want to leave with cars that do!

Compare that situation to a gourmet restaurant, where customer satisfaction depends on a complex mesh of personality, ambience, taste, cuisine, and many even less tangible factors. Here, specification of service is best left to the owner or the chef, and learning to manage the business takes years of subtle observation and experience—luxuries new franchisees simply do not possess.

The second factor in franchising simplicity is organizational structure. In its basic form, franchising is a bilevel marketing system comprised of the franchisor and franchisees. Within this structure, policies and decisions can be made quickly and passed along easily from one step to the next. Likewise, royalty payments and advertising fees can be collected directly from franchisees without using intermediaries.

But not all franchises are so elemental. Take, for example, subfranchising. Here, a master franchisee buys exclusive rights to a territory, then acts as the franchisor, selling franchises and servicing franchisees in the territory. The master franchisee oversees the day-to-day problems that arise with individual units and receives an ongoing percentage of the royalties for his or her troubles.

Area development franchising resembles subfranchising in that territories are involved. However, area developers own and develop the franchises on their own. They don't sell franchises and don't provide the services typical of a franchisor. Under area development, franchisees are multiunit owners in a territory that was granted by contract.

Because subfranchising involves a third party, it tends to be more unwieldy than simple area development arrangements. Jiffy Lube, the fast oil-change and lube specialists, illustrates this point. The company's only master franchise agreement was terminated in April 1986, with the repurchase of 35 subfranchises for more than $500,000. "The middle party created a problem in communicating with in-field operators," says Neil F. O'Shea, vice-president of franchising for the company. O'Shea believes that the additional management level made it difficult to implement decisions and strategies. "The situation was like making a date through a friend; the logistics were often confused," he explains.

But Jiffy Lube's area development program, established in 1983, has met with terrific success. "In franchising, there is a gap between the time costs start to accrue and income starts to flow," says John Sasser, chief financial officer of the company. "For us, substantial area development fees bridged that gap, allowing the company to finance its rapid growth without having to wait for royalties to flow." Area development fees provided Jiffy Lube with $2.2 million in revenue in 1985, and about the same in 1986. Sasser is frank about what this cash has meant to Jiffy Lube. "Without this additional source of income, the company would have been in serious financial straits."

It's impossible to say whether subfranchising or area development could work for your company. But it's important for you to realize the problems inherent in both systems before venturing into either. Chief among these problems is loss of control.

Under subfranchising you add another level of management over which you have limited control. Master franchisees are semiautonomous contractors. They agree to sell franchises and service franchisees. As long as the master franchisees meet the terms of the agreements, you, as franchisor, retain limited recourse as to how they represent your business. For example, master franchisees may not provide the degree of service that new franchisees need to succeed. They may make income projections or engage in other practices that the franchisor expressly forbids. Remember, their actions are difficult to police; you can't be with them every day, and you can't structure a contract to cover every contingency. You're dependent on the master franchisee's abilities and honesty, which are sometimes undermined by conflicting goals and interests. Whereas franchisors often seek only qualified prospects to join the system as franchisees, master franchisees may accept less competent applicants in order to gain initial license fees. There are even reports of master franchisees supplying franchisees with unauthorized products and permitting operation of side businesses that compete with the franchised company.

And there are other difficulties. Both subfranchising and area development franchising tend to create pockets of power throughout a business that in troubled times can strike death blows to struggling organizations. One unfortunate example was Arthur Treacher's Fish and Chips, one of the large franchises of the 1970s. Started in the late 1960s, the company grew to some 700 units by 1980. Much of the expansion came through concentrated area development that saw individual franchisees owning large numbers of franchised units.

The arrangement worked well when times were good and competition was light. However, as more and more fast-food outlets crowded the market and as the franchisor's level of service began to decline, powerful splinter groups formed and convinced other franchisees to break from the company, stop paying royalties, and stay in business without the centralized decision-making of the franchisor. Costly and disruptive litigation resulted, during which franchisees refused to pay royalties.

With no source of income, the franchisor filed bankruptcy. Ironically, the powerful franchisees soon learned that independence was no paradise. Lacking management and organizational skills, eventually many of them also faded from the fast-food scene.

Arthur Treacher's presents powerful testimony to the perils inherent in portioning out your franchise in large doses. Complex franchises can sometimes win faster growth and quick cash, but they also wield a dangerous backlash. Beware! By giving away power, you sacrifice a degree of authority, control, and leverage important in everyday operation and critical in tough markets or fierce competition.

Complex franchise systems also bring marketing problems. In most franchise arrangements, you sell to two consumers—the public and prospective franchisees. However, in trilevel franchise organizations, there is a third consumer—the master franchisees or wealthy investors seeking area development rights. The added market level increases the scope of your sales programs and often causes confusion among these three distinct target markets. "Area development sales are much different than mom-and-pop sales," says O'Shea of Jiffy Lube. "Well-capitalized investors are knowledgeable businesspeople, who often have previous franchise experience. They aren't looking for the self-satisfaction of owning and operating a small business. They are more concerned with financial projections—cash flow, profits, and returns-on-investment."

Before committing to a trilevel or area franchise program, consider your business. Can it afford to broaden its marketing effort? Is it the type of opportunity that would attract large investors? Do you want the larger fish or the small, local owner/operator to be the heart of your organization?

Finally, there is a credibility problem that trilevel franchise systems face. By adding management levels, you isolate franchisees from the franchisor. In essence, you tell the people with the most to lose that the company doesn't stand behind them. Instead, problems, inquiries, and concerns must be routed through a third party, who probably has neither your expertise nor experience. Franchisees often don't appreciate this arrangement. You developed the program. They want you to solve their problems. When things get tough, they want to talk to the guy on top, not a go-between.

With time and proper management, you may be able to overcome all these disadvantages. But for most novice franchisors, simplifying will sidestep these and a wealth of other concerns.

A BICYCLE BUILT FOR TWO

Your franchisees require one thing above all else—the ability to make money. Can your business give them this opportunity? Is it profitable enough for two to share in the booty? These are basic questions in the franchise success formula. Remember, most franchisors take a significant portion of franchisees' ongoing sales. Royalties, advertising fees, rent, and other payments quickly amount to a sizable portion of revenue—anywhere from four percent to 25 percent! Some businesses cannot support this expense and still provide franchisees a profit. The most obvious example is supermarkets, which make just one percent to three percent profit from sales. Tack on another four percent for the franchisor, and the business becomes unprofitable.

The key to deciding whether your business is profitable enough to franchise is to determine what a typical franchisee could earn from your business—a task more complicated than just taking the net income from last year's financial statements. Many of your booked expenses may accord fully with generally accepted accounting principles, but may not apply to a franchisee's business. For example, let's take an imaginary printing business that last year had gross sales of $200,000 and total expenses of $180,000. At first glance, the profit appears too low to attract a franchisee, even without considering payments to the franchisor.

However, many of these costs simply don't apply to a franchisee. To calculate a franchisee's potential income, you must subtract any costs that a typical franchisee would not assume and then add royalty, advertising, and any other fees that a franchisee would pay. For our printing firm, we'll assume the owner will operate the store, which has royalty fees of $10,000 (.05 × $200,000) and advertising payments of $4000 (.02 × $200,000):

Gross Sales		$200,000
Expenses (from income statement	$180,000	
Less expenses not inherent to the franchisee:		
R&D	$ (5,000)	
Legal fees for franchising	(10,000)	
Company cars	(6,000)	
Entertainment	(4,000)	
Manager's salary retained by owner/ operator	(25,000)	
Total		(50,000)

Expenses from financial statement inherent to franchisee		130,000	
Additional Expenses for franchisee:			
Royalty	10,000		
Advertising payments	4,000		
Total		14,000	
Less franchisee's expense			144,000
Yield to franchisee			$56,000

As you can see, the printing company's income statement contains many expenses that a typical franchise would not accrue. Franchisees rarely experience significant research and development, legal, entertainment, and similar expenses. Likewise, a manager's salary should not be included in the example because the franchise owner will also manage our fictitious business, thereby negating that salary. Once these costs are eliminated and royalties and advertising expenses are included, the profit a franchisee can expect from owning and operating the store is $56,000. This sum suggests that the business generates enough money for the franchisor to gain a reasonable royalty—$10,000—while the franchisee could live relatively comfortably with a $56,000 annual income.

This type of analysis answers basic profitability questions, but it's based upon identifiable, reasonable expenses. It doesn't account for one great imponderable—greed. Avaricious franchisors who seek to maximize their own fortunes at the franchisee's expense only undermine their own businesses. "The best advice I can give a new franchisor is not to be greedy," says Arthur Karp of The Original Great American Chocolate Chip Company. "You can't have a system that makes money for you and strangles the franchisee. If anything, the program should be skewed toward the franchisees, because if they succeed, you will succeed. Franchising is a partnership— not in the legal sense, but in the practical sense that requires the effective participation of both parties to work properly."

That's why your business must generate enough profit to keep both parties happy. A one-sided system that earns windfalls for one party and causes ruin for the other is doomed to fail. The program must be mutually beneficial. "Keep franchisees making money, and they will keep your sign above the business," says MAACO's Martino. The moral is clear: The bicycle must be built for two!

REASONABLE CAPITAL INVESTMENT REQUIREMENTS

The next critical financial determinant in franchise success is the initial capital requirement. How expensive can your opportunity be and still attract franchisees? There is no set number. New franchisees of Kentucky Fried Chicken spend an average of $675,000 to set up shop. Domino's Pizza franchisees spend anywhere from $56,000 to $132,000. New owners of a Pilot Air Freight franchise require from $30,000 to $60,000 to get underway. Franchisees of The Hair Performers pay between $45,000 and $125,000 to start the business while the cost of establishing a 1 Potato 2 (a food franchise based in Minnesota) is only $20,000. The numbers vary according to the idiosyncrasies of the respective business—what's excessive for one may be modest for another. Your task is to create a franchise opportunity that reasonably reflects the capital requirements of other businesses and franchises in your industry. Logically, if your business requires expensive freestanding buildings and extensive capital equipment, then costs can run into the hundreds of thousands of dollars. On the other hand, if your franchise is operated by a single employee out of the home, it should sport a modest price tag.

Although a necessity for some industries (particularly fast food), high initial investment requirements often slow growth for new franchisors. The market for franchisees can be illustrated by a pyramid. The lower the initial investment costs, the greater your base of prospective franchisees. Conversely, the higher the expense of getting into business, the fewer prospects you will attract. "By keeping our business reasonably priced, we attract prospective franchisees who simply cannot afford other opportunities," says DeLuca of Subway Sandwiches & Salads. The company's $7500 initial fee is one of the lowest in the fast-food industry. Total costs, which range from $30,000 to $60,000, are kept in check by a simple menu and basic shop design. "Our mainstays of the business—sandwiches and salads—don't re-

NUGGET #5

Initial Capital Investment of 14 Major Franchises

Name	Product or Service	Range of Capital Required
Athletic Attic, The	Athletic Footwear and Related Apparel	$117,000-$142,000
AAMCO	Transmission Repair	$75,000
Rent-A-Wreck	Auto Rental and Leasing	$5,000-$50,000
Nutri/System Weight Loss	Weight Loss Program	$10,000-$75,000
Pearle Vision Centers	Eyecare Centers	$175,000
Mr. Build	Remodeling, Maintenance, and Repair	$10,000-$40,000
Comprehensive Accounting	Accounting, Bookkeeping, Consulting, and Taxes	$25,000-$35,000
American Advertising Distributors	Direct-Mail Advertising	$10,000
Sanford Rose Associates	Employment Search and Recruiting	$15,000
Proforma	Business Forms, Printing, and Computer Supplies	$4,500
McDonald's	Hamburgers	$300,000-$337,000
Subway Sandwiches and Salads	Specialty Sandwiches and Salads	$22,000-$72,000
Lawn Doctor	Automated Lawn Care	$22,500
Merry Maids	Professional Home Cleaning	$9,500-$14,500

quire fryers, grills, or large ovens, which are expensive pieces of equipment. And the simplicity of the shop's design makes it applicable to a wide variety of locations at minimal costs," DeLuca explains.

High initial investment requirements also may strap new franchisees for working capital. Remember, franchisees have to finance the business startup plus a few months' expenses while the business is getting established. If your business requires too much up-front investment, franchisees may skimp on early service, advertising, and marketing—the kiss of death for new businesses.

To keep costs reasonable, you will need to pare your franchise package down to its essentials. This doesn't mean you should underestimate the actual requirements of your franchise business. It does, however, entail careful selection of equipment, inventory, furnishings, and other early assets. Initially, franchisees need only those items immediately critical to success. The costly add-ons and expensive frills can come later as the business grows and matures. In the beginning, your goal is to offer new franchisees a thrifty yet effective program that maximizes potential but minimizes costs. For example, if you own and operate a three-bay automotive service business, examine what a franchised two-bay operation would mean in terms of costs and profits. The downscaled business might be more manageable, practical, and affordable for the new franchisee. Similarly, if you run a computer service firm that employs six salaried salespersons, see whether a smaller, more focused salesforce could still be effective in the formative stages of the franchise. Franchisees need conservative startup operations that require reasonable initial investments but don't undermine potential sales.

Many of these opportunities fall in the service-producing sector of the economy.

A SERVICE BUSINESS

Service businesses offer franchisors many advantages that businesses in other sectors of the economy simply to not possess. Chief among these is low initial investment. Service businesses often require only modest capital investment to establish and maintain. For instance, new franchisees of The Maids International, a major domestic cleaning franchise based in Omaha, Nebraska, need only $30,000 to $40,000 in total startup capital, $11,500 of which goes to the initial fee. The balance pays for a comprehensive equipment and supply package, rental for office space, and early salaries. "The thirty-thousand-dollar to forty-thousand-dollar range is the total turnkey cost for starting operation," says Becky Bishop, director of marketing for the company. "This includes uniforms, supplies, equipment, training, and even postage-paid, direct-mail pieces." Bishop believes the low initial investment opens the door for a broad range of people who otherwise could not afford to buy a business. "We see a lot of couples going into business together who simply can't finance high up-front costs," she says.

The same holds true for many business-service franchises. "Our total cost for a new franchisee is anywhere between sixteen thousand dollars and twenty-five thousand dollars, which is low for franchising but competitive in our industry," says Doug Bugie, director of franchising for Management Recruiters, an executive search firm with 380 franchises across the country. "A large portion of those costs goes for three or four months of working capital. The remainder covers the initial fee and office setup, which includes furniture, rent, telephones, salaries, and some advertising."

This type of low initial investment is unknown to businesses outside the service sector, yet very conducive to successful franchising. Domestic cleaning services, employment agencies, executive search firms, home improvement businesses, travel services, as well as day-care companies have all found comfortable (and profitable) homes in franchising.

Low initial investment offers an additional advantage for franchisors: flexibility. By now, most businesspeople are familiar with the saga of the U.S. steel and automobile industries which, tied to huge capital investment in antiquated plants and equipment, were unable to adapt to changing consumer tastes and desires. Compare that situation with a temporary service agency or computer service firm that needs only two inexpensive assets to make money—a desk and a telephone. Untethered by costly past investment decisions, these companies are free to change direction and make rapid corrections in constantly evolving markets. As MAACO founder Tony Martino explains, "Success often depends on being able to make sudden, midcourse adjustments. You must understand that no plan is ever absolutely right. It must be open to constant review and change. At MAACO, we do things differently today in marketing and service than we did last month or even yesterday. Granted, some business fundamentals never change, but the vast majority of decisions we make are later reviewed, improved, and upgraded."

Service industries provide the degree of adaptability that franchisors need to succeed in today's turbulent business environment. Their low capital requirements reduce the financial risks of exploring new opportunities and abandoning dated, less profitable markets.

Although risks are minimized in most service businesses, potential is not.

A common cliche in franchising is that the market is limited only by a franchisee's energy and willingness to work hard. But for many service businesses this is absolutely true. "We grant exclusive territories with twenty thousand to twenty-five thousand qualified customers in a specific geographical area," says Bishop of The Maids International. "To be successful, franchisees need only penetrate two percent to three percent and many do much better. Once they exploit this area, we encourage them to buy a second territory. Granted, there is a comfort level many franchisees reach at which they stop expanding, but for the true entrepreneur, growth is virtually boundless."

Robert Snelling, Chairman of Snelling and Snelling, the world's largest employment agency, seconds that assertion. "Only fifteen percent of people changing jobs use an employment agency," says Snelling, who has been franchising since 1956. "We have not even begun to approach that finite number." Snelling is quick to note that the business services industry is the second fastest growth industry in the United States. "This growth has prompted us to move back into the temporary personnel service industry," he says. To indicate the mammoth size of that market, Snelling quotes studies that show 98 percent of the companies that use temporary personnel services plan to use such services more in the near future. "U.S. business is being forced to manage labor as effectively as it does capital and equipment. Part of that efficiency can come from using temporary employees as needed, instead of retaining more costly full-time workers."

Steve Pataky, area vice-president for Adia Personnel Service based in Menlo Park, California, makes a similar point. "Business is beginning to realize that outside contractors can perform many functions more efficiently than in-house personnel," he says. "In temporary and full-time employment, the time and money spent advertising, screening, processing, and checking credentials of applicants is simply more than most companies can handle."

Other service industries are also experiencing significant growth. The air-cargo industry, for example, has grown every year since the early 1980s, according to Dan Herron of Dynamic Air Freight. Herron believes the growth is due to the changing American economy. "Decentralization, a shift to high technology, and the need for rapid delivery of parts and inventory mean that American manufacturers need things faster than ever before. Our segment of the air-freight market showed about a ten percent increase in

NUGGET #6

Can Your Business Succeed As a Franchise?

The answer is difficult to determine. But the more of these questions you can answer affirmatively, the more likely you'll succeed.

1. Do you presently own a profitable business?
2. Have you been in business long enough to develop an efficient operating procedure that poses minimal problems?
3. Do you want to expand your business rapidly?
4. Can your business be readily systematized, broken into its essential components?
5. Is your business in a disorganized industry, characterized by a great many small mom-and-pop operators?
6. Is your industry lacking a significant number of large franchises or company-owned businesses?
7. Is your business in an established market? Has the validity of your product or service been proven?
8. Does your product or service fill a legitimate consumer want or need?
9. Is your business relatively simple to operate? Could it be learned quickly and easily by other businesspeople?
10. Does your business generate enough revenue for both the franchisee and franchisor to share in the wealth?
11. Could your business be easily duplicated? Could it be cloned for a reasonable amount of money?
12. Is your business replicable in any of a number of locations? Could the concept work in markets nationwide?
13. Is your business in the service sector of the economy?
14. Can your business be operated on a modest inventory?
15. Is your business based on a trend rather than a fad (trends are long-term; fads are fleeting)?
16. Could a copy of your business break even in a reasonable amount of time (a year or less)?

NUGGET #6 (Continued)

---

17. Could your business generate enough revenue to attract potential franchisees? Would a reasonable man be happy working for the return your business could provide?

18. Does your business offer something new or improved? A better product or service?

19. Does your business lend itself to public relations? Could it generate interest on its own?

20. Have you ever been approached by someone interested in buying your business as a franchise?

21. Is your business prepared to enter long-term business relationships with independent operators?

22. Can you offer franchisees training, advice, other support services, and administer a network of independent businesses?

23. Can your business afford to invest in a franchise program?

1985 compared to 1984, and there is no reason this trend won't continue well into the 1990s."

There is little question that service-producing industries provide the lion's share of jobs and wealth in today's economy, and the trend shows no signs of abating. The United States has moved from a manufacturing to a service economy. Many of these services are designed to improve efficiency and convenience for U.S. business as well as for the general public. Franchising is a leader and an integral part of this shift.

SUCCESSFUL FRANCHISING

As I warned, there is no simple formula for franchise success. The marketing system is too complex for rudimentary analysis. Yet the points articulated here provide guidelines in determining whether your business can grow and prosper as a franchise company. All the indicators of success need not be present. But the more criteria you meet, the greater your chances of finding success in franchising today.

CHAPTER 6

THE REWARDS OF FRANCHISING

As an intellectual exercise, historians often take real events from history and add fictitious propositions, asking, What if? What if Columbus had not discovered America in 1492? Would the development of the New World have been set back for years, decades, or centuries? What if the South had won the Civil War? Would a separate and independent nation now sit below the Mason-Dixon line? Such inquiries are designed to increase understanding of historical consequences. Perhaps a similar investigation aimed at business can uncover the consequences and rewards of franchising.

For example, what if some of today's biggest and best companies had never franchised? What if Ray Kroc hadn't met the McDonald brothers in 1954 and the business had never grown? Certainly, Kroc, a milkshake machine salesman, never would have become a multimillionaire. But more importantly, one of the world's biggest and most effective corporations would never have been born. McDonald's could have been limited to that tiny roadside diner, and thousands of jobs and opportunities the company provides would never have been created.

And what if AAMCO had never franchised? What if Robert Morgan and Tony Martino had not worked to build a franchised transmission empire? Both, no doubt, still would have achieved business success, but it's doubtful

71

whether each would have attained the national prominence they now enjoy, and the motoring public would have been the worse for it.

And where would Neil Balter be today without franchising? Only 10 years ago, Balter was a rowdy high school kid from Southern California, whose only ambition was to party and have a good time. But even then, his mischief showed signs of entrepreneurial brilliance. For example, there was the time his parents went on vacation and Neil decided to throw a party—for 500 people! Charging a dollar a head, the young man managed to cover his costs and have a good time to boot.

When a neighbor informed Neil's parents of the party, beer, and cops, Neil was given an ultimatum: Clean up your act or move out of the house. He opted to move and soon enrolled at Pierce Community College in Los Angeles. To support himself, he got the idea to remodel closets. "I saw a friend's closet that had been outfitted with shelves and dividers, making efficient use of space," he recounts. "It seemed like something everyone would want done."

Neil borrowed money for tools and started to sketch and diagram closet designs for customers he found in the San Fernando Valley. California Closets was born and grew quickly. In 1981, the young entrepreneur had sales of $100,000, of which $15,000 was profit. In 1982 the company started to franchise. Today California Closets claims more than 80 franchises throughout the country. And Neil's parents now work for the company—"A son and father operation," Neil quips.

Balter is frank about what franchising has done for him. "I believe strongly in franchising. Without it, the company never would have achieved the degree of success and national exposure it now enjoys." He's equally candid about its disadvantages. "Franchising is a tough way to go. It requires a lot of work, energy, sweat, and sacrifice. But looking back, there is nothing I would have done differently."

GROWTH AND DEVELOPMENT

So the moral is clear. Franchising lets businesses grow more quickly than they otherwise could. And there lies its greatest reward. The marketing system allows small companies to expand beyond local and regional markets. It takes medium-sized companies and transforms them into giants. Franchising is a proven vehicle for growth that few business systems can rival. "It may sound clichéd, but franchising allows your company to grow fast using other people's money," says John Edwards of Pilot Air Freight. "The marketing system releases you from many of the costs associated with expansion and places them on franchisees," he explains.

Arthur Karp of The Original Great American Chocolate Chip Company also believes expansion is an important advantage of franchising. "When Michael Coles and I started the company, we had neither the capital nor the access to the cash we needed to expand. Without franchising, we would have relied on the profits of one store to help us open the next. It would have been an extremely slow process. But the initial fees of franchising allowed us to speed that growth and gain many more mall locations."

Franchising provides companies with legitimate tools for business growth and development. Initial license fees generate revenue that can be poured back into the franchise company and used for investment, diversification, marketing, advertising, research and development, and a wealth of other functions vital to success in today's market. Moreover, by displacing expansion costs onto the franchisee, you liberate your own capital for investment or development. "It costs me one hundred and twenty-five thousand dollars to open a company-owned California Closet center," says Balter. "Under franchising, I don't spend a dime, and I get twenty thousand dollars in license fees—about five thousand dollars of which is pure profit!"

And under franchising growth is self-perpetuating. "I like franchising because it gives you built-in growth," says Robert Snelling of Snelling and Snelling. "Many of our franchisees own more than one office. They are independent operators who want their business to expand. They know there is a lot of potential in the marketplace and are willing to work for it. And this process doesn't stop when someone retires. We have many families involved with Snelling and Snelling that have passed the business to a son or daughter once a parent leaves the company. This type of ongoing growth and development simply does not exist at company-owned operations."

Growth is the bait that lures many small business owners into franchising. But there are other advantages to franchising that are no less valuable.

COMMITTED AND LOCAL LABOR

"Franchising secures for you the energy, talents, and ambitions of people who, because of their entrepreneurial instincts, would not otherwise work for you in the traditional sense," says Fred DeLuca of Subway Sandwiches & Salads. DeLuca believes that the very quality that attracts franchisees to own and operate a business would keep many from working for company-owned operations. "We look for people who want, almost need, to go into business for themselves," he says. "They have a degree of confidence and ability that requires the pursuit of their own opportunities."

Joan Barnes at Gymboree explains the same phenomenon in slightly different terms. "Franchising is a terrific way to bring enthusiastic and competent people into your organization. Many of our franchisees look at Gymboree as a personal- and career-growth opportunity. Employees at company-owned operations don't view their jobs in the same light," she says.

Franchisees provide a loyal and committed work force. Their investment is not based solely on dollars and cents but also on self-esteem and pride. Theoretically, they are more willing than paid employees to invest the time and concern needed to succeed. "Franchising gives the Hair Performers more competent and caring managers," says company president John Amico. "I can't hire a manager who works as hard as a franchisee. The incentive to perform simply is not there."

For some companies, franchisee commitment has tipped the scale in favor of continuing to franchise. "We have reached a level of success where we no longer need franchising to grow," says Arthur Karp. "Banks will gladly lend us the money we need to expand. Yet we're staying with franchising because, aside from the capital it generates, the system gives you committed labor that you just can't employ on the open market. For instance, I could hire a very bright young man for twenty-five thousand dollars a year to manage a cookie store. But if he is offered thirty-thousand dollars to manage the tobacco shop down the mall, the guy is history. It's simple economics. However, you give this manager a piece of the action and let him own the shop, and he is much more committed to you and the company."

This type of dedication frees the franchisor from many direct oversight responsibilities, lowering management costs. On the local level, the franchisees are the bosses. They hold the reins over salesclerks or cooks, secretaries or delivery people. They take care of the trivial, time-consuming problems that would cost you manpower and money. "McDonald's statue held for ransom," reads an article that recently appeared in the *Philadelphia Inquirer*. The article chronicles how high school students in Delaware swiped a 7-foot plastic statue of Ronald McDonald and demanded 8891 Chicken McNuggets in exchange for its return. The caper serves as a lighthearted example of the types of ongoing difficulties businesses face. But there are many more serious problems franchisees handle everyday. There are inventory decisions, personnel problems, advertising and marketing dilemmas, customer relations concerns, cash flow issues, and scheduling quandaries. As a franchisor, it's your job to set up policies to mitigate these problems by providing effective operating and marketing procedures, advice, forecasts, and new products and services. Direct supervision, however, is left to the franchisee.

PERSONAL SATISFACTION

Don't let anyone ever tell you that franchising is not a tremendously rewarding business undertaking. To clone your business on a regional or national scale means your concept is valid and works, not only in one particular location, but in a variety of towns and cities. Successful franchising provides tangible evidence that your product or service fills a real need in the marketplace, and that it can attract the imagination, interest, and dollars of the American public.

"The ability to successfully replicate your business often evidences a sound concept coupled with competent management," says Brian Thomas, president and founder of Thomas James Associates, an investment banking firm based in Rochester, New York. "Successful franchising often plays a major role in our decision to take a company public."

The business community looks fondly on people of vision and daring who can package their success and pass it to others in the way of franchise opportunities. A certain mystique surrounds today's Ray Krocs, Tony Martinos, Gary Goransons, Neil Balters, and other franchise entrepreneurs. This type of recognition, in the right measure, can be extremely rewarding.

But there is more to personal satisfaction than what others think. Self-esteem can only come from within. And here, franchising again plays a role. "The most rewarding part of franchising is watching the transformation of franchisees. In the beginning, they are full of doubt," notes Les Charm of Docktor Pet Centers. "They are just crawling along, barely making it, and you can see this in their appearance. Their shoulders are stooped and eyes downcast. It's a trying and difficult time. But then a metamorphosis takes hold. Franchisees begin to taste success. They become more animated and jaunty. They are on the verge of making it big and become more confident and secure. It's a terrifically exciting and rewarding experience."

Providing people with the means for success, giving them legitimate opportunities, and improving their life-styles are all part of the franchise process. As a franchisor, you will play an integral part in the lives of others. You will stick by franchisees from the outset; see them struggle; revel in their success; and you will laugh, work, and sacrifice together. Franchising creates a large, extended family. As the head of the household, you will experience the same pride, concern, and interest as does any parent.

"We had a franchisee who lost her partner," Bud Hadfield of Kwik Kopy says. "She didn't let us know about her trouble, but we found out, and gave her a call. She said she was going to make it. Later we discovered she gave up her apartment to save money and moved a cot into the back of the store. It was touch-and-go for a while, but she is making it. As a businessman, it's an honor and privilege for me to be associated with such courage and commitment. It's immensely satisfying, and I am extremely grateful to be a part of these and other success stories."

POOL OF TALENT

"I consider one of the great advantages of franchising to be the pool of creative thinkers you gain in the form of franchisees," says Neil Balter of California Closets. "Success often depends on creativity and imagination. Franchisees represent a never-ending fountain of ideas and opinions."

By gaining numbers, outlets, or stores, you share the vision and foresight of businesspeople who have many of the same goals as the franchisor. "A large part of my job is listening to franchisees," says Charm of Docktor Pet Centers. "I go to franchisee seminars, not to lecture, but to see what's going on out in the field. After all, who knows more about the business than the people running the businesses? Good franchisors take creative and profitable ideas from franchisees, refine and systematize them, and then make them available to the system as a whole."

By franchising, you gain the talents and energies of a diverse and competent group of people—a resource and strategic advantage your company alone would never possess. As a franchisor, it's your responsibility to capitalize on this asset by motivating and energizing your franchisees to identify new market opportunities and operating efficiencies, and then providing channels for communication. Newsletters, franchisee advisory boards, seminars, and conferences can all be used to pass along company policies and news. Once franchisees understand the importance of their contributions, they often become more open to sharing their experiences and ideas with you and other franchisees.

The combined talents within your franchise system are a tremendous resource. Identify them early and utilize them often, and you will capitalize on the strength that comes with numbers.

TRANSFERRING THE RISK OF LOSS

Anytime a company opens a new store or unit, there is an investment of financial and human resources. And with that investment comes risk. In the event of a failure, the company risks losing time, energy, money, and market share. There also are contingent liabilities. If the unit fails, you still are responsible for future rent, startup debts, and other costs that continue to drain company resources well after the unsuccessful unit has shut its doors.

In franchising, however, the franchisor's risk is greatly reduced, because franchisees bear 100 percent of a new unit's financial liabilities. Franchisees sign the leases and are responsible to landlords. They assume all the expense of inventory, construction, early promotion, hiring employees, and other startup costs.

NUGGET #7

The Hows and Whys of a Franchise Advisory Board

Are you considering the establishment of a franchisee advisory board? The International Franchise Association offers its insight into the task.

Do have a written set of bylaws or a constitution that spells out the ground rules of your council.

Don't consider the bylaws unchangeable. Times change, so include a by-laws provision for making amendments.

Do set down some broad goals and objectives when forming your council. They'll serve to delineate the direction of your organization.

Don't limit attendance at council meetings strictly to franchisees, owners, or top executives. Be sure to invite key people to discussions concerning their particular area.

Do have someone responsible for taking minutes at each meetings and for distributing them to council members.

Don't let your national council get bogged down in a flood of tasks that can more appropriately be handled by a standing committee or a regional council.

Do set an agenda for every meeting and stick to it. It's the only way to avoid gripe sessions.

Don't waste the experience of your council's past presidents. Ask them to serve on a special advisory board, and draw on their knowledge at appropriate times.

Do have the franchisor's top management personnel at the meetings, if the franchisor is involved in the council. The presence of lower echelon people signals to franchisees that their opinions and problems are not taken seriously.

Don't invite hassles regarding who pays for what meeting expenses. Determine in advance which expenses the franchisor will pay and which the franchisees will pay.

Do have a follow-up mechanism that keeps council members and non-members informed of activities. It builds the council's reputation as an effective organization.

Don't create legal problems. Be aware of the legal implications of forming a council and of running meetings.

Thus, if the unit folds, creditors have no recourse to the franchisor. The old axiom that franchisees are in business for themselves but not by themselves extends as far as financial insolvency. Then, franchisees are completely on their own. The franchisor owes no greater financial duty to the unsuccessful franchisee.

Take, for example, a hot dog franchise. If a single unit fails, the franchisor loses market share and royalty payments. Yet the value of both are minimal for a struggling outlet that has failed to gain customers and sales. Moreover, the franchisor can resell the location or territory, collecting a second initial license fee from a new operator. If the new franchisee succeeds, market share is regained and greater sales generate higher royalties. So by transferring the risk of individual units to franchisees, the franchisor creates a win/win situation, reducing its financial liabilities and retaining potential growth and expansion.

But there are reasons to be cautious. A record of franchisee failure makes future franchise sales a difficult proposition. Moreover, some disreputable franchisors have fallen into legal trouble by encouraging unit turnover to retake markets for company-owned operations or to gain additional initial license fees by refranchising. As a general rule, resale of a franchised unit is a viable option only if a franchisee fails outright, and sale by the franchisee is not feasible. Preying on franchisees only builds dissension and animosity within the franchise system. Franchisees often have their own informal network of communication. Force out an owner in Birmingham, and word quickly spreads to Boston, Butte, and Baltimore.

But stand behind a struggling franchisee, take the extra step some people need to succeed, and you'll have helped two people to succeed—the franchisee and yourself!

WIDESPREAD COMPREHENSIVE ADVERTISING

Except for those who foot the bill, few people realize the tremendous expense of comprehensive advertising. The U.S. public is so inundated with print, radio, and television advertising that there is a tendency to forget that someone pays for each message. Making an impression on consumers costs money—and lots of it. You have to reach into tens of millions of living rooms and then speak convincingly, clearly, and often enough for consumers to begin to recognize your product or service. One minute of prime time television can cost hundreds of thousands of dollars. And even then, only a small portion of the potential audience sees your message!

But reaching the consumer is only half the battle. Once you get their attention, you have to educate them about your product: what it is, how it's used, and why it's better than your competitors'. It's not enough to simply create awareness; you also must express an urgency that motivates consumers to act. To create a taste, stir a desire, or feed a need requires full-blown advertising programs that are comprehensive in scope, thorough in coverage, and extremely expensive.

For example, a one-time shot at reaching every home in the United States through television would cost about $1.5 million, according to Jon Seitz, a media director with a leading Philadelphia advertising agency and expert in media scheduling and purchasing. "But rarely does an advertiser want to reach every home in the country. Instead, companies target their advertising toward particular audiences. Here, frequency is important to reinforce the advertiser's message, and this adds substantially to costs."

Alternative media are often no less expensive. For instance, in order to reach a significant percentage of the population through radio, time must be purchased on a market-by-market basis. "When you add up the expense of buying radio time in the top two hundred markets, the costs equal or exceed an equivalent television campaign," Seitz says. "And contrary to popular opinion, radio time is not cheap. A minute on the 1987 Super Bowl, for instance, costs four hundred thousand dollars," he points out.

The economics of advertising in newspapers is similar. "There are literally thousands of newspapers throughout the country that can't be eliminated from your campaign if you seek to achieve total penetration of the nation," Seitz states. Frequency is particularly important here because of competing ads and the low retention quotient of newspaper advertising in general. Still, that doesn't mean a single print ad is inexpensive. In 1987, a single-run, full page ad in *The Sunday New York Times* cost $50,000. Similar high costs hold true in magazine advertising.

Direct mail, which often achieves impressive results, also comes with a high price tag. Much of this medium's success is due to comprehensive testing of coverage and message. More than television, radio, and newspaper advertising, direct-mail campaigns can be analyzed, tested, and evaluated. Mailing lists can be divided by demographic and psychographic parameters. Campaigns can be refined and updated.

But all this takes time and money. Researching markets, developing lists, testing campaigns, writing messages, and designing and redesigning layouts are all highly labor-intensive undertakings. And that doesn't include the cost of printing, distributing, and mailing the individual pieces. After all this, many people consider direct mail junk and toss it straight into the waste basket!

So what can you do? How can a small businessperson finance a comprehensive advertising program? It seems a Catch-22 situation. You need advertising to grow. But you can't afford to advertise because you are small. Is there a solution? Certainly, and it is franchising. Virtually every major franchise company pools franchisee resources to finance regional or national advertising programs. For instance, Super Cuts, a 470-unit hair-care franchise based in San Rafael, California, charges franchisees five percent of gross sales for advertising. McDonald's franchisees pay four percent of their gross. At Precision Tune, it's a hefty nine percent. Other companies work off a flat fee. Dial-A-Gift, a franchise that sends gifts by wire, charges franchisees $100 a month toward advertising the service. Franchisees of Miami-based Dryclean U.S.A., pay $200 a month to the company's advertising pool.

Don't underestimate the value of these advertising arrangements. McDonald's spends some $500 million on advertising each year, all of which comes from franchisees. And even for small franchises the benefits can be dramatic. For example, if your product or service is targeted toward a male audience, the best place to advertise may be on major sporting events in your local market. But such exposure comes with a price tag well beyond the reach of most small businesses. Let's suppose, however, you're a 10-unit franchise based in Philadelphia, and each unit contributes five percent of gross sales ($350,000 on average), for a total advertising budget of $175,000. If all this is used to buy media time, you probably have enough money to purchase a 30-second commercial on a season's worth of televised Phillies' games, or three 30-second spots on each 76ers' game, or five 30-second spots during each game in the Flyers' season. And that's not all. Your budget may be high enough to entitle you to an advertiser's sponsorship, which includes special mention during the game, promotions throughout the season, special merchandising packages, season tickets, and premiums for distribution to your customers. Not a bad way to gain regional recognition of your product or service!

CONSIDERING ALL THE POSITIVES

Okay, so you have read all the pluses and are impressed. You know that franchising could lead to regional or national growth. You realize the marketing system attracts other people's capital, and loyal, committed labor. It all appears immensely rewarding, and you'd love to gain the print and broadcast exposure that franchise advertising programs provide. But does it sound too good to be true? Shouldn't there be some negative aspects? There are. And Chapter 7 is devoted to a candid discussion of the disadvantages of franchising.

CHAPTER 7

THE DISADVANTAGES OF FRANCHISING

Ask knowledgeable businesspeople to name the greatest disadvantage of franchising and many will respond, "Regulation."

Put the same question to a general-practice attorney and you'll often hear a similar, if not more technical answer.

Even some of today's most successful franchisors cite regulation as the largest impediment to franchising.

Well, I'm here to tell you, it just ain't so! Sounds incredible, but of all the issues in franchising, the most misunderstood is the effect of regulation on the marketing system.

Those who broadcast the evils of franchise regulation are either misinformed or too removed from franchising to understand its full scope and impact. These individuals form part of the conspiracy of misunderstanding that surrounds franchise law today.

So let's correct a few misconceptions right now. Franchise law does not restrict your access to the open market. It doesn't discourage the free-market system or limit your ability to grow, win market share, and make money. The mere health of franchising in today's economy proves that regulation has not thwarted its growth or inhibited its potential. Franchise law simply is not the monster it's perceived to be.

So what is franchise regulation? Regulation is a condition and expense of doing business as a franchisor. It is a reality that successful franchisors must study, address, and overcome. It takes some time and entails some expense, but franchise compliances and disclosure should not consume an inordinate length of time or number of dollars. "Quite frankly, regulation has very little effect on our company," says Les Charm of Docktor Pet Centers. "I believe if you're sincere in your commitment to your franchisees, you won't have to worry about franchise law. It's the disreputable franchisors who have to beware."

REGULATION: ITS HISTORY AND IMPACT

Franchising today lies in an era of progressive regulation. Laissez-faire is over. Many of the hucksters and fast-buck artists who preyed on unsuspecting franchisees have either turned and run or are in jail. Today, franchising is regulated in the public interest, much as the railroads fell under government restrictions at the turn of the century after robber barons reaped huge rewards from unfair practices.

To understand how bad certain franchising abuses were, let's go back to the 1960s, when franchise hysteria swept the nation. "Make $1,000 A Week For the Rest of Your Life," read franchise ads in *The Wall Street Journal*. "A Millionaire After Only Six Months!" trade journals promised prospective franchisees. America became enamored with self-contained business opportunities called franchises. For instance, when McDonald's stock went public in April 1965, its price more than doubled in one month, skyrocketing from $22.50 a share to more than $50 a share.

People were hungry to buy into success, and a new stream of franchise opportunities, some legitimate and others less reputable, popped up to meet the demand. Perhaps the most notorious was Minnie Pearl's Fried Chicken, which failed so miserably that it added the expression, "Minnie-Pearling it," to the U.S. vernacular. And there were a host of fraudulent schemes that promised the world and delivered shattered dreams. Franchising for a time became the domain of high-pressure sales and exaggerated claims of unbridled income from limited investments. The problems led to increased cries for government intervention in the way of regulation.

California was the first to heed the call. Realizing that many resident franchisees were suffering substantial losses at the hands of unscrupulous franchisors, the state enacted the nation's first franchise investment law in 1970. It required a franchising company to register prior to the offer or sale of franchises in California or to its residents, and imposed a cooling-off period before a sale could be finalized. It also compelled franchisors to provide prospective franchisees with a copy of the franchise agreement, a company financial statement, and a detailed disclosure document, which in effect reduced the franchise offer to a written formal agreement, reviewable by the state.

The law discouraged disreputable operators from doing business in the state and forced many legitimate franchisors to seriously evaluate their offerings in terms of a franchisee's increased right to know. It also served as a precedent for other state regulations. Today 15 states have laws specifically relating to franchise disclosure. Many other states possess laws that indirectly affect the marketing system.

The federal government began to regulate franchising in 1979, when the Federal Trade Commission (FTC) promulgated a comprehensive, nationwide franchising rule. Like the regulation in California the FTC rule dealt with a prospective franchisee's right to reliable information regarding the franchisor's business. The FTC rule made it unlawful to offer or sell a franchise anywhere in the United States without first providing a disclosure document at either the earlier of (1) the first personal meeting to discuss the sale of the franchise; or (2) at least 10 business days before the signing of any franchise or related agreement; or (3) at least 10 business days before any payment to the franchisor.

Although today the FTC rule applies throughout the nation, state laws that impose more rigorous standards than the federal law take precedence over FTC rules.

Preparation of a disclosure document can follow either the FTC's basic disclosure format or the Uniform Franchise Offering Circular (UFOC). The UFOC, which is the more comprehensive and more widely used of the two, is comprised of 20 items about the franchised business and its principals. For example, UFOC Item #3 asks for a description of any litigation brought against you or the people in your organization for fraud, violation of franchise laws, embezzlement, fraudulent conversion, restraint of trade, or unfair or deceptive practices. Similarly, Item #4 asks whether you or any principals of the company have been adjudicated bankrupt or have reorganized due to insolvency. Other items listed in the UFOC deal specifically with the franchise company, including: company history, product purchase requirements, initial license and other fees, investment in the franchise, exclusive areas, service obligations to the franchisee, training, and length of the franchise agreement.

Another important franchise document is the franchise agreement, which is the contract that governs the terms of the relationship. Your contract will vary according to your specific business, but it will cover many of the same issues specified in your UFOC, such as: the fees involved in buying and operating the franchise, termination and renewal of the agreement, description of your company's training program, a franchisee's obligations to buy inventory or materials from the franchisor or others, and size of the territory awarded.

Together with a financial statement, a completed UFOC and franchise agreement allow you to sell franchises in unregulated states.

Obviously, franchising brings with it a variety of legal paperwork. But don't despair! A lot of good comes from taking the time to prepare these documents.

By forcing franchisors to define the scope of their businesses through disclosure documents, regulation has caused franchise companies to better plan and develop their goals and methods—a sensible exercise for any business. Committing plans to paper allows for objective appraisals of strategies and tactics. It forces management to separate fact from fantasy and provides a realistic portrayal of the undertaking. It also offers a well-conceived business plan that can serve as a valuable road map for the ever-changing fiscal terrain. This business blueprint gives franchise entrepreneurs a huge advantage over less-prepared competitors.

Regulation also reduces the franchisor's risk of disgruntled franchisees prevailing in or even attempting litigation. By clearly defining your offer in properly written franchise documents, and by stating costs, services, and income potential beforehand, you increase mutual understanding and shield yourself from improper claims of fraud and other business violations. A signed legal document provides solid, tangible evidence as to what was offered and what was accepted. Franchisors accused of misrepresentation often need only present the signed documents to prove the franchisee had full knowledge of the costs and risks before undertaking the venture. Regulation, therefore, limits false accusations on both sides of the house—the franchisor's and franchisee's. As proof, consider that since the FTC rule was implemented, franchise litigation has decreased—a rare occurrence in our litigious world.

Yet for all the good that regulation has brought, there is still some bad in terms of time and expense. Complying with franchise regulation is a serious undertaking that requires the help of an expert knowledgeable in both business and law. To save time and trouble, you need a competent franchise attorney who can sidestep costly problems.

Just how much will compliance cost? That depends on the complexity and condition of your business. But a typical business that has a relatively clean operating history should be able to obtain a basic franchise program for between $10,000 and $15,000. This program should include preparation of a Uniform Franchise Offering Circular or a FTC Disclosure Document, a franchise agreement, and an elemental outline on the structure and operation of the franchise.

However, be cautious. Business savvy is critical in the preparation of your legal franchise documentation. The $10,000 to $15,000 price range I described assumes you are working with an expert franchise attorney, who not only knows the legal aspects but also the business aspects of franchising! Many lawyers don't, and franchisors are worse because of it.

"Franchise law is an area of specialization unto its own," says Brian Thomas, president of Thomas James Associates. "It's amazing the number of franchise companies we see wanting to go public that don't have the correct legal paperwork. It's imperative that franchisors work with franchise attorneys and not just general practice lawyers."

Thomas is not alone in his opinion. "The first thing I would tell a prospective franchisor is to find a competent franchise lawyer," says Peter Shea, of Stained Glass Overlay. "You don't need the attorney on staff, but you do need him or her on call to see you through the early compliances and disclosures."

The lawyer you choose should have a solid and diversified list of franchise clients and be able to present sample disclosures and agreements for your in-office inspection. When interviewing franchise attorneys, you should ask specific questions regarding their experience. Too often prospective franchisors move forward on a "We'll find out" basis, permitting their attorneys to avoid specific questions by saying, "I'll do some research, make some telephone calls, and we'll find out." This approach simply does not work in franchising, where regulation is too exacting and demanding for the novice.

This is particularly true in complying with state regulation, which varies greatly according to the jurisdiction. State compliance and registration is often the most tedious and demanding aspect of legal franchise work. A qualified franchise attorney is a must.

How much will state registrations cost you? Again, the answer is a function of the scope and history of your business. But it also depends on the demands of the individual states. Some states such as Illinois and New York impose rigorous requirements to obtain franchisor approval. Others such as Hawaii and Michigan have less exacting legal requirements.

Although not feasible for every company, my suggestion to you in developing a state compliance program is to invest in a national program that covers every state in the union. This may seem overly ambitious and an unnecessary early expense, but generally it's not. You must understand that franchising is a national phenomenon that knows no artificial boundary. It's fine to target an immediate geographical area for growth. But what happens when a prospect calls from outside that area? Can you sell him? Not until you are registered in that state. Sixty to 90 days later, when your legal work is complete, your hot prospect has either cooled or has bought a competitor's franchise.

It's a common scenario. Shortsighted businesspeople, aiming to save a dollar up front, lose bundles. The loss is unfortunate, because one lost sale could finance your entire state compliance program! The $15,000 to $25,000 you lose in one licensing fee is what you could expect to pay for a properly completed national registration program, including state mandated filing fees.

But again, beware. Some lawyers quote much lower prices. Here, you can be sure the attorney doesn't know the quantity and quality of the work involved. State registration is a complex process that demands mastery of various state regulation requirements. Maryland, for instance, requires sep-

NUGGET #8

Twelve Key Questions to Ask a Franchise Attorney

Finding a competent franchise attorney is priority number one for new franchisors. Here are some of the questions you can ask to help determine your attorney's experience with and understanding of the marketing system:

Questions	Desired Answers
1. Have you personally drafted franchise disclosure documents for at least three franchisors or served as counsel with franchising responsibility for an established franchisor?	Yes. (The details should be provided to you.)
2. What percentage of your practice is devoted to franchising?	Your attorney should invest at least one-third of his or her time in franchising.
3. Do you maintain a nationwide collection of franchise laws and regulations? If so, what is the resource?	The premier resource is the *Business Franchise Guide*. If your attorney can't name a source, you should wonder why.
4. Can you handle my filings with the Federal Trade Commission?	This is a trick question. There are no FTC filings. Your attorney should know this.
5. In which states do you have franchisors registered to sell franchises?	An experienced franchise attorney should have clients registered in most registration states.
6. What is the UFOC?	The UFOC is the Uniform Franchise Offering Circular, a basic franchise disclosure document. If your attorney doesn't know about it, find someone else to quarterback your franchise legal program.

NUGGET #8 (*Continued*)

7. What are the principal differences between the FTC and UFOC disclosure documents?	The UFOC is more comprehensive and widely accepted. Specifically, the UFOC requires audited financial statements and disclosure of a franchisor's obligations as well as a franchisee's initial investment.
8. What states regulate franchising?	California, Hawaii, Illinois, Indiana, Maryland, Michigan, Minnesota, New York, North Dakota, Oregon, Rhode Island, South Dakota, Virginia, Washington, and Wisconsin, and Texas, under certain circumstances.
9. I don't have a federally registered trademark. How does this affect my franchise sales capacity?	You'll need to register in Connecticut and North Carolina and, under certain circumstances, in a few other states.
10. How long will it take to complete an average registration after filing?	If it's more than 60 to 70 days, it's too long.
11. Which items of the UFOC disclose territorial issues, trademarks, and termination rights?	Territorial issues come under FTC #13 and UFOC #12; trademarks are FTC #1 and UFOC #13; termination are FTC #15 and UFOC #17.
12. If I'm selling a franchise to a Virginia prospect for a location in Maryland, and doing so from my Pennsylvania office, in which state do I have to register?	In Maryland, because Virginia law doesn't apply and Pennsylvania doesn't regulate franchising.

NUGGET #9

Franchise Regulatory Agencies

The federal government, 15 states, and a Canadian province have laws that could potentially influence your franchise offering. Here's a list of their addresses along with the cost of filing or registration for each.

State	Fee
Federal Trade Commission	n/a
Franchise Program Advisor	
Division of Enforcement	
Bureau of Consumer Protection	
Pennsylvania Ave. at 6th St., NW	
Washington, D.C. 20580	
(202) 376-2805	
California	$450
Department of Corporations	
600 South Commonwealth Ave.	
Los Angeles, CA 90005	
(213) 736-2741	
or	
1390 Market St.	
San Francisco, CA 94108	
(415) 557-3787	
Hawaii	$50
Department of Commerce and	
Consumer Affairs	
1010 Richards St.	
Honolulu, HI 96813	
(808) 548-5317	
Illinois	$500
Franchise Division	
Office of Attorney General	
500 South Second St.	
Springfield, IL 62706	
(217) 782-1279	

Indiana $500
Franchise Division
Indiana Securities Division
Secretary of State
Suite 560
One North Capitol St.
Indianapolis, IN 46204
(317) 232-6681

Maryland $250
Maryland Division of Securities
Fourth Floor
The Munsey Building
7 North Calvert St.
Baltimore, MD 21202
(301) 576-6360

Michigan $250
Consumer Protection Division
Antitrust and Franchise Unit
Michigan Department of Attorney General
670 Law Building
Lansing, MI 48913
(517) 373-7117

Minnesota $250
Minnesota Department of Commerce
500 Metro Square Building
St. Paul, MN 55101
(619) 296-6328

New York $500
Bureau of Investor Protection and Securities
New York State Department of Law
120 Broadway
New York, NY 10271
(212) 341-2211

North Dakota $250
Office of Securities Commissioner
Third Floor

Capitol Building
Bismarck, ND 58505
(701) 224-2910

Oregon   0
Corporation Division
Commerce Building
Salem, OR 97310
(503) 378-4387

Rhode Island $200
Securities Section
Banking Division
100 North Main St.
Providence, RI 02903
(401) 277-2405

South Dakota $250
Division of Securities
910 E. Sioux Ave.
Pierre, SD 57501
(605) 773-4013

Virginia $250
Franchise Section
Division of Securities and Retail
Franchising
11 South 12th St.
Richmond, VA 23219
(804) 786-7751

Washington $500
Department of Licensing
Securities Division
Business and Professions Administration
PO Box 648
Olympia, Washington 98504
(206) 753-6928

Wisconsin $400
Registration Division
Franchise Investment Division

NUGGET #9 *(Continued)*

Wisconsin Securities Commission
PO Box 1768
111 West Wilson St.
Madison, WI 53701

Canada $250
Alberta Securities Commission
10th Floor
Capitol Square Building
Edmonton, Alberta T5J 3B1 Canada
(403) 427-5201

---

arate disclosure of any arbitration in which you or your company have been involved. If your lawyer omits this one requirement from the initial filing, your franchise program will be delayed 30 to 60 days while the state requests further disclosure. And even then, your attorney may not know how to properly respond to the state's request.

An experienced franchise attorney should steer you away from costly and time-consuming errors, getting you registered in virtually every state in less than 90 days. If your filing process takes longer, ask your attorney specific questions regarding the delay. And do not allow the blame to fall on state agencies.

After 10 years of franchise experience, I have found most state regulators to be highly competent professionals with a sincere concern in protecting local consumers and businesses. They neither care to see you fail nor wish to cause you delay. They do, however, expect you to provide the information a prospective franchisee needs to make an accurate judgment on your business. Fail to supply the necessary information and prepare to finance a costly review-and-rewrite process that could drag on for months, maybe even years.

And that is the reason that the competency of your attorney is so critical. A shoddy disclosure document, a poorly written franchise agreement, or an incomplete state filing can cost you plenty in time, money, market share, and frustration. You can avoid many of these problems by finding a qualified legal professional who knows the inner world of franchising.

So there are disadvantages to franchise compliance. It costs money and time. A typical business can expect to spend about $30,000 for proper completion of the basic franchise documents, a national program of state compliances, and some advice and guidance on franchise structure and development. It's no small amount, but it pays for itself in results. If you are genuinely interested in expanding your business, if your long-term goal is to break out of local or regional markets, then the costs of franchise legal work is a small investment in success.

INCREASED EXPOSURE TO POTENTIAL LITIGATION

A franchisor sells a complicated, emotionally charged product. Franchisees buy opportunities, life-styles, and the chance to succeed on their own. They take the ultimate risk, quitting their jobs and investing most of their savings in your franchise. The risk is no small gamble. The big winners will hold you in deepest gratitude. The losers, no doubt, will deny their role in the failed venture and cast blame on you. It's inevitable. Even the most generous and concerned franchisor opens itself to possible litigation brought by unsuccessful franchisees.

You must determine now whether expanding your business through franchising is worth risking an occasional lawsuit. If not, forget about franchising. But if you are willing to face the possibility of a day in court, then franchising poses no greater threats than many other forms of business.

How can you reduce the likelihood of litigation? By being honest with prospective franchisees and telling them exactly what lies ahead. No venture is risk-free. You must articulate this fact early, before a franchisee signs on the dotted line. You also need to be realistic in your estimations. Franchisees deserve to know the facts about your business and the true costs of going into it. They should have accurate figures on which to base their decision.

Your franchise agreement and disclosure document detail the costs of buying your franchise, as well as its operational requirements. But in order to make the offer more enticing, some franchisors conveniently overlook ad-

NUGGET #10

How Franchise Regulators Review State Filings

Mark Forseth, franchise examiner for Maryland's Division of Securities, offers his insights.

"Basically, I use two criteria in reviewing franchise filings. First, I check to see that the franchisor has complied with the rules and regulations of Maryland law. Next, I assume the role of a franchise prospect and determine whether the franchisor has supplied the information material to making an educated and informed purchasing decision. I ask myself: What would I want to know about this franchise opportunity? What is missing from this picture? What important details are being glossed over? What obligations am I assuming and what obligations is the franchisor assuming?

"In Maryland, we review a total of about six hundred initial franchise filings, amendments, and renewals a year. The most common problem is that people don't take the time to read the rules and regulations before filing. For instance, documentation is often missing and financial statements outdated. They simply don't pay enough attention to detail. Consequently, about seventy-five percent of initial filings are returned to the franchisor or its attorney with additional information requested.

"As regulators, our objective is not to slow your filing process. Instead, it's to get you registered as quickly as possible according to the laws of Maryland. We must ensure that the information you provide is what a prospect needs to make a reasonable purchasing decision, by staying alert to possible fraud in the offering circular, as well as in the offer and sale of the franchise.

ditional expenses and facts that detract from the business. This is highly improper and only increases your chances of winding up in court. If franchisees need six months' working capital, state that fact. If new owners won't draw early salaries, let prospects know about such sacrifices. Your disclosure document and franchise agreement need to reflect the true economics and dynamics of the undertaking. Underestimating initial investment costs or overstating income potential are two fast ways to end up in court.

The U.S. public is an extremely litigious bunch. Businesspeople, by virtue of their public position, open themselves to the increased threat of lawsuits and court cases. No strategy can protect you completely. But if you are honest in conducting your business, sincere in your goals, and committed to mutual success, then your chances of facing serious legal liability are minimized.

CERTAIN RESTRICTIONS PLACED ON FRANCHISORS

Few businesspeople realize that franchisors are not allowed to set prices. As a franchisor, you can suggest retail prices to your franchisees, but restraint of trade laws prohibit you from establishing systemwide pricing. To many businesspeople, this represents a minor concern. They believe that local owners, situated closer to the consumer, are more capable of adjusting prices according to the market and competition. In other industries, however, price reflects the quality and image of the product. Here, discounting is tantamount to destroying product image and consumer loyalty. It also risks triggering all-out price wars that decrease an industry's total revenue.

Similarly, in the typical business format franchise, franchisors cannot force franchisees to buy products from them. You can make the products available and strongly recommend their purchase, but getting franchisees to buy your product often depends on simple, old-fashioned salesmanship.

The same is true of promotion. A franchisor can spend big money on developing a new promotion, only to find some franchisees refusing to take part in the campaign. As a franchisor, there's no way to force participation. That's why many commercials for franchise products or services limit the offer with "at participating dealers" taglines.

Restricted authority is a tremendous disadvantage for some businesses. If your company lacks the flexibility franchisees bring to an organization, then it may not be right for franchising.

A LONG-TERM RELATIONSHIP

A prime consideration in franchising is the duration of the relationship, which tends to be lengthy. "Once you get into franchising, it is extremely difficult to get out," says William Cherkasky of the International Franchise Association. "Sure you can stop franchising, but you still have to service the franchisees you have sold. The only real way out is a buy-back, but this is an extremely expensive strategy."

The length of your franchise agreement depends on the needs of your business. But for psychological security, many franchisees look for long-term agreements that indicate the stability of their investment. A common term is 15 or 20 years, which can seem a particularly long time in franchising—where initial goodwill between the franchisor and its franchisees can vanish. "There is a common thread that runs through franchising," says Gary Goranson of Tidy Car. "I call it the 'What Have You Done For Me Lately' syndrome. It usually strikes after the initial honeymoon period has ended."

Goranson believes once franchisors teach franchisees the bulk of the business, a period of unrest and discontent frequently follows. "After a few years in the system, franchisees start questioning your commitment to providing quality services. But at this stage, the franchisees have everything they need to succeed. For the franchisor, this is a real test of understanding and requires extremely broad shoulders to handle the continuing demands."

Servicing long-term franchisee relationships may be the greatest challenge you face as a franchisor. The demands to increase sales, develop new markets, and create better products are constant and ongoing. Last year's big coup is quickly forgotten in a market that changes by the week, day, and hour. You will need to constantly upgrade ideas, concepts, and approaches. "People know that it costs money to get into franchising, but they often don't realize it also costs to stay in," says Stanley Bresler of Bresler's 33 Flavors Ice Cream. "Providing ongoing services to franchisees is a costly but important part of the franchise game."

Sometimes these services come in the form of motivation. Franchisors are often confronted with franchisees who reach a certain level of success and then just coast. "One of the biggest disadvantages of franchising is not being able to break through a franchisee's comfort level," says Robert Snelling of Snelling and Snelling. "If they were company employees, you could command them to act. But franchisees own the shop. They don't snap to attention very easily."

Snelling and Snelling overcomes franchisee apathy by showing owners the value of expanding their business. "Franchisees may make very comfortable livings off a single franchise, but if they had ten, they would gain real security for retirement or as an investment," Snelling notes.

LOSING THE LION'S SHARE OF THE PROFITS

There's money to be made in franchising. Just take your company's profits from last year and multiply by 10, by 100, by 1000, and you'll see how quickly the dollars can accumulate. But all that money won't be yours. The franchisee will retain the majority of the cash while you'll receive only a percentage. That's okay for many businesspeople. By their calculations, a small percentage of a great big pie is much better than a large percentage of a tiny pie! For other business owners, however, the thought of sharing the profit runs against their business sense. "If I developed the company and made it successful, why should I give away some of the profit?" businesspeople often ask. It's a good point. If you have the resources and desire to expand your business on your own, by all means do so and keep the booty for yourself. Neil Balter of California Closets is doing just that. After selling scores of franchises, Balter is turning to company-owned expansion for future development. "We will continue to franchise in marginal markets. But in major cities we are opening company-owned units because the company only gets five percent of a franchise. With company-owned stores, however, we keep all the profits of a unit that could gross one million dollars a year!"

Certainly, sharing profit is a primary concern to any businessperson. But in franchising, sharing the spoils is the price franchisors pay for fast growth. If that price is too high, then franchising is simply not for you.

THE NEGATIVES ARE OVER

So the negatives have been stated. Franchising is a regulated marketing system that demands both state and federal registrations and compliances. And as your business grows, you will open yourself to possible litigation and complicated relationships with franchisees. But perhaps the most important reality of franchising is that it's a communal system that diminishes your independence.

As a prudent businessperson, you should consider all these concerns before franchising your business. Certainly, an objective appraisal of the disadvantages will better prepare you for the future. But if you are among the intrepid businesspeople who wish someday to see their company's sign hang in every town in America, then these concerns are only minor barriers to overcome. And the second half of this book will show you exactly how that can be done.

CHAPTER 8

STRUCTURING YOUR FRANCHISE—AN OVERVIEW

Franchising your business is like waging war! To succeed, you'll need to assess troops, plot strategies, calculate risks, marshall resources, and prepare an attack. As in any combat you'll want brave and loyal soldiers, a corps of fierce, strong warriors ready to do battle for your cause.

How big a force? Certainly a fleet of ships stands a better chance than a few sailboats. A division brings better odds than a lone soldier. But remember, bigger doesn't necessarily mean better. History is full of the Davids who have slain the Goliaths. In the late 1500s, for example, the tiny British Navy, employing small and nimble sailing vessels, repelled the massive Spanish Armada.

But there's another way small can win and that's by growing. People forget that even the Western world's largest army started as a ragtag troop of colonists fighting for American independence.

So small can grow and small can win. If leadership is effective and implementation skillful, size is secondary to strategy and commitment.

Franchising is no different. it would be nice to wage your franchise battle fully armed with a staff of experienced franchise specialists. Who wouldn't choose to wade into battle alongside an in-house franchise attorney, a Harvard-trained chief financial officer, and veteran franchise sales and operations experts? But for the vast majority of us, that's simply unrealistic. Few companies possess the capital to hire such personnel, at least in their formative stages. Most successful franchises begin on a more modest level, with a core of skilled and resourceful individuals who are willing to learn new assignments and assume new responsibilities.

A similar principle holds true in developing franchise programs. Your initial franchise program could be founded on four-color brochures, extensive marketing programs, videotaped training and sales presentations, handsome newsletters, ongoing motivational and professional development programs, toll-free hot lines, workshops, seminars, and conferences. Certainly, all hold merit. But they also cost thousands of dollars to develop and implement. Moreover, many simply aren't necessary early in your franchise undertaking. Many big-ticket items can be deferred—shelved until your franchise starts to grow and generate revenue.

Other programs, however, simply cannot wait. They are too integral to franchise success to be delayed. What are the essential elements of a franchise program? Every new franchisor, no matter how big or small, rich or poor, needs a franchise marketing mechanism, training provisions, written policies and procedures, basic franchisee control methods, a legal program, and service capacity to resolve in-field problems.

It all sounds formidable. But remember, many of these basic components overlap. For example, franchise policies and procedures cover a portion of your legal documentation and also warrant a major section in your operating manual and your training program.

Needless to say, the size and scope of your initial franchise program depends on the energies, means, and talents you and others in your organization possess. What's critical, however, is that this program facilitates growth and expansion without crippling your primary profit center—your current business. Here is a brief introduction to the essentials of an effective franchise program, which serves as an overview to the remainder of the book.

ESTABLISHING THE FRANCHISE PRODUCT

First, you must define your product! Any effective marketing program starts with an initial evaluation of the item you intend to sell. And in franchising, that item is your business. What are the scope, dimensions, and extent of your franchised business? Is the franchise an exact replica of your current business or prototype? If not, how should it differ in appearance, operation, and profitability?

For example, to make their franchised units more manageable and profitable, some full-menu restaurants streamline their offerings before franchising. Likewise, a full-service computer store that programs, repairs, and sells personal and mainframe computers may only franchise its personal computer sales.

Thus, before franchising, you need to establish the boundaries of your franchised business. What will you sell? And, just as importantly, to whom?

Because the success of your franchise depends on the people who buy your product, you must analyze your customers by identifying their needs, wants, and desires.

And the evaluation continues with an objective appraisal of your competition and market position. What other businesses (both franchised and nonfranchised) offer products or services similar to yours? How do these businesses compare? Do they offer quick service? More convenience? A better product? Higher quality?

Don't forget image. Like beauty, image is difficult to describe but obvious when seen. Every business gives off a certain aura or persona that attracts or repels consumers. Furniture discounters, for instance, often use their warehouses as showrooms to connote rock-bottom prices. Franchised automotive repair centers cut windows in their garage walls to allow waiting customers to view the speed with which attendants service their cars.

Image is an intangible quality that bridges cold, hard facts, and speaks to customers in emotional terms. It's the human voice behind the corporate combine—proof that living, breathing human beings stand behind a product or service.

Image is critical in franchising, because the decision to buy a franchise is a tremendously emotional one. Prospects are searching for new and exciting life-styles. They follow their hearts as well as their brains, searching for opportunities that fit some ideal concept of themselves.

Thus, newly franchising companies need to project a single, cohesive image that speaks directly to the prospective franchisees. From the way employees answer telephones, to store layout and design, to sales literature and brochures, your company should express a friendly and consistent image.

But there is more to a product than position and image. Price represents a third critical factor. In franchising, price relates to consumers and franchisees alike. Just as smart shoppers compare price tags so, too, do prospective franchisees. And here, initial license fees and ongoing royalty payments represent the price. As a franchisor, you must decide how much to charge new franchisees as well as the cost of continuing the association.

LEGAL REQUIREMENTS

As discussed in the previous chapter, before you can sell your first franchise, you must comply with state and federal franchise regulations. You and your attorney must develop a disclosure document, contend with state registrations, and decide on the fundamental terms of your franchise agreement. The considerations include: site selection, training, advertising, the use of and adherence to operating manuals, accounting records and procedures, quality standards, termination, services provided, noncompete covenants, territories, fees, and royalties.

DEVELOPING FRANCHISEE POLICIES
FOR OPERATIONS

The control of franchisees is a major concern that many franchisors never fully address. In a typical business, the boss directs employees' actions by riding roughshod over day-to-day operations, constantly correcting and modifying behavior. But control is not as simple in franchising, where franchisors and franchisees are both independent businesspeople, separated by both distance and philosophies. Here, policies dictate franchisee behavior.

The policies you set should be comprehensive, covering such issues as:

Design and setup of the unit
Staffing and personnel issues
Inventory and equipment

Marketing and advertising

Customer relations

Sources of supply

Grand openings

The extent of your services

Special services offered to struggling franchisees

Pricing recommendations

Assuring legal and contractual compliance

Maintenance and upkeep of the franchised unit

OPERATING MANUALS

Once you have defined your franchise product, complied with legal requirements, and written basic policies on the operation of the franchised unit, your operating manual is two-thirds complete! Operating manuals take general policies and guidelines and further refine them into easy-to-follow steps. Whereas policies determine a range of behavior, operating manuals spell out specific acts franchisees should perform in the operation, promotion, and advancement of their businesses.

For example, an operations manual tells franchisees how to order, receive, store, account for, and use inventory. It explains how to motivate, manage, attract, and retain personnel. It describes the steps involved in advertising, promotion, and public relations.

Operations manuals represent the master plan by which franchisees synchronize their operations. They are a fundamental and integral component of any franchise program.

SALES, MARKETING, AND PUBLIC RELATIONS

More than any other factor, sales determine the success of your franchise program. Fail to find and win prospects and you fail in your primary objective—to grow big.

The first step in sales is building awareness, and advertising is a logical start. Some franchisors advertise in the business opportunity section of regional and national newspapers. Others use national business magazines such as *Entrepreneur, Inc, Success,* and *Venture.* No matter how modest your budget, you'll need to set some funds aside for planning an advertising campaign and buying ad space or time.

And there are other ways to build awareness. Public relations is the art of gaining something for nothing. By placing telephone calls to newspapers, by writing and distributing news releases, by meeting with reporters and writers, franchisors often win exposure in local, regional, and national media that serves as an invaluable source of *free* lead generation.

Then, once you catch the public's eye, you'll need to respond to their interest. Most franchisors send prospects information packets or sales brochures. The effectiveness of each is debatable. Rarely are sales consummated on the basis of indirect communication. But franchisors need some method of building relationships with prospects, especially if they live at a distance, and sales brochures often serve this purpose.

More imperative, however, is personal contact. Once a prospect shows interest in your franchise, you'll need to reach out and personally cement a friendly working relationship. Sometimes it's done over the telephone. Sometimes a personalized letter suffices. Other times a face-to-face meeting is called for. Whichever method suits you, know now that a sales response system is imperative for franchise success.

You'll also need to develop a sales presentation and program. Prospective franchisees expect and deserve a full dog-and-pony show. They will want as much information as possible before making a decision. The sales meeting is crucial in alleviating a prospect's fears and anxieties and often sets the stage for the all-important close.

BUILDING A TRAINING PROGRAM

Training serves two purposes in franchising. First, it supplies you with talented and competent franchisees. Second, it sells franchises. Prospective franchisees are business neophytes. Their greatest fears concern their abilities to learn to operate a new business effectively and efficiently. Training programs pacify these fears. "I wouldn't worry about ordering inventory just yet," franchisors tell prospects. "We cover that thoroughly in our ten-day training program."

How do new franchisors train early franchisees? Some hire professional trainers to develop in-depth and comprehensive instructional courses. Most franchisors, however, start by offering one-on-one instruction in the home office using staff on hand. This is perfectly acceptable, if new franchisees gain the knowledge they need to succeed.

The subjects your training program should cover depend on the needs of your franchisees. However, every franchisee training program should include a basic introduction to customer relations, sales, consumer advertising, the product, personnel management, accounting and miscellaneous paperwork, sources of supply, and basic inventory management.

ESTABLISHING A SERVICE CENTER

Once your franchisees are in the field, you need to service them. In the beginning, much of this service will come in the form of advice and guidance. For efficiency and effectiveness, new franchisors need to systematize the response procedure, creating a channel through which problems and inquiries can be funneled quickly and appropriately. Sometimes this entails designating one person to field minor, incoming messages and advance them to appropriate personnel for resolution. Larger, more difficult problems, however, often require more thorough and thoughtful evaluations. Here, on-site visits and in-depth analyses are often the only means of unraveling latent, potentially disastrous dilemmas. New franchisors must be prepared to travel to the scene of the problem, examine the difficulties, and suggest possible remedies.

Franchisees don't expect brilliant solutions to every problem. They do, however, demand an immediate helping hand in return for the hefty sum they pay in fees and royalties. Keep your end of the bargain by developing an in-house mechanism that triggers the best and quickest answers possible.

THE PREREQUISITES

So these are the basic elements of a franchise program. A quick review shows you need to define your product—its position, price, and image

—set policies and procedures, write an operations manual, develop a sales and marketing program, create a training program, and establish an in-house service center.

Sound difficult? Well, it is and it isn't. What some companies find troublesome, others find simple. Your company may delight in teaching new franchisees the specifics of your business. Then again, it may find the task tedious and unrewarding.

Whether your franchise development program includes all or just some of the elements laid out in this chapter is less important than whether it properly meets the needs of franchisees. Structuring that program depends on learning the intricacies of franchising. Chapter 9 begins that process.

DEFINING YOUR FRANCHISE OFFERING: SOME BASIC ELEMENTS

The Caterpillar and Alice looked at each other for some time in silence:
at last the Caterpillar addressed her in a languid, sleepy voice.
"Who are you?" said the Caterpillar. Alice replied,
rather shyly, "I–I hardly know, sir, just at present—at
least I knew who I was when I got up this morning, but I
think I must have changed several times since then."
—Alice in Wonderland
Lewis Carroll

Unfortunately, the bewilderment expressed by Alice in her escapades through the looking glass is the same confusion many businesspeople communicate when they describe their company's goals and objectives. Sure, they can offer generalities regarding their products or services. But when pressed to define their market, image, or position, many rely on nebulous terms that show a lack of serious analysis.

"Who is your competition?" I often ask business owners. "A couple of places in the neighborhood," is a usual reply.

"Is their product better than yours?" I continue.

"No, ours is much better," is the response.

"How is it better?"

"It's just better."

And so it goes with many successful businesspeople. Their businesses prosper, yet they haven't taken the time to analyze how their business fits a particular market niche.

Why the confusion? Well, many businesspeople know more than they articulate. Entrepreneurs often are so intimately linked with their operations that they lose the ability to objectively describe their business decision-making processes.

For example, I once asked a restaurant owner why he chose to decorate his restaurant in pastel colors and play novelty tunes from cartoons and movies of the 1930s and 1940s. His response was a limp, "It seemed to fit the business." But behind this inadequate explanation rested a more profound answer.

In actuality, the business owner understood from experience that his restaurant attracted families with small children. The pastels added to the cheery environment, and the music set an easygoing atmosphere. Even though the business owner found it difficult to describe the rationale behind his decisions, an intuitive understanding of the restaurant, its image, and its customers led him to create a product that meshed well with the market.

But not all entrepreneurs are as instinctive as the restaurant owner. A more common explanation for lack of market knowledge is simple ignorance. Entrepreneurs start businesses to serve particular markets. Over a period of time, the markets change and evolve. To keep pace, the businesses also adjust and shift. After a few years of turbulence, the businesses end up much like Alice in Wonderland, knowing who they were this morning but not who they are this afternoon.

DEFINING IMAGE AND MARKET POSITION

"Many times a business will fall into a market and never take time to analyze its customers," says Burton Brodo, associate director at the University of

Pennsylvania's Wharton School of Business. Brodo feels this is a common occurrence in franchising, where a business becomes successful on the local level and then must better define itself in preparation for growth.

"At this juncture, a company can undertake postintroduction research," Brodo states. This research doesn't have to be expensive. It can consist of a simple questionnaire you have prepared and distributed in your place of business with the purpose of constructing a consumer profile.

To be effective, the questionnaire should include both general and specific inquiries. For example, questions regarding age, sex, marital status, number of children, income level, home size and location, and type of job are examples of the specific information you should gather.

You also want to discover the motivating forces behind your customers' purchasing decisions. Why do they buy your product or service? What is the most important attribute of your product or service? How does your product or service compare to the competition's? Who do your customers consider to be your competition? These subjective questions yield deep insight into how your product relates to the consumers' needs and wants.

"Most entrepreneurs don't have the money for in-depth, costly market research," Brodo says. "But properly developed and analyzed questionnaires often give the business owner a clear idea of his customer and market."

Once research is complete, you must further define your marketing plan and company image—two closely related business tools. A marketing plan represents the master blueprint by which you sell your product or service. It uses much of the research you gained in the questionnaire to construct a single path to reaching the consumer. Image flows from your marketing plan and provides focus and cohesion—a single voice by which the consumer recognizes your product or service.

Development of an image begins by first deciding basic marketing questions such as: Who is your market or market segments? How do you reach these people? How do your customers behave? What do they expect? Will they accept your product or service? Will they buy into your company's concept?

Once these issues are resolved, you must synchronize other aspects of your business accordingly. Some things to evaluate include:

1. *Merchandise Strategy*—What type of products or services do you sell? What is the price of your merchandise? What is its primary attribute?

Quality? Selection? Service? Convenience? How do you communicate these attributes?

2. *Physical facilities*—What image does the physical environment of your store project? How well does store layout and design appeal to your target market? Does your storefront, logo, and signage reflect your image? Is your location accessible? Should it be accessible?

3. *Advertising and Promotion*—What is your promotional strategy? Ad strategy? What media are you using? What is the message? Is the message expressed or implied?

In all these considerations, your primary goal is consistency. "Nothing destroys a well-conceived image more quickly than inconsistency," warns Brodo. "Your advertising should reflect the true value of your product or service. Your merchandising strategy and physical facility should fit the target market." If not, Brodo believes, consumers lapse into cognitive dissonance—a state of disappointed expectations where consumers' emotional associations are destroyed by their conscious evaluation of your business. The phenomenon occurs when customers' brains contradict their hearts—when the fantasy of happy, helpful salespeople collides with the reality of insensitive, uncaring employees. Such inconsistencies guarantee quick alienation of your customer. Beware!

Once your market is defined and your company's image established, market position is the next major consideration. Here, franchise entrepreneurs must evaluate their company's standing relative to competitors—both franchised and nonfranchised.

Where can you find information regarding the enemy? For nonfranchising competitors, the Small Business Association and the Department of Commerce can supply you with lists of companies by industry. Likewise, the annual reports of public companies (available upon request) and articles in trade journals often provide a wealth of information on the performance and future plans of other companies.

For information on competing franchises, the International Franchise Association provides lists of member companies. The Department of Commerce's *Franchise Opportunities Handbook* and the Info Press's *Franchise Annual* are other good sources. Likewise, *Entrepreneur, Money, Success,*

Franchise, Venture, and *Income Opportunities* magazines run regular features concerning the country's top franchise companies.

Perhaps your best resources are your competitors. You can gain valuable information by writing a brief note to your competitors requesting sales literature. These inquiries are usually answered with franchise brochures and other materials complete with valuable data regarding your competitors' operations.

After identifying other companies in your industry, you must determine how your business compares. One simple method uses a 2-axis diagram to graphically represent the market. For this example, consider the franchised submarine sandwich market. On the horizontal axis, we'll plot the total investment costs of the franchise (a vital consideration to franchisees). On the vertical axis, we'll plot the number of franchised units (a supposed indicator of the franchise's health). That market would appear as follows:

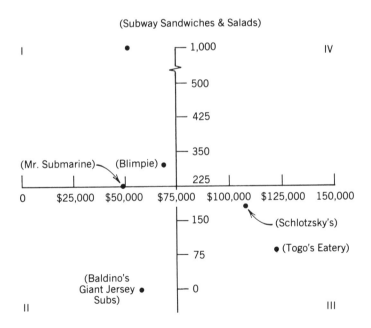

From the diagram, you can see that the market for submarine sandwich franchises varies greatly according to costs and number of units. Quadrant I shows Subway Sandwiches & Salads to be the clear market leader with more than 1000 units—more than four times the number of their nearest competitor—and total investment of about $45,000. In that same price range, Blimpie and Mr. Submarine own about 260 and 220 units, respectively. On the other end of the scale in quadrant III, Togo's Eatery and Schlotzsky's are positioned in the high-cost end of the market with total investment costs of more than $100,000, yet each with fewer than 200 units. It's probably no coincidence that quadrant IV (high costs, many units) remains vacant.

Small submarine sandwich entrepreneurs seeking to compare their operations to other franchise companies need only place their businesses along the horizontal and vertical axes to gain a quick overview of how they stack up against the competition.

But the evaluation need not end there. Other graphs could be constructed for a myriad of variables, including royalties, services, products, advertising, promotion, geography, convenience, and image. Such exercises provide easy insights into the markets businesspeople compete in every day.

ESTABLISHING A PRICE: SETTING INITIAL FEES

In defining any product, price is the critical attribute. Set the price too high, and you lose sales. Set it too low, and you forfeit profit, and discount the perceived value of your product. In franchising, you face similar risks. For a new entrant, a $40,000 initial fee significantly limits the pool of prospects. On the other hand, a $500 initial fee leaves no money to cover the costs of franchising. It also raises serious questions as to the validity of your franchise opportunity.

How much should you charge for the initial fee? There are two schools of thought. The first assumes that to provide the quality of services franchisees require to succeed, initial fees and franchisor profits need to be high. Stained Glass Overlay, which charges $30,000 in initial fees, exemplifies this approach and openly admits the importance of these revenues.

Conversely, The Athlete's Foot, based in Atlanta, attributes its success to a modest initial fee ($7500). "The Athlete's Foot believes that to grow big and, hopefully, rich in franchising we need a program funded through the royalties of successful franchisees and not from the sale of franchises," says Paul Modzelewski, director of franchise sales for the company. "Although the fee should convey the perceived value of the opportunity, it should not hamstring franchisees for working capital. Also, startup costs are significant in The Athlete's Foot. The additional burden of a high initial fee could discourage many of our potential franchisees."

How do franchisors set initial licensing fees? Although the exact figure you set depends on the nature of your business, there are criteria to help show the way. First, you should remember that an initial fee theoretically includes payment for the right to do business under the franchisor's trademark and business system. But in the real world of profit and loss, the fee also should bear some relationship to the direct costs of franchising your business, as well as establishing the individual franchised unit. As a franchisor, you need to determine the expenses of marketing your opportunity and paying commissioned salespeople. These costs serve as a floor above which initial fees can be set.

But don't expect early franchisees to pay all overhead costs associated with the startup of your franchise. Remember, average marginal costs of opening franchised units decline as you amortize fixed startup costs over more and more units. In other words, your $60,000 initial investment in legal and marketing fees is immense if charged solely against your first franchisee. But those same expenses spread over 10 franchises equal only $6000 per unit, and over 100 units the costs drop to $600 per store.

The next criteria in setting initial fees is competition. Logically, you would not want to charge $25,000 when other franchisors in your industry require only a $10,000 initial fee. Without a proven track record, it's extremely risky to set your fee higher than or even equal to established names in the industry. To compensate, many new franchisors undervalue themselves early in the game. Then, as interest builds and success grows, they increase their fees according to demand. There's real merit in this strategy, if not taken to an extreme, thereby reducing the value of your franchise opportunity.

Finally, profit plays a part in setting initial fees. All businesspeople have the right to earn a return on their investment. Franchising is no different. If you can turn a profit selling franchises and still remain competitive in your industry, by all means do so! Regardless of which option you choose, don't expect to live off franchise sales. Ongoing royalties are the true measure of a franchise company's health.

COLLECTING INITIAL FEES: WHEN, WHERE, AND HOW

Some franchisors choose to collect initial fees by categories according to services rendered. They charge separately for training, marketing, advertising, and site selection. In one instance, I saw a franchisor charge a franchisee for the commission paid to its own salesperson on the sale! Breaking out costs may appear to provide franchisees with a comforting accounting of their investment. In reality, it's a shell game that creates more problems than solutions.

Franchisees want and ought to receive services under the umbrella of a single fee. They don't expect to pay separately for marketing, advice, sales, and so on. Training presents a good example. To tell franchisees that you intend to provide a complete program for business success and then charge a separate fee for a most elemental component of that success is incongruous and problematic. Franchisees purchase an intangible bundle of rights. For simplicity, you should package this bundle in simplest terms, which is a single fee that covers most reasonable expenses.

But there are exceptions to the rule. As a franchisor, anytime you contract with a third party to provide franchisees with needed services, you're entitled to compensation for those costs. Take, for example, advertising and promotion costs for a grand opening. These two integral components of any new business venture call for experienced management. Consequently, many franchisors contract with local advertising agencies directly, ensuring the effective coordination of media purchases and public relations. Here, an additional charge to the franchisee is easily justifiable, because the franchisor is incurring expenses to perform a task outside the bounds of the usual franchisee/franchisor relationship.

How do franchisors collect fees? Some ask for the full amount up-front upon signing the franchise agreement. However, to entice more prospects, other franchisors break the payments into portions—say 50 percent down and 50 percent at the time of training.

Because some franchise deals are contingent upon site selection and location, payment arrangements also can involve a nonrefundable consultation fee, which can be credited toward the initial license fee. Here, a franchisor actively works to find a location for a prospect, and then covers out-of-pocket expenses by charging a few thousand dollars regardless of whether the search is successful. This arrangement is perfectly ethical and becoming more common within franchising.

Whichever fee collection structure you implement, always follow one cardinal rule: Never allow franchisees to open until initial fees are paid or financed in full. Your trademark is an extremely valuable asset that requires constant vigilance. Granting free use reduces its value and could upset other franchisees who paid dearly for their right to use it. Moreover, once franchisees open, it's not always easy to make them pay this debt. You could get stuck holding an empty bag while they fill their wallets using your business program.

DEVELOPMENT OF A ROYALTY STRUCTURE

The dictionary definition of royalty is a payment made to an inventor for each item sold. In a way, franchise royalties can be viewed in the same manner. The weekly or monthly royalty fees franchisees pay are compensation for sales made from the franchise invention, which is the trademark and business program the franchisor has developed. Royalty payments, minus the cost of services provided, also comprise the profits franchisors earn for efforts and the capital risked during the start up, expansion, and operation of the franchise.

These franchisee payments can be quite generous. Consider a small franchise with six units grossing $300,000 apiece and paying a 5-percent royalty. After one year, the franchisor will have earned $90,000—and that's exclusive of initial license fees. The numbers climb dramatically as the franchise grows. The same franchise with 50 stores, for example, will receive royalties of $750,000; 100 stores would generate $1.5 million in a year! And these calculations don't assume increasing sales. A modest 5-percent increase per unit yields an extra $75,000 for the 100-store franchisor.

Do all franchises use a percentage of gross sales to determine royalty payments? No. Some set flat fees. And although these fees appear less cumbersome and more viable to administer, they contradict a basic precept of franchising.

To understand, you first must realize that franchisors implicitly promise to provide expanded services as chains grow and develop. As your company expands into regional and national markets, advertising, marketing, and product research and development efforts should broaden to support more ambitious strategies. The very nature of percentage royalties provides funds for these programs by increasing total payments to the franchisor proportionally with system-wide sales.

However, flat fees offer no such mechanism. A franchisee pays the same amount regardless of whether he or she grosses $100,000, $200,000, $300,000, $400,000, or $500,000. The sum you receive in royalties remains static. Flat fees provide little incentive for the franchisor to finance services franchisees need to grow.

So why are flat fees used? Supposedly because they appeal to prospective franchisees. "We don't penalize your success," franchisors tell prospects. "You pay us the same amount no matter how big you grow." They also eliminate many reporting and financial burdens, while providing the franchisor with predictable income.

But in counseling prospective franchisees, I strongly warn against accepting flat fee arrangements because they undermine the franchisor's interest in seeing franchisees grow and prosper. Under flat fees, the franchisor's revenue is fixed. Its only incentive to make more money is to open more franchises, not to provide franchisees the marketing know-how they need to increase sales. Don't send prospects this message. Establish a percentage royalty that links their growth with your success.

SETTING ROYALTIES

The first step in establishing royalty fees is to determine the relative profitability of your business. If profit margins are low, high royalties may shatter the fragile operating health of your franchisee. If margins are high, however, a greater royalty may be warranted.

Typically, franchise royalties range from three percent to 10 percent of gross sales. One notable exception on the high side is Jazzercise, with a 30-percent royalty—one of the highest in all of franchising. There is an obvious danger in this extreme. Because royalties are paid on gross sales, a 30-percent interest makes the franchisor a full partner in the business. For example, a business that grosses $100,000 a year and pays 30 percent or $30,000 in royalties, still must cover operating expenses, which could easily run 40 percent, or $40,000. The franchisee's remaining $30,000 equals the franchisor's interest in the business. Such arrangements tend to discourage talented, top-notch prospects from joining your franchise and can also breed discontent among present franchisees. (A Jazzercise spokesperson claimed the average franchisee leaves the chain after five years, a relatively short franchise lifespan).

Sometimes, however, high royalties mask increased or innovative services. For example, Pilot Air Freight charges franchisees a 12 percent royalty fee. The relatively high rate helps finance an innovative billing program that has the home office front each franchisee a weekly income based on the franchise's actual business transactions. In essence, Pilot's Lima, Pennsylvania office operates as a bank, advancing franchisees money on bills that have yet to be paid by their customers. "The system's great advantage is that it yields an immediate cash flow for franchisees," says company president John Edwards. "At the end of their first week, franchisees get paid for their efforts. They don't have to wait until bills are collected."

At the other end of the spectrum, some franchisors choose to set low royalties (one or two percent of sales), and there's nothing intrinsically wrong with this approach. However, in my own practice, I advise prospective franchisees to carefully investigate franchises with suspiciously low royalties. Remember, bona fide franchisors live and make their profits off royalties. If this income stream is too low, franchisees must question (1) whether the franchisor will earn enough royalty revenue to provide the promised services, and (2) whether the franchisor is using cut-rate royalties as a sales come-on to make profits off excessive license fees.

Here is an anonymous but reprehensible example. A prospective franchisee once asked me to evaluate a retail franchise that charged an initial license fee of $35,000 and royalties of only 1.5 percent. Included in the fee was a long list of general advertising and promotional services, as well as a limited opening inventory. The franchisor further enticed prospects by flaunting its low royalty as an advantage few of its competitors offered.

After careful examination, however, it became obvious that the franchisor overvalued the worth of its marketing services (which were comprised mostly of banners, posters, flyers, and lapel buttons), and its inventory (which was being supplied well above its cost). Thus, the franchisor could afford to sacrifice royalties because it made money off the franchise sale. Moreover, the franchisor shrewdly worded its agreement so that royalties could be increased after three years, thus guaranteeing itself the best of both worlds. If the franchisee failed, the company didn't care because it had its money. If the franchisee succeeded (despite the minimal marketing services), the company would simply increase its cut in the franchisee's prosperity.

How should you set your royalty? Because an initial mistake in setting royalties could significantly impair your company's future income, the calculation proves exceedingly important. First, check your competition and the percentage they take. Unless you offer expanded services, try to be competitive—don't offer a royalty that exceeds the established names in the industry. But be cautious not to copy your competition to the point of duplicating their mistakes. Instead, the level of your royalties must depend on the future financial goals and projections of your company. And here, no one can help more than an attorney or accountant familiar with your past and present operating performance.

Yet you may not have to set any royalties, per se. Instead, you may make money solely from profit earned off products sold to franchisees if you operate a product franchise. Under product franchising, the name of the business and the product are identical, and the consumer perceives them to be the same (see Chapter 2 for a full discussion).

Product franchising is playing a less important role in the U.S. economy as the number of such arrangements decreases, according to the Department of Commerce. For example, Neal's Cookies, a 22-unit cookie, muffin, and brownie chain, started as a product franchise in 1984. "Neal's original intent was to make money off the batter sold to franchisees," says Virginia Wise, director of marketing for the Houston-based franchise. "But after our first year, the company found that many franchisees resented buying product from the company only. So we instituted a 5-percent royalty for new franchisees to conform with traditional business format franchising, and to create a partnership that provided incentive for both the franchisees and franchisor to work toward mutual growth and development." The company also liberalized its product purchase requirements. Today it still has franchisees that abide by the original contract of buying batter and paying no royalties.

And although product franchising is losing favor, it does offer one major advantage: flexibility. Unlike royalties, which are set by contract, products are priced according to current market conditions. Thus, product franchisors can more easily adjust the level of income (and profit) they receive from franchisees.

ESTABLISHING ADVERTISING ROYALTIES AND PROGRAMS

Establishing advertising royalties is a seemingly no-win proposition. Commit your company to a large-scale, consumer advertising program and you automatically increase royalties, which tends to alienate prospective franchisees. On the other hand, establish a modest advertising program and you deprive your franchisees of the growth and profits that advertising generates.

Ad campaigns harbor similar problems. No ad agency can guarantee results. They sell ideas, creativity, and hunches—not concrete solutions. Advertising represents a plunge into the unknown, one of your business's biggest gambles. To play the game, you spend your money, spin the wheel, and hope the ball falls on your number. Sometimes it does. Other times it ricochets. For those footing the bill, it's an intensely anxious, pray-as-you-pay experience.

What type of advertising programs work in franchising? The most basic arrangement is a centralized program, administered by the home office. Here, the franchisor collects a separate advertising royalty from franchisees and wields near total control over creative and strategic development and implementation of the program. Many franchisors believe the system promotes uniformity of concept and professionalism in presentation.

"We collect the advertising money because leaving it to a franchisee or group of franchisees can be fatal," says Gary Goranson, of Tidy Car. "Each franchisee will undertake a unique ad campaign that simply does not work for the system as a whole." Goranson recalls a group of Texas franchisees who, after listening to a local advertising agency, invested their entire budget in producing and running a single advertisement during an episode of the television show *Dallas*. "No single ad is powerful enough to stand on its own. Ad agencies are often too involved with this type of hocus-pocus—to the detriment of sincere franchisees."

How has Goranson structured Tidy Car's consumer advertising? "I believe you have to achieve a certain amount of market penetration to be successful," he states. "In our case, the ad program is designed to achieve five-percent penetration of the market in any area where we have franchisees. To finance that extensive a program, we collect one thousand dollars a week from each franchisee, ninety percent of which goes back into their respective market area."

But centralized advertising also presents major drawbacks. In concentrating decision making at the home office, you deprive franchisees of an important feeling of participation and deny yourself their valuable input. As the ears and eyes of the company, franchisees often possess the insight you need to make strategic marketing and advertising decisions. Isolating them can undermine your own effectiveness.

Moreover, centralization forces franchisors into the costly necessity of developing and administering advertising programs for differing locations—an unwieldy assignment for veteran franchisors and a nearly impossible task for inexperienced ones.

To circumvent these problems, franchisors often establish ad programs that centralize creative development, but leave campaign implementation to individual franchisees or groups of franchisees. The home office produces advertising copy and radio and television commercials, financed through a modest monthly fee of typically between $50 and $300. Franchisees then agree to spend a percentage of gross receipts to place these materials through local ad agencies or directly with the appropriate media.

AAMCO uses a variation of this approach with great success. In the company's franchise agreement, it locks franchisees into paying a proportionate share of national creative advertising in accordance with a formula developed by a committee of company and franchisee representatives. These payments cover the company's expense of creating print and broadcast advertisements, as well as administering the program.

In addition, the company commits franchisees to spend a percentage of gross receipts on local advertising, often in conjunction with other AAMCO franchisees in the same or adjoining areas.

The establishment of a national creative program allows franchisors to retain control and consistency over critical input. It also frees franchisors from the complex and costly chores of buying print space and broadcast time in a variety of disparate markets.

In addition to creative programs, franchisors often establish advertising pools (or cooperatives) among franchisees to promote regional advertising efforts. In pool arrangements, the advertising royalties that once flowed to the franchisor now pass directly to regional committees comprised of company and franchisee representatives. These committees administer the funds and tend to regional advertising needs.

For the franchisor, advertising pools maximize the benefits of decentralization and franchisee involvement in local decision-making. They also liberate franchisors from many of the more tedious and costly chores of advertising. However, problems still arise.

By their very nature, advertising pools breed conflict by mixing together franchisees who don't always share the same advertising goals or objectives. The advertising needs of a successful, multiunit franchisee, for example, differ greatly from those of a new franchisee battling to stay afloat. Likewise, the metropolitan newspaper ads that pull shoppers for your franchisee at Broad and Main Streets may prove less effective for suburban locations, where customers read local newspapers instead.

As a franchisor, you should be aware of these problems and avoid them through careful establishment of pool territories. Decide what franchisees join what pools. For instance, does your California franchisee in Riverside join with franchisees 20 miles north in San Bernardino or 40 miles west in Los Angeles? Or does Riverside and its immediate vicinity constitute its own pool? In Maryland, should franchisees in Annapolis advertise with Baltimore franchisees during Oriole games or with Washington franchisees during Redskin games?

And what about power within the pool? Should each franchisee get one vote or should franchisees be represented according to the number of units they own? Likewise, how will the pool be managed? By majority vote? By two-thirds' vote?

How will the pool be financed? Will contributions be based on gross receipts? Should every franchisee make an equal contribution? Can the pool vote to increase or decrease rates and contributions? Will allowances be made for franchisees who need or want to supplement the pool's efforts with advertising in peripheral media?

Ad pools should be established with an eye for problem prevention. The trick is to identify as many contingencies as possible and then provide for them in your franchise documentation. However, new franchisors rarely foresee the type or scope of conflicts ad pools create. Here, it's wise to deal with a competent franchise attorney who has developed procedures and contracts for other advertising pools. The experience he or she brings to this area will save you plenty in hassle and heartaches in years to come.

In sum, establishing advertising programs is a difficult but necessary part of successful franchising. Whichever system you choose—centralized, decentralized, national creative, pool, or any variation thereof—the program should be developed to:

1. Ensure substantial franchisor control of the company's image and advertising message.
2. Provide some mechanism for franchisee input.
3. Use ad dollars cost effectively.
4. Reach your target market through the best available media.

OTHER FEES

Many businesspeople wrongly believe that the only fees involved with franchising are initial fees, royalties, and advertising expenses. In actuality, there are other fees, payments, and transfers that a franchisor can impose on franchisees.

Perhaps the most controversial of these are security deposits. In franchising, security deposits are used to ensure that monies owed the franchisor are paid by franchisees. They can be collected up-front with the payment of the initial license fee or as a small percentage of early sales or any combination of the two methods.

Many franchisors shun security deposits, believing they cast an unfavorable first impression on the franchisor/franchisee relationship. To some degree, this is a valid point. Asking for a security deposit suggests a lack of confidence in the franchisee's intentions to pay his or her fair share.

But there is another side to the coin. Franchisors hold a legitimate interest in protecting their revenue stream. And rightly or wrongly, nothing better guarantees the stream's continued flow than the threat of some financial loss. In this respect, security deposits often provide important, if only psychological, leverage in the struggle to keep franchisees current in their payments.

Finally, security deposits can serve to reimburse franchisors for costs, fees, judgments, or liabilities incurred relating to franchisees' operation of their businesses or for actions taken to enforce franchise agreements. For example, security deposits can cover a franchisor's costs in defending liability claims brought against the company by a customer of the franchisee. They also can finance the legal costs of actions taken against the franchisee for breach of contract.

So although security deposits seem an unnecessary evil, they serve a real function in protecting the franchisor's financial and legal interests.

Warranty payments represent another fee franchisors often impose. For many franchise companies, chainwide warranties are vital to their image, as well as to attracting today's highly mobile consumers. As most consumers know, a major advantage to servicing your car at a Midas Muffler franchise in Akron is that its warranty is backed by Midas shops nationwide. The same principle holds true in other automotive aftermarkets, and, to a lesser degree, in the return policies at clothing, furniture, and similar retail businesses. And many other companies are experimenting with nontraditional warranties. For example, Snelling and Snelling, the employment agency franchise, offers a guarantee on employees who quit within the first 100 days of a new assignment.

How are warranties financed? Through a variety of methods, but typically using intra-network transfers and payments. In other words, the Midas shop owner in Akron needs to compensate other franchisees that honor the guarantee.

To expedite these transfers, some franchisors establish procedures for franchisees to contribute monies to a warranty program. Others impose no up-front contributions, but later, when reasonable claims surface against a

NUGGET #11

Should a Franchisor Provide Financing?

Many do, for at least part of the initial license fee. If you can afford such an arrangement, it usually works to close more deals. For the balance of a franchisee's initial investment, however, franchisors often work with banks and other financial institutions. For instance, a franchisor may offer to finance a franchisee's investment of $80,000 and then sell the obligation to a bank for less than face value (say $72,000). Of course, the franchisor could then be held accountable if the franchisee defaults, so these relationships need to be carefully structured.

Alternatively, a franchisor may work directly with a financial institution to help franchisees obtain financing. "Initially, we meet with the franchisor and decide whether their concept is sound and the management is effective," says Donna Feinhandler, vice-president of Franchise Capital Corporation, a firm located in Van Nuys, California, which is dedicated to providing franchisees financing through limited partnerships. "If we satisfy ourselves as to the franchisor's financial stability and prospects for continued success, we then work to provide its qualified franchisees with financing."

When evaluating individual franchisees, Feinhandler says her firm evaluates three critical criteria. "First, we look at the franchisee's financial strength, evaluating net worth, liquidity, and other important financial measures. Second, we consider the franchisee's past experience to see if he or she possesses a successful business history and work experience in a related industry. Third, we carefully analyze site selection to determine whether we believe the franchisee can succeed in the chosen location."

How can franchisors help their franchisees during this selection process? By providing prospective franchisees with detailed business plans that show projected cash flows, sales revenues, costs, and break-evens, as well as by helping franchisees select appropriate locations for their businesses.

Finally, Feinhandler warns that some financing companies may show less interest in working with new franchisors because of their relative inexperience. However, she encourages rookie franchisors to contact financing companies to investigate options. "You never know how receptive a financing company will be until you inquire," she says. "What you may consider a negative in your business, we may consider a positive."

particular franchisee, they mandate and supervise the transfer of funds to cover the cost of repair and replacement.

Two other typical fees are transfer and renewal fees. Transfer fees are the monies franchisees pay the franchisor for the right to sell the business to an agreed-upon party. Renewal fees are a bit more complicated and form part of the next section's discussion.

TERM AND RENEWAL OF THE FRANCHISE

Franchise terms can be granted for nearly any length of time, from one year to 10 years, to 30 years. However, the term of most franchise agreements spans 5, 10, 15 or 20 years. Setting the term for your company requires the finesse of a chainsaw juggler to avoid the lethal consequences of failing to balance many opposing forces that often enter into the decision.

From the franchisee's perspective, long-term contracts provide better investment protection by limiting the franchisor's ability to reclaim trademarks and operating systems. They also permit the franchisee to benefit from the long-term appreciation that growing businesses experience.

For franchisors, lengthy contracts prove more problematic. On the one hand, long-term agreements promote stability within the company and reduce the franchisor's risk of losing locations or units when franchisees leave the system. On the other hand, they reduce flexibility by limiting how often franchisors can alter contract terms, increase fees, or demand that franchisees upgrade physical facilities and operational programs.

In determining the exact length of the agreement, franchisors need to choose periods that address franchisee concerns and still provide ample stability with maximum flexibility in system operation and design.

Along with contract length, renewal terms should be decided early in your franchise development process in order to avoid problems that arise once an agreement has expired. In the typical arrangement, franchisors condition renewal upon the franchisees' compliance with the contract and past operating record, particularly payment of royalties. But there are other concerns. For example, upon expiration of your agreement, will you allow franchisees to simply renew their present contracts or must they sign new contracts that reflect the business's then-current standards? This seems a minor point; however, imposing additional fees and requiring upgrading or modernization often angers franchisees who don't plan on these expenses.

Finally, you must determine whether you'll charge a renewal fee, and if so, what the fee will be. Some franchisors set the renewal fee equal to the then-current initial license fee. Others make it only a percentage—say 25 percent—of the initial fee. Still others waive the renewal fee altogether.

In setting your renewal fee, always remember that franchisees strongly resent paying twice for something they have spent the last 10 years building. Requiring substantial renewal fees may win franchisors quick cash and long-term animosity.

FRANCHISEES' INITIAL INVESTMENT

Simply defined, initial investment represents the total cost of your franchise opportunity. It's the bottom line your franchisees must pay to open the business and keep it operating until profits start flowing. Initial investment is also a basic and critical determinant of franchise success. To attract prospects, your initial investment must be competitive with other franchise opportunities in your industry. Likewise, to guarantee successful franchisees, your initial investment must give franchisees a fair estimation of the capital they need to start the business. Undercapitalization is the leading cause of business failure in America, according to the Department of Commerce. A realistic appraisal of total costs assures your franchisees of having the cash to pay their bills. It also limits your legal liability.

Courts frown on franchisors who understate total investment costs in an attempt to attract franchise prospects. You're responsible for the accuracy of the information franchisees use to make enlightened decisions. Misrepresentations of this information opens you to serious liability in case of franchisee failure.

Determining initial investment requires careful analysis of the costs inherent to your business, as well as those specific to the franchised unit. Clearly, many expenses you currently incur in the day-to-day operation of your business will similarly affect franchisees. Inventory, labor, equipment, supplies, rent, utilities, and telephone service are all generic business expenses that you could estimate for franchisees by using records from your current operation.

However, in addition, you need to estimate costs unique to franchised units. For instance, the franchisee may have to pay an architect to adapt standard plans to a specific location, as well as contractors to upgrade physical facilities. Other franchisee expenses may include complying with zoning and other local ordinances, purchasing insurance, leaving deposits on utilities and telephones, preparing signage, developing and implementing grand-opening promotions, retaining an accountant or attorney, acquiring *Yellow Pages* advertisements, printing business cards and stationery, and placing employment advertising. For the most part, franchisors have little trouble estimating these tangible, easily definable expenses. However, inaccuracies are far more common in assessing one final, but critical cost of franchising—working capital.

In traditional accounting, working capital is defined as total current assets (cash, inventory, and accounts receivables) minus total current liabilities (accounts payable, income tax payable, and short-term notes payable). In other words, it's a measure of a company's short-term health.

In franchising, working capital refers to the amount of money franchisees need on hand to support the business and themselves until the franchised operation turns a profit. It's a survival fund that finances the early costs of doing business. For example, if a franchisee's total costs (including the franchisee's salary) run $4000 in the first month of operation and revenue equals only $1900, working capital finances the $2100 difference.

Some less reputable franchisors employ a wealth of tricks to underestimate working capital requirements. For instance, a franchise may optimistically target break-even for the first or second month of operation. Others conveniently omit franchisees' early living expenses and salaries from working capital estimates. These manipulations are unethical at best and illegal at worst. To succeed, franchisees need accurate cost projections on which to base management decisions.

How do you determine working capital requirements? By developing simple break-even and shortfall analyses. Break-even occurs when:

$$\text{Revenue} = \text{Fixed costs}[1] + \text{variable costs}[2]$$

[1]Fixed costs are costs that remain constant, in total, regardless of sales or level of production. Examples are rent, insurance, and wages paid to salaried employees.
[2]Variable costs are costs that vary in direct proportion to changes in sales or the level of production. Examples are sales commissions, inventory costs, and royalties.

If revenue exceeds total costs, profit results. If costs exceed revenue, a shortfall develops that must be financed with working capital from the franchisee. The extent of these shortfalls can be identified by projecting costs and revenue for the first year of operation.

In this example, we'll assume that, based on your pilot store's performance, a franchisee will break even in the sixth month of operation and that first-year revenue equals $210,000. We'll also assume that rent, the owner's salary, insurance, and other fixed costs total $5250 a month. Variable costs—royalties, commissions, and cost of goods sold—equal 70 percent of revenue (you should calculate your variable costs according to your pilot store's performance).

	Revenue (assumed)	Fixed costs (assumed)	Variable Costs (.70 of revenue)	Working Capital Required
January	$10,500	$5,250	$7,350	$2,100
February	12,000	5,250	8,400	1,650
March	13,000	5,250	9,100	1,350
April	15,000	5,250	10,500	750
May	16,000	5,250	11,200	450
June*	17,500	5,250	12,250	0
July	18,000	5,250	12,600	0
August	19,000	5,250	13,300	0
September	20,000	5,250	14,000	0
October	21,000	5,250	14,700	0
November	23,000	5,250	16,100	0
December	25,000	5,250	17,500	0
	$210,000	$63,000	$147,000	$6,300

*Break even

In the above example, a franchisee would need $2100 to finance the first month of operation, $1650 in the second, $1350 in the third, $750 for the fourth, and $450 for the fifth, for a total of $6300 in working capital for the year. Break-even occurs in June, and a profit is produced in July.

But your working capital analysis is still not complete. To the $6300 shortfall, you must add other expenses that franchisees pay to support their early operations. Such costs as transportation to and from training programs, cash on hand at opening, rent prior to opening, and labor costs during training must also be considered. Once tallied, the total is added to initial fees, as well as opening inventory, supplies, construction, renovation, equipment, and other typical business expenses to determine the total initial investment required of franchisees.

PRODUCT PURCHASE REQUIREMENTS

Earlier I briefly described my first exposure to franchising as a young boy who enjoyed the consistent quality and service of Howard Johnson Restaurants during the 1950s. Today uniformity of product and service is still the pillar on which successful franchising rests. One way franchisors provide for that consistency is by controlling the supply of products to franchisees.

Most people mistakenly assume that franchisors directly sell franchisees products. They believe McDonald's serves as a middle man, acquiring beef from Midwest ranchers and potatoes from Idaho farmers before distributing the products to franchised units. In reality, McDonald's doesn't provide products to franchisees. Instead, the company, like many business-format franchisors, uses contractual techniques to control the quality of the franchised product.

There are three techniques to choose from: supplier designation, supplier approval, and issuance of specifications. How do you know which to use? By applying a subjective/objective criteria to the product in question.

For example, if the supplied product holds significant importance to the franchised business, particularly where subjective taste decisions are involved, then the franchisor can designate a specific supplier from which the franchisee must buy. Thus, a fast-food franchisor may designate that Coca-Cola be used in its restaurants, rather than a generic cola. Likewise, a health spa chain may require franchisees to purchase equipment from Nautilus or Universal because the companies' products meet some subjective criteria of quality. Designating suppliers often wins volume discounts for franchisees and is legal to the extent that the franchisor does not derive income or kickbacks from the arrangement.

If the product, though important, requires less control over the supplier or is open to more objective evaluation, the franchisor may choose to identify major sources of supply, allowing the franchisee to choose a specific supplier from the approved list. So the fast-food franchise now provides franchisees with a listing of 13 bakeries from which they may buy hamburger buns, and the health-spa chain approves 20 suppliers of exercise mats and warm-up gear. Supplier approval provides flexibility in product acquisition but also calls for increased monitoring of product quality and uniformity by the franchisor.

As with designated suppliers, franchisors can face legal difficulties if they seek to derive income from franchisee purchases from approved suppliers. Other legal problems arise when franchisors, whose real intentions are to sell franchisees products, promise to review alternative suppliers but provide no meaningful mechanism for approval or simply refuse to do so.

The third and final control mechanism is issuance of specifications, which is used where no subjective analysis is required and written requirements can direct franchisees to buy from any of a number of suppliers. In our fast-food example, the franchisor may specify the types and size of the cooking utensils required, but leave supply sources to the franchisee. For the health-spa chain, franchisors may detail the weight and construction of dumbbells, but allow the franchisee to find an appropriate supplier.

Yet some franchisors are product suppliers and profitable ones at that. Docktor Pet Centers, for instance, provides its franchisees with store-brand pet foods, toys, and supplies. "Product is a big part of our concept," says Les Charm. "We are a specialty retail store that provides franchisees with products that can't be obtained by mom-and-pop outlets. I find most franchisees are very receptive to the Docktor Pet Centers name brand. They judge it as quality merchandise that yields real competitive advantages. And for our company, name brands add another profit center to the business."

Yet other franchisors are less enthusiastic about supplying products. "We supplied product in the beginning," says Goranson of Tidy Car, "but found the practice generated ill will within the system. Franchisees suspect every product you sell them of being inferior and another way for you to make money. Now, we just negotiate with suppliers to lower cost to the point that when added to royalties, total operating costs are equal to what independents pay."

Goranson illustrates the extent of franchisee skepticism with an event that occurred during a Tidy Car convention. "The company contracted with the hotel for a so-called package rate. But a few franchisees didn't mention they were with Tidy Car and received the hotel's cheaper transient rate. Word soon got around and the franchisees were outraged. They believed we were making money off the deal. The experience drove home the point that franchisees really look at company-supplied products—even hotel rooms—with a jaundiced eye."

Aside from the business implications, product supply in franchising also bears legal consideration in its relationship to the Sherman and Clayton Acts, which encourage competition and discourage tying arrangements. Tying arrangements occur when a seller bases the sale of a desired product on the buyer's purchase of a second, less wanted product. An illegal tying arrangement may exist where the two products are obviously separate and distinct, a substantial amount of interstate commerce is involved, and the seller has sufficient economic power with respect to the desirable product to appreciably restrain competition in the market for the less desirable product.

In franchising, the courts often view the trademark as the tying product franchisors use to sell extraneous items to the franchisee. The exception, obviously, is product franchises, where the trademark and the product are one and the same.

In business format franchises, however, the trademark and product are usually separate and unique. Franchisors who tie their franchise opportunity to purchases of product, profiting on royalties and product sales, may infringe upon the spirit and letter of antitrust law. If your franchise idea relies heavily on product supply for success, you need a competent attorney to review your program in light of recent antitrust court holdings.

TERRITORIAL ISSUES AND CONCERNS

Territorial questions are a vital concern to franchisors, primarily because of the importance franchisees place on the issue. "At Rampart, the designation of territories was irrelevant from an operational standpoint," begins Tom Fleisher, former chief operating officer of Rampart Industries, a burglar and fire alarm franchise. "Franchisees were free to follow leads from anywhere. But psychologically, assigning specific geographical areas proved an important selling point. Franchisees wanted to know the nature of the competition they would face. They wanted a definable territory to call their own," explains Fleisher, who is now a Philadelphia-based consultant. "We understood this and used it as part of our package."

There are, however, situations where franchisors need exclusive territories to assure operational effectiveness. In businesses where repeat personal contact is critical to success, the designation of a single person or office to service area accounts helps build sales relationships. Likewise, in regions where the customer base won't support competing offices, exclusive territories may achieve more efficient market exploitation by limiting intrabrand competition. And exclusive territories can also help franchisors limit the duration of the sales effort by restricting the number of franchises they must sell.

But what exactly is included in an exclusive territory grant? Franchisors and franchisees alike often mistakenly assume exclusivity applies to all aspects of a business in a particular geographical area. And although territories *are* often exclusive, franchisors are free to qualify what that exclusivity really means. For example, Haagen-Dazs, the ice-cream franchise, retains the right to distribute its product through nonfranchised outlets such as supermarkets and convenience stores.

Franchisors also use market segments to distinguish what businesses franchisees may service. Pilot Air Freight franchisees, for instance, have exclusivity only for domestic business; the franchisor may still compete for international cargo. Distinctions can even be drawn between customer types. For instance, a computer company that wishes to franchise sales to high schools and universities could structure its agreement so the company retains large industrial accounts.

However, the effect of exclusivity on competition raises legal questions. Traditionally, the courts have distinguished fair from unfair practices according to the market level where restrictive grants are employed. If the territorial and customer restrictions are imposed vertically, such as a franchisor and its franchisees, the grant of exclusivity is legal. However, if the restrictions are imposed horizontally, such as a group of franchisees who allocate territories among themselves, exclusivity approaches collusion and is deemed illegal. Hence, sensible franchisors should *never* give franchisees a say in the allocation of territories.

In an attempt to distance themselves from legal difficulties, some franchisors label exclusive areas "areas of primary responsibility." For the most part, these are the same as exclusive areas. However, they can differ if the franchisor states that the territory is primarily entrusted to one franchisee but not protected from the sales efforts of another.

Some franchisors attempt to deal with interterritorial competition with profit pass overs and income-splitting, whereby a franchisee that wins business in another territory pays the resident franchisee a percentage of receipts or profits. Although a possible administrative monster, the techniques work well when managed effectively.

Concurrent with exclusive territories are minimum performance requirements, which stipulate a level of sales franchisees must achieve to retain their exclusive right over the territory and/or continued use of the trademark and business program. Franchisors employ performance requirements out of necessity.

No matter how careful your selection process, franchisees who are less than capable businesspeople will occasionally slip into your system. For a myriad of personal and professional reasons, a significant percentage of franchisees languish in the never-never land of wasted potential and lost opportunity. It's a sad fact of franchising that 20 percent of franchisees achieve 70 percent of the results, while the middle 60 percent generates about a quarter of company revenue. That leaves a scant five percent of sales for the final 20 percent of franchisees, who usually rank as malcontents—unmotivated, careless, or confused.

These underachievers are an especially dangerous breed when protected by exclusive territories. With a substantial territory tied down, they display a degree of nonchalance or incompetence that lets vastly profitable markets go unattended or underexploited.

In defense, franchisors establish minimum performance requirements according to the size and potential of the territory awarded and the performance of franchisees in similar markets. The requirements are not intended to represent a sales goal or objective. They are, instead, guidelines which if franchisees cannot attain, they should consider new careers.

Franchisors use many techniques in structuring minimum performance requirements. For example, some waive the obligation for the first year of operation. Others state the requirement for the first year or two of business and reserve the right to subsequently increase the minimum on an annual basis, according to the performance of the franchise as a whole.

Similarly, franchisors react differently when minimums are not attained. Many franchisors treat an initial failure leniently, or grant compliance periods. They also may offer remedial training or special services to correct legitimate problems. The penalty for continued poor performance can range from loss of exclusive right over the area to immediate termination of the franchise agreement.

When writing your franchise agreement, it's best to take a firm stand in defining the penalties franchisees face for missing minimum requirements. When managing your business, however, a more lenient posture can help turn struggling owners into successful entrepreneurs.

As a final note regarding minimum requirements, franchisees usually display extreme sensitivity to minimums and often try to negotiate their waiver before signing a franchise agreement. They also may request contractual provisions that suspend or defer minimum performance requirements for a specified time.

In representing franchisors, I strongly recommend against accepting such terms. The royalties that flow from a franchisee's sales are the fiscal lifeblood of a properly managed franchise. To allow poorly performing franchisees to divert, delay, hinder, or impede that stream of royalties means opening the floodgates to possible financial peril. Protect your royalty flow by hedging the risks of exclusive territories through careful development of and adherence to minimum performance requirements.

Other techniques franchisors use to protect their interests in exclusive territories include area development requirements. Here, franchisors places stipulations on the development of large multiunit areas. (See Chapter 5 for a full discussion of area development.) The requirements usually commit franchisees to open an agreed upon number of units within a specified time. The practice is intended to guarantee franchisors timely penetration of a market. But there are drawbacks.

An overly ambitious opening schedule may force franchisees to bring new units on stream too quickly, or to grow faster than customer acceptance will support. Franchisors who use area development requirements often seek well-capitalized, investment-oriented franchisees that possess the resources to finance large multiunit programs.

But what if you're not interested in granting exclusive territories? What if your franchisees don't need to be protected from one another? Are there any alternatives? Certainly. Location grants are one. Under location grants, franchisees receive a location without a guaranteed buffer zone between other franchisees and themselves.

Yet these franchisees are, to a degree, protected by laws that restrict franchisors from intentionally placing units that harm franchisees' chances of success or that otherwise unfairly compete with them. However, the measures of intent, harm, and competition are difficult to measure. Many franchisors find that location grants permit adequate exploitation of the market without stirring up legal trouble.

Franchisees are extremely conscious of the business territory they service on a daily basis. They want, often demand, firm, definable limits placed on the scope and bounds of intracompany competition. Some franchisors meet these concerns halfway by tying location grants to a zone or radious surrounding the franchise. Unlike exclusive territories, these zones are usually small—a block or neighborhood rather than a town, city, or region.

Other franchisors tie locations to population or other minimum standards. For example, a maid service grants no absolute exclusivity, but agrees not to establish more than one franchise per 50,000 qualified customers in an area. So in areas of 100,000 customers, the franchisor could sell two franchises next door to one another.

These arrangements work well in alleviating franchisee apprehension and yet still providing franchisors substantial control over the placement of franchised units.

YOU'RE HALF FINISHED!

So you have begun to define your business—you've established an image, analyzed your competition, and developed a marketing plan. Moreover, you've decided on a license fee, royalty level, and other miscellaneous fees outlined in this chapter. But you're only half finished. Many of the most important components are still to come. As a franchisor, you must determine the services you'll provide franchisees, a subject discussed in Chapter 10.

CHAPTER 10

WHAT OBLIGATIONS TO ASSUME: THE FRANCHISOR AS SERVANT

In franchising, no other issue demands as much forethought and planning as the services you will provide franchisees. Your franchisees' success, their ability to earn profits, is critically linked to the attention and guidance you offer. You have an awesome responsibility.

As a franchisor, you commit yourself legally, ethically, and morally to providing all reasonable assistance a business neophyte needs to succeed. Being a franchisor represents an obligation that far and away exceeds the typical business association. It's an alliance that more closely approximates a marriage than an economic relationship.

But how much is enough? What services should you provide? Generalizations are difficult because the answer varies according to the business. Remember, from a legal standpoint, you should never commit to more than you can realistically provide. Even if you intend to offer extended services in the near future, or if you sporadically perform some of these services now, your franchise agreement and disclosure statement should only commit to those services you currently provide on a uniform and regular basis. Never make written promises based on hopes or expectations. There is nothing wrong with discussing company plans for broader marketing, greater advertising, and improved product research and development, but to commit to eventualities is to blueprint your downfall. In structuring your franchise program, I urge you to follow one golden rule: Always perform more services than you are committed to perform. The converse to that advice is equally important: Always commit to less than you intend to perform.

Bear in mind that there are some fundamental services every franchisor must provide. Broadly, they can be separated into five categories: business specification and operating manuals, training, site selection or analysis, opening assistance, and subsequent management and marketing services.

WRITING BUSINESS SPECIFICATIONS AND OPERATING MANUALS

The most basic but critical information you should offer franchisees is detailed specification of your business's operation and an operating manual. Most franchisees have no previous experience in the business they buy. They are rank amateurs, pure novices. They need the instruction sheet, the nuts-and-bolts discussion that describes how to: greet, service, and appease customers; order, store, and prepare product; hire, motivate, and manage employees; promote, develop, and advertise the business, as well as handle hundreds of other basic business issues. But how do you specify your business? How do you detail your operation so franchisees can understand? How do you prepare and write an operating manual?

"The process begins by testing yourself," says Jerry Cusack, an expert on franchise operations development and a consultant based in York, Pennsylvania. "You should ask yourself, 'What are the critical points I have to tell a franchisee about my business?' And then make absolutely no assumptions regarding the franchisee's level of knowledge."

Cusack's knowledge of restaurant operations dates back to his early years working at his father's restaurant in the Wall Street district of Manhattan. There, he gained an intuitive understanding of the food and beverage industry that later led to degrees in business and hospitality management, as well as executive positions with Arthur Treacher's and Taco Belle.

As an exercise in how franchisors assume too much regarding their franchisees, Cusack pulls a pen from his shirt pocket during a recent interview and enlists the interviewer's assistance.

"Imagine I have never written," he begins. "Give me instructions on how to write."

Obligingly, the interviewer commands Cusack to place the small tip of the pen against a piece of paper sitting on his desk.

He does so successfully, and is then directed to move the pen in a small circle.

Again he follows the commands; however, his movements are jerky and the resulting circle is oblong and deformed.

"The problem," Cusack begins, "isn't in your directions but rather with your assumptions. You assumed I picked up the pen with my writing hand. I'm right-handed but grabbed the pen with my left."

Such are the challenges you will face in specifying your business for franchisees. No assumptions, no matter how inconsequential, should be made. You must constantly remind yourself that what seems obvious to you after years of business experience is far from apparent to beginners.

"Once you have identified the correct level of assumptions, the next step is to define the operations of the business," Cusack says. "What are the steps people must take to prepare or sell the product?" Even something as seemingly simple as preparing a ham-and-cheese sandwich involves a wealth of steps that must be defined, Cusack notes. For example, how many ounces of ham should you use? Of cheese? How big is the bun? Is the sandwich heated? If so, for how long? In a microwave oven? A toaster oven? On a grill? Is the product served with condiments? If so, are they placed on top of the sandwich or served separately? How is the product presented? On a tray or a plate? Is it wrapped? In what? Should it be placed in a bag? Can it be held under a warming light or must it be served immediately?

The questions go on and on, but all must be answered if the franchisee is to understand how to properly operate the franchised business.

Once you start answering questions, you'll need a way to organize the information, which is the first step in assembling an operating manual. The organization of a manual differs according to the business. A franchise that sells office supplies operates quite differently than a health spa or a travel agency. Your manual needs to account for such variations. However, there are some basic requirements that every operating manual should include. Five of these are:

1. *An Introduction*—Your introduction can serve to reiterate your commitment to the franchisee, business, and consumer. Consider developing a short statement on company goals, objectives, and philosophies, and including them as a springboard into more complex and tangible issues of operating and managing the franchised unit.

2. *An Operational Analysis*—Every manual needs a practical discussion of how to run the business. If it's a sales call-oriented business, you must tell franchisees how to generate leads, schedule appointments, and close deals. If it's a retail store, you'll need to explain how to greet and service customers, display merchandise, and manage inventory. Some operating manuals walk a franchisee through a typical business day.

For example, the directions start by telling the owner to arrive at eight A.M., open doors, place $50 in change and small bills in the cash register, and turn on office equipment.

Next, the manuals spell out morning operations. A typical operating manual may read: "Employees must report by eight-thirty A.M. From nine A.M. until ten-thirty A.M., their primary duty is to check inventory and order stock for the day. At the same time, the franchisee should contact yesterday's customers to see whether orders were received."

The remainder of the day is also scheduled: "Sales calls are made in early afternoon, after which customer complaints and special orders are cared for." Finally, closing tasks are explained, and a quitting time is specified.

3. *An accounting overview*—The in-house controls and accounting procedures you develop for your franchisees are a critical component of the overall success of your franchise system. As novice businesspeople, franchisees need step-by-step instructions on recording, reporting, and managing the income they receive in the normal operation of their businesses. As a franchisor, you must provide specific instructions on such issues as:

Revenue management—which includes how to account for cash register receipts; when to deposit cash in banks; how to accept and verify credit cards and personal checks; when to reconcile invoices; and how to record hourly, daily, weekly, and monthly sales figures

Inventory management—which covers receiving and accounting for product, recording its use, tracking pilferage, declaring its value on balance sheets, and avoiding spoilage

Managerial accounting—which details calculating break-evens, preparing profit-and-loss statements, developing budgets, determining fixed and variable costs, and accounting for special promotions and programs (i.e., cents-off coupons and direct mail campaigns)

Payroll accounting—which relates to withholding state and federal income taxes from employees' earnings, payments to the Federal Insurance Contributions Act (FICA), and deductions for state unemployment insurance, as well as employer benefits such as health and group life insurance, and investment and employee stock ownership programs

Franchising accounting—which involves tabulating royalty and other payments to the franchisor, as well as a description of when, where, and how the payments must be made

For many of these simpler items, such as inventory management, franchisors provide easy-to-follow forms for franchisees to fill in. For more complex issues, such as payroll deductions, franchisors require franchisees to retain an accountant's services through stipulations in the franchise agreement

4. *Customer service*—We live in the age of the consumer, and to succeed, businesspeople must prepare to meet the needs and desires, hopes and expectations of the market with diligence and care. An effective operating manual explains the importance of the consumer to the overall success of the enterprise. Consider how one operating manual from a major franchise company begins: "Customers are our life line, and effective customer relations is your primary responsibility as a franchisee. . . . If all your employees remain keenly concerned that the customer enjoys the product in comfortable and clean surroundings, our mutual success is inevitable."

Sales is also key to customer relations. And a good-quality operating manual should outline the key points of salesmanship. "Purchasing decisions are usually not based on an idea, but on the person who effectively sells the idea," reads the introduction to a fitness franchise's operating manual. The manual goes on to explain, "Effective salespeople are not pushy or aggressive. They are energetic, forward-looking, enthusiastic, and knowledgeable about their product and/or service."

What other topics should be included? Franchisees need to know how to deal with customers in a range of scenarios, from answering the telephone to diffusing angry patrons. For example, many service franchises refuse to quote prices over the telephone, believing that no job can be properly priced without a thorough review of the work involved. But how is this policy explained to a telephone caller who just received a price quote from a competitor? As a franchisor, you'll need to establish guidelines and procedures that franchisees can use in customer relations. Some policies are as simple as developing scripts for franchisees to follow. Others entail the establishment of corporate philosophies that deal directly with the integral role the consumer plays in U.S. business.

5. *Personnel Management*—One of the greatest problems new franchisees face is managing personnel. As former employees, they have little conception of the frustration, tribulation, and satisfaction that comes from being the boss and having other people work for them.

That's why personnel is often the most referred-to section of a properly written operating manual. It requires a detailed and comprehensive examination of such topics as:

Job descriptions—the tasks that must be accomplished in operating the franchised business

Hiring—where to find qualified employees

Interviewing—how to evaluate whether a prospective employee fits a job opening

Training—how to prepare new employees to work effectively

Motivation—how to inject enthusiasm and care into the work force

Leadership—how to direct employees in the efficient and effective operation of your business

Performance review—how to evaluate the skills and talents of employees

Continuing management—how to retain good employees and dismiss poor workers

And there are other considerations. Franchisors must develop rules and regulations for employees to follow while working at franchised businesses.

Policies on dress codes, employee discounts, breaks, vacation, behavior, sick leave, and tardiness must all be defined so franchisees can employ them quickly and appropriately.

You also may want to establish general personnel policies. For example, some franchisors recommend that franchisees continue to actively interview even when staffing is at 100 percent. "In many ways, hiring should be an ongoing process," says Jerry Cusack. "This prepares the franchisee for employee turnover, which is constant for cooks, waitresses, and other minimum-wage jobs. But it also lets the franchisee see the pool of available labor from which he could upgrade his work force."

Together, these five items—introduction, operational analysis, accounting overview, customer relations, and personnel management—represent the keystones on which an effective operating manual can be built. The list, however, is not exclusive. Some manuals detail advertising programs franchisees should develop. Others describe promotion and public relations techniques. For example, the manual for a major weight-loss franchise outlines a public relations program that directs clients to donate clothing to local charities as they shed pounds and clothes sizes. Speedy Transmission Centers' operating manual urges franchisees to meet with community groups to educate them on transmission repair.

The topics to include in your operating manual are linked to the nature and scope of your business. Offering a definitive statement on their compilation proves an impossible task. In broad terms, your goal is to provide franchisees with an easy-to-follow guidebook that adequately explains crucial components of your business.

DEVELOPING A TRAINING PROGRAM

In a perfect world with no profit and loss, I would counsel most franchisors to offer an in-depth, one-year training program for franchisees. Not only would this provide competent owners, but it also would afford you a degree of protection against franchisees prevailing in lawsuits brought against you for improper training.

In the trench warfare of business, however, where even minor delays cost a great deal of money, extensive training programs simply are not feasible.

NUGGET #12

Some Critical Components of an Operations Manual (A sample index)

I. Introduction and Background
   A. Corporate history
   B. Corporate philosophy
II. Operational Analysis
   A. The product
   B. In-office or in-shop procedures
   C. Supplies and inventory management
   D. Business hours
III. Customer Services
   A. The market
   B. Customer relations
IV. Sales
   A. Procedures
      1. Telephone script
      2. In-store or in-shop sales methods
      3. Overcoming objections
      4. Generating leads
   B. Supervising and motivating salespeople
      1. Techniques
      2. Calculating commissions
V. Advertising
   A. National advertising and promotion fund
   B. Regional advertising
      1. Radio
      2. TV
      3. Print
   C. Regional promotion
      1. Community relation programs
      2. Cents-off coupons
   D. Measuring results

NUGGET #12 *(Continued)*

VI. Personnel Management
   A. Staffing
      1. Job descriptions
      2. Hiring employees
   B. Establishing personnel policies
      1. Salaries and wages
      2. Raises and promotions
      3. Benefits
   C. Supervising staff
      1. Maintaining personnel records
      2. Performance reviews
VII. Accounting Procedures and Forms
   A. Basic accounting overview
   B. Revenue management
      1. Visa and Mastercard accounts
      2. Recording sales
      3. Justifying receipts
      4. Making change
   C. Payroll accounting
      1. Withholding taxes
      2. Withholding benefits
   D. Franchising accounting
      1. Submitting royalties
      2. Submitting other fees

Success depends on quickly moving new franchisees into the field to tap their share of the market. And franchisees, too, demand decisive action. Having left their jobs, they can ill afford a year's apprenticeship. They need money to live and support their families.

But here rests a bitter trade-off. The less time you invest up-front in new business owners, the more time you lose later assisting hapless franchisees.

What's the dividing line between too little and just enough? One word—effectiveness. Your training program should be structured to develop effective businesspeople who can hold their own in business's tough operating environment. This doesn't mean you need to instill new franchisees with the knowledge of a Harvard MBA. It does, however, mean you're responsible for providing an overview of the franchised business, as well as an accurate presentation of what to expect as a small business owner.

Not only must you provide this training, but you also have to make sure it's absorbed. In other words, you will want to pre- and post-test your franchisees to verify their mastery of your business. Why? To satisfy yourself of their competence, but also to prove you made the effort. A successfully completed exam supplies evidence that you provided franchisees with a measure of competence before unleasing them into the cruel, hard business world.

How rigorous should the tests be? Keep in mind that their value lies in establishing a standard. Those who fall below the standard should receive additional attention, not failing grades.

And tests serve an additional purpose: They break down the self-professed know-it-alls. "One of the most difficult tasks in training is getting new franchisees to accept your system," says Cusack, our operation's consultant. "Many believe they already know the answers and that the instruction is for the other guy. But tests—and especially pretests—shock trainees into realizing how little they know about running a business. After failing to correctly answer even basic operational questions, trainees become more involved in learning the correct way to conduct a business."

What other elements should an effective training program include? "Motivation is high on the list," according to Terry Greenhut, president and founder of Automotivation Unlimited, a firm based in Mount Kisco, New York, that trains managers and employees of both franchised and nonfranchised companies. "We spend roughly a fourth of our time trying to make trainees realize they are worth more than what a customer pays, that their self-worth depends on the job they do as professionals, not just the dollar they receive for a job."

Greenhut's firm also spends a large portion of time on sales. "We use role-playing and videotapes to show trainees how to react to customers and make sales," he says. "We show them how to take a personal interest in a customer's problem, make an effective sales presentation, diffuse objections, and close deals." Greenhut believes that salesmanship is a talent that can be practiced and improved. "In the automotive repair industry, price objections represent the hardest aspect of sales. Many businesspeople believe they must give in or lose the sale. We don't subscribe to that thinking. Consumers search for the best value for their dollars, not necessarily the cheapest prices. In training, we show shop owners and franchisees how to present their service as quality workmanship, commanding a quality price."

But the sales training doesn't stop there. Greenhut also teaches trainees how to deal with the more unpleasant aspects of selling a product or service. "We also show businesspeople how to handle rejection." For instance, Greenhut notes, if a salesperson makes one $100 sale per 10 sales calls, that's a fairly high rejection rate. But broken into pieces, the same figures could be interpreted as earning $10 per sales call, which psychologically seems a better payoff.

Surprisingly, Greenhut's training programs cover one last business topic: ethics. "The automotive repair industry isn't held in high regard by many customers. We teach our trainees to be fair and honest with consumers. It's okay to get top dollar for your work only if your work is top quality and you deserve it."

What other topics should you include in your training program? Certainly, you'll want to familiarize franchisees with your product or service. But remember, the owner may or may not be involved with actual production or sales. For instance, the owner of a domestic cleaning franchise probably won't push a mop. Likewise, print shop franchisees may spend their time making sales calls and servicing accounts, not setting type.

It's often this way in franchise training—product or service knowledge taking a backseat to management expertise. And you'll want to structure your training program accordingly, because new franchisees have to learn how to *manage* independent businesses.

They must see, learn, and experience the day-to-day tasks that drive a business forward, before venturing out on their own. Nowhere is this knowledge more obtainable than in an operating franchise, company store, or mock shop. After covering general business issues in a classroom, many franchisors move their trainees to the real world, having them make sandwiches, meet customers, direct employees, schedule inventory, order parts, or work cash registers. If managed properly, the experience offers franchisees the real-life training that classroom study simply can't provide.

Obviously, you should structure your training program to fit the needs of your business. No single design can accommodate all possible contingencies, and this discussion is meant merely to offer suggestions. Every training program demands careful forethought and preparation if it intends to produce caring and competent franchisees. Here are some further points you may wish to consider before teaching your first franchisee:

Whom will your program train? Will you train the owner? Spouse? Manager? Or any other employees? If not, can the franchisee pay for these individuals to attend training?

What are the objectives of your training program? To cover the nuts-and-bolts of the product? To introduce the franchisee to sales and marketing? To energize and motivate new business owners? To teach management?

How will you test? Will evaluation take place in an actual unit? Will there be a written examination? Multiple choice? Essay? Who will grade it?

How long is your program? Will it span a week? Two weeks? A month? Will continuing education be part of your program? If so, who pays for these annual refresher courses? The franchisee? The franchisor? Are the costs shared?

Who will conduct your program? Do you have the personnel to teach new franchisees your business? Are they experienced? Can you perform this task? If not, can you afford to employ experienced trainers?

Where will the training course be held? At your home office? In a company-operated unit? On location at a franchised unit?

What materials and/or facilities do you need to conduct the course? Workbooks? Audio or videotapes? A classroom? A mock shop? Desks? Chairs? Chalkboards? Flip charts? Video cassette recorders or other audio-visual equipment?

Where will your franchisees stay while attending the course? At local hotels? With franchisees? Will you arrange accommodations?

When will the training course take place? Immediately after signing the franchise agreement? Ninety days before opening? A month before opening? A week before opening?

NUGGET #13

Training Employees

What are the steps in training employees? At least one franchisor believes it's a 4-step exchange between the franchisee or manager and the new employee:

1. *Explanation*—The initial explanation gives new employees an overview of their jobs and working environment. It includes a tour of the physical plant and a general briefing on company policies and procedures.
2. *Demonstration*—Here, the trainer offers a step-by-step walk-through of the job. Nothing is assumed, and the demonstration is repeated until the new employee understands the procedure.
3. *Performance*—It's the employee's turn to perform the task under close supervision of the trainer, who offers immediate feedback until the operation is performed correctly. The employee must then repeat the job at an accelerated pace.
4. *Follow Up*—The trainer continues to observe new employees, verbally testing their knowledge and offering appropriate rewards or recognition for acceptable performance.

What must the franchisee do prior to the course? Complete work sheets or homework assignments? Visit operating franchises? Choose territories or locations? Analyze regional markets?

How will you deal with poor performers? Can franchisees wash out of your program? Will you offer a remedial program? Can franchisees be required to repeat the course?

FINDING BUSINESS LOCATIONS: A SHORT PRIMER

Location is an essential precursor of small business success. Perhaps more than anything else, franchisees will look to you for advice and guidance on finding and selecting commercial real estate. And with good reason. For a new business, a proper location represents that crucial first step in the long race for profits. It makes a good business better. It turns marginal enterprises profitable. In fact, even mediocre business concepts can succeed if customers can patronize the business easily, with minimal inconvenience.

And there are two ways you can help. First, through site selection, which maximizes your role in location decisions but also opens you to travel, costs, and inconvenience. Under site selection, the franchisor ventures into the field and conducts research on specific locations. It's expensive and time-consuming. It also exposes you to possible litigation. "The franchisor chose the site," a disgruntled franchisee could testify in court. "The franchisor should have had the expertise to know I couldn't have succeeded at that location."

The second alternative is site approval, which limits the franchisor's involvement and liability. Here, the franchisor provides in-depth specifications on the type and cost of locations franchisees should be investigating. The franchisee then undertakes the legwork and submits his finding for franchisor approval.

Whichever method you choose, you'll need to learn as much as possible about real estate selection for strategic and marketing reasons. More and more, prospective franchisees are hinging their purchasing decisions on finding acceptable locations. Even service-oriented and home-based franchises must be situated in the thick of things or risk failure. "If you can't offer prospective franchisees at least a formula for finding an acceptable location, hot leads turn real cold, real fast," says Speedy Transmission Centers' D'Arcy Williams.

But finding those locations isn't always easy—especially in today's commercial real estate market where many of the very best properties have already been claimed. And those left undeveloped are often so expensive that even the big boys of franchising—the Burger Kings, Midas Mufflers, and ComputerLands—know to keep their distance.

But good deals can still be found, and it's the job of opportunistic franchisors to help sniff out these bargains for franchisees. Sound like a difficult task? It is, if you don't know the secrets to securing quality sites.

Surprisingly, the process begins not on the highways and byways of the American landscape but perhaps in your own backyard. Before evaluating sites you first must evaluate your company to determine its physical needs.

Where will your business succeed? Does it need a freestanding building? A mall location? A strip mall? An office park? An upscale or downscale environment? "We're in an impulse business," says Arthur Karp of The Original Great American Chocolate Chip Cookie Company. "So we need the wide exposure to people that malls provide. Our concept just wouldn't work if shoppers had to make special trips to purchase the product." The Athlete's Foot, however, is seeking to avoid high mall rents by targeting more strip malls. "The rents at many suburban malls are so high that it's a gamble whether the franchisee will break even," says Hamer Phillips, the company's vice-president of real estate. "But secondary locations also present problems because they cost more to advertise once opened."

After analyzing your business's general needs, the next step is to specify your space requirements. In an office franchise, this includes the number of work stations, reception areas, and waiting rooms you'll want. In a retail store, it encompasses room for inventory, product display, and office space. For food, you'll need to consider prep area and a dining room. Automotive repair shops must provide for bay space, parts storage, and perhaps a receiving dock.

But space requirements don't end at the building's four walls. Many businesses require on-site parking, drive-through lanes and windows, and room for industrial-sized Dumpsters and equipment as well as for signage and displays.

By determining the site's optimal type and size, you significantly narrow the number of appropriate locations. But making that final location decision is still a difficult one.

Take, for example, a hypothetical case based on a real experience. After searching for locations in the Pittsburgh area, a major breakfast franchise chose a suburban site just outside Monroeville, Pennsylvania, along the eastbound lane of a major highway.

Demographics showed the area supported a large population of middle-class families, the traditional patrons of breakfast establishments. Also, an encouraging competitive analysis revealed major food franchises successfully operating in the area, but no other breakfast restaurants.

Strangely, however, after 10 months of operation, the location's franchisee was still struggling to break even, and the future looked bleak. On Saturdays and Sundays, business was brisk, with more than enough hungry customers stopping to grab pancakes, coffee, and home fries. On weekdays, however, the steady stream slowed to a trickle as only a handful of breakfast-eaters walked through its doors. Even heavy promotion and extensive advertising failed to turn the tide.

The problem rested not with the concept, management, or owner, but rather with the seemingly idyllic location. Monroeville sits east of Pittsburgh, and morning traffic flowed away from the suburb toward the city. Unfortunately, the restaurant was located on the opposite side of the highway. Strapped for time, commuters refused to fight oncoming traffic first thing in the morning, and passed the restaurant for more convenient locations.

So in site selection, even minor oversights can result in major shortfalls, which is a frightening realization when considering the importance of location to the success of your franchisees. Securing accessible, high-traffic properties in areas that reflect the demographic needs of your business represents that crucial link in developing profitable franchised units.

Remember, other franchise companies may be larger and better capitalized than you are. But you can diminish the hardships by finding the right place to conduct your business!

So how exactly do you find these all-important locations? "When I first began franchising," begins D'Arcy Williams, "I relied heavily on commercial realtors to do the legwork." For example, if Williams had a franchisee interested in locating near Syracuse, New York, he'd call four or five local commercial realtors and explain exactly what he needed. "I told them I would be in town on a specific date and that I needed a map of the area with the properties charted, along with traffic counts and flows, zoning information, and demographic statistics on the surrounding neighborhoods. Most realtors willingly obliged, accompanying me and the prospect on a personal tour of the properties."

But there's a risk, since realtors have been known to overestimate a property to gain a commission. Meeting with several real estate agents provides a truer account of what's available. But you still must conduct your own research to verify their recommendations. Where do you begin? "You start by making two critical assessments," says consultant Cusack. "First, you must decide whether the specific trading area has the potential customers you need for a successful business. Second, you should determine what specific locations within the area are most suitable for your business."

To help with the first determination, Cusack recommends obtaining pop-ulation density and census track maps from the local chamber of commerce and the post office, respectively. The maps show where the majority of the local population lives, as well as the average income for residents of specific regions. They can also help pinpoint any nearby traffic generators, such as large apartment complexes, office buildings, schools, colleges, civic and sports arenas, hospitals, as well as malls and other commercial hubs.

Next, you should gather as much information as possible on the area's general economic climate. What is the unemployment rate? Who are the major employers? Is growth forecast? Is there planned business expansion in the area? The local city planning commission can answer many of these questions. But you should also speak with businesspeople in the area to gain their insight into the local economy. Do they expect to increase sales next year? Have many businesses failed during the past few years? What do these businesspeople see as the region's economic future?

Once through with generalities, it's time to focus on specific sites, and here your research should be no less thorough. A first consideration is inter-nal competition. Are there other company franchises operating in the same area? How close are they? Will one cannibalize the sales of the other? Prox-imity isn't necessarily a bad thing. A strong, combined market share is your company's best defense against outside competition and helps finance large, cooperative advertising programs. But how near is too near? For obvious reasons, franchisors like to see their units packed more closely together than do franchisees. What's the closest you can place a new franchised unit to an established franchised unit without harming the established unit's owner?

Next, you need to analyze outside competition. Who in the area provides products and services similar to yours, and where are they located? Surpris-ingly, many franchises locate across the street from their strongest rival. "We have no qualms about locating next to an AAMCO," says Williams of Speedy Transmission Centers. "In fact, we find it wins business. I don't know whether people like to comparison shop or if there is just that much overflow, but AAMCOs bring us business."

Other companies follow the pack only to the extent that neighboring businesses complement one another's offerings. For example, an ice-cream franchise might open next to a hot dog stand and a salad shop to offer hun-gry passersby an assortment from which to choose.

In such arrangements, competitors' sales volumes represent a true test to whether the location is profitable. How can you determine how much a nearby business grosses? Many business owners hold vested interests in developing neighboring properties and may gladly discuss their own prosperity, if it could profitably affect their enterprises. However, a more reliable method is to hire location feasibility consultants, who often work with local commercial realtors.

With the competition accessed, the site's physical attributes must be analyzed, and here the evaluation begins with traffic patterns. More than anything else, your location needs a high level of pedestrian and/or vehicular traffic to succeed. However, all traffic isn't necessarily good traffic. Small businesspeople need a higher-than-average number of passersby they can convert into customers.

For sheer traffic volume, you should contact the area's department of transportation, city planning commission, and local chamber of commerce. They offer up-to-date traffic counts for most major roadways and can also provide statistics on planned roads and construction projects, as well as any neighborhood renewal plans.

Determining the quality of traffic is a bit more difficult. Good quality traffic means a higher concentration of local traffic from the immediate area, as opposed to transients from outside the specific region. By the same token, passenger automobile traffic generates more customers than truck traffic, and pedestrian shopping traffic produces more serious buyers than a commuter or business clientele.

Other factors that influence the quality of traffic include visibility and accessibility. In other words, your business must be easy to see and simple to reach. In visibility, the primary concerns include proximity to highway or pedestrian traffic, size of frontage, restrictions on signage and building placement, lot size, and the number of competing businesses. Remember, you want your business to stand out and draw attention. An obscure building, shrouded by the neon signs of competing businesses, stands little chance of being found and recognized by customers. However, a structure with attractive signs and frontage commands attention and has a much better shot at attracting passersby.

Accessibility relates to the ease with which customers can reach your location—in short, convenience. The customer must be able to enter your business simply, with a minimal amount of bother. Ease of entry and departure, parking availability, and traffic levels are all important considerations. Things to avoid include sharp street grades or curves that limit easy access, high-speed traffic flows, one-way streets, divided highways, hidden locations, and traffic backups.

What constitutes an accessible site? That depends on whether your business is freestanding or in a strip or suburban mall. Many of the best locations are busy corner lots—more specifically, far corner sites along main traffic flows, such as the one shown in Figure 4 below:

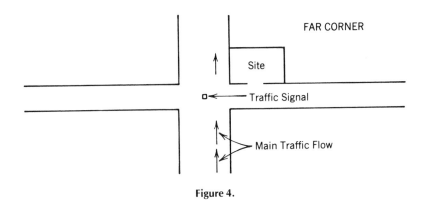

Figure 4.

As you can see, the far corner site offers easy access to the main traffic flow. Moreover, the stoplight allows cars to enter and exit freely and provides a wait for consumers to make purchasing decisions. Compare the far corner location with the near corner site in Figure 5 that creates problems because of traffic backups:

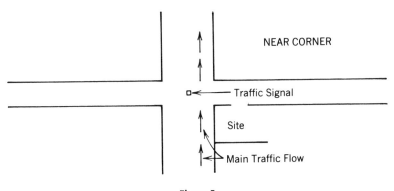

Figure 5.

The location still provides access to the main traffic flow; however, because the sites sit on the nearside of the stoplight, traffic backs up in front of the building's entrances, discouraging easy access.

Three other sites are the turn corner, wraparound, and middle of the block. The turn corner, shown in Figure 6, possesses many advantages of the far corner:

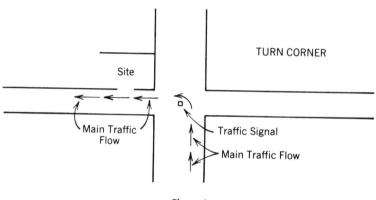

Figure 6.

Again, the location possesses simple access to the main flow of traffic while the stoplight allows easy passage and adequate recognition time.

With many of these prime corner locations disappearing, some franchisors are opting for wraparound sites (Figure 7) that offer many corner site advantages:

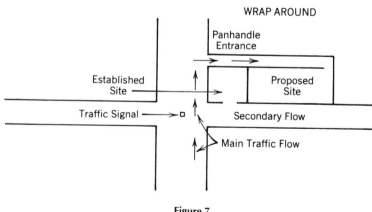

Figure 7.

Here, the panhandle entrance offers access from both major thorough-fares while the stoplight buys recognition time for consumers in the main traffic flow. The recessed location along the secondary traffic flow avoids the traffic backups experienced in front of the corner location.

Finally, middle-of-the-block sites are becoming more valuable as corners and near corners fill up. Here, it's imperative that your frontage measure wider than corner locations to attract a less captive audience. Also, you must make certain that medians don't disrupt opposite-lane access and that speed limits are low enough to allow easy access (less than 40 m.p.h.). Finally, if the block is short, you should make sure that traffic backups don't block your entrances. Figure 8 shows the typical middle-of-the-block location with bro-ken medians:

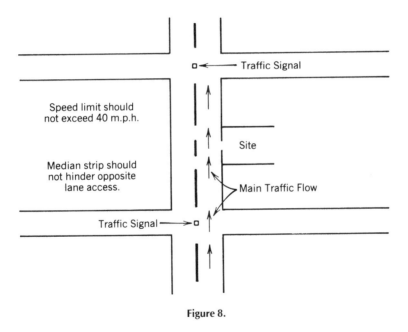

Figure 8.

Choosing mall locations presents fewer decisions for one disturbing rea-son: Mall space is often difficult to come by. According to the International Council of Shopping Centers, the vacancy rate for midsized, enclosed malls (200,000 to 399,000 square feet) is about five percent. For large malls (more than 800,000 square feet) the rate drops to about two percent. After allowing for natural turnover, the numbers reveal only a scant number of mall locations open for lease.

Despite the drawbacks, many franchises require the wide exposure and easy access that large regional malls provide. If you operate one of these franchises, you'll have to work doubly hard to find available space, and once found, you'll have to research the site: its potential and fit with your business. The management offices of most malls can supply you with customer profiles, pedestrian counts, traffic patterns, parking specifications, average gross per store, rent schedules, and failure rate for past enterprises. But beware! Malls are selling themselves. You will want to conduct your own research to verify their figures. (Many of the sources cited in the preceding discussion can also help you.)

Once you find an appropriate mall, you'll need to evaluate locations within the building. Let competition be your compass. Logically, you won't want to locate next to your strongest rival, and most franchises don't. For instance, The Athlete's Foot franchises try to locate as far away as possible from Foot Locker stores. Similarly, Computerland shops prefer to operate some distance away from Entre Computer Centers.

However, some competitive franchises do quite well in close proximity. Women's clothing stores often prosper next to each other. Food courts actually stimulate demand for fast food by providing a wide selection of fare in a comfortable setting.

In malls, the general rule on competitive placement is that stores carrying the same name-brand products (such as records, sporting goods, or electronics) should try to locate away from each other. On the other hand, businesses that carry similar but distinguishable merchandise (i.e., women's clothing stores) show less concern about their competitors' proximity.

But competition represents only a single factor in choosing the right mall location. You must also consider shopper traffic flows. Like seats at a basketball game, center court is the most sought-after mall location. It's estimated that the center of many malls see 40 to 50 percent more shoppers than locations in the wings or hallway exits.

Proximity to anchor stores is another concern. Some franchised businesses try to locate as close as possible to the big draws of a Macy's, Sears, or J.C. Penney. Others find these retailers siphon off customers by offering credit cards and a wider merchandise selection.

Also consider visibility. Malls closely control the size and placement of signage, displays, and front-of-the store promotions. If your franchise concept relies heavily on any of these factors to draw consumer attention, you would be wise to check and double-check any restriction with the landlord or mall management association.

Finally, you'll want to note the distance of your location to major entrances, movie theaters, food courts, and other traffic magnets to see how they affect your in-mall position.

THE FRANCHISOR AS LANDLORD

No discussion of franchise real estate would be complete without mention of the hardy and profitable breed of franchisor that owns the franchised land or building. More and more franchisors are turning to real estate as an additional profit center. And it's going to become an even more common practice for a wealth of investment and strategic reasons.

We have already discussed the difficulties businesspeople face in finding prime commercial real estate. In franchising, the dilemma is further exacerbated by timing: The franchisor finds a hot prospect but can't find property, or the franchisor finds a hot piece of property and can't find a serious prospect.

To mitigate these problems, some franchisors continually search for good commercial property, buy and develop it, and then find a franchisee during construction or even after the business has been opened as a company-owned unit.

The advantages here are many. In purchasing the property, the franchisor locks in real estate that could otherwise end up in a competitor's hands. Likewise, it reaps the capital gains and rental incomes that commercial real estate generates.

But a more compelling reason for franchisors to own real estate is control over the franchisee. In Chapter 5, we looked at Arthur Treacher's Fish & Chips, the large fast-food franchise that failed in the early 1980s after franchisees broke from the company and attempted to stay in business as a loose cooperative of independent operators. Because the franchisor didn't own the property, its only recourse was a long, painstaking lawsuit, during which

---

NUGGET #14

Favorable and Unfavorable Competitive Factors in Site Selection

Favorable

1. No strong competition and little likelihood of future competitors due to zoning, scarcity of sites, or both.
2. Most or all competitors in the area are minor players, inferior in size, location, and facilities.
3. No other similar business in the area.
4. High competitive sales values, despite modest facilities or secondary locations.
5. Heavy foot or vehicular traffic.

Unfavorable

1. Excessive general competition for potential business in the trade area.
2. Other similar competitors in the area.
3. Low competitive sales, despite first-rate facilities and excellent sites.
4. Existing competitors controlling all viable sites.

---

the franchisees refused to pay royalties—the kiss of death to a franchise company.

If, however, Arthur Treacher's had owned the property, it likely could have evicted the troublemakers and found new franchisees to take over the then still-profitable franchises. Futhermore, the company would have gained new initial license fees for its trouble.

Remember, real estate investment is also a speculative venture that requires substantial initial capital investment. It makes money for many franchisors, particularly food franchises where rents are based on a percentage of gross sales.

Take, for example, a typical fast-food franchise/real estate venture. The franchisor buys a small corner lot for about $20,000 in an undeveloped area that holds potential commercial value. The company then borrows to build on the lot—say $300,000—and outfits the business with all needed signage and equipment. Before the unit is finished, the company finds a franchisee who agrees to pay $25,000 in initial license fees, plus eight percent of gross sales as rent and another four percent as royalty.

If over 10 years, the franchise averages sales of $1 million a year (not out of the ordinary for many major food franchises), the franchisor stands to earn $800,000 in total rental fees—an annual 25-percent return on its initial investment of $320,000.

And the windfall doesn't end there. The franchisor can depreciate the building and deduct interest payments on the loan. Plus, the franchisor retains ownership of the property and garners all of the capital appreciation that goes hand in hand with commercial real estate development.

So real estate can prove an important revenue source for many of today's best, brightest (and biggest) franchise companies. However, because of the initial expense, the practice is well beyond most small, modestly capitalized franchisors.

PROVIDING OPENING ASSISTANCE

First impressions are lasting, especially in business, where customers' initial experiences with a product or service influence their perceptions for years to come. That's why grand openings are important to small businesspeople. Many of a business's best, long-term customers enter the front door in the first few months of operation. These consumers are doubly important because they can form the core of repeat business who can influence others to try your product or service. Marketers often refer to a diffusion of innovation that sees an inquisitive, trend-setting percentage of people inform and influence less adventurous consumers. Alienate innovators through poor service or an inferior grade of product and you lose their patronage, as well as the 8, 9, or 10 other consumers they influence.

Even more serious is when innovators are the press. More and more, the role of community informant is being usurped by print and broadcast journalists who influence thousands rather than dozens. Movie reviewers and restaurant critics represent two obvious examples, but even business journalists and news writers serve to enlighten their readers on what's new and valuable.

To win early customers, your franchisees need to follow detailed operating plans that outline all needed steps for successfully opening a business.

First, the plan should set forth timetables so franchisees know exactly when and what must be done to get their units open. For instance, there may be permits and licenses to obtain, employees to hire, suppliers to find, signs to erect, shelves and racks to stock, inventory to store, equipment to lease, insurance to purchase, accountants to contact, advertisements to place, associations to join, telephones to connect, stationery to order, cash registers to install, uniforms to order, garbage removal to arrange, bank accounts to open, utilities to install, employees to train, office furniture to lease, records to keep, meetings to hold, and schedules to prepare.

It all needs to be done, and the franchisee won't do it unless you spell it out. Your plans must be complete, down to the most minor detail. For example, every business requires a listing in the *Yellow Pages*, but how many new franchisees would remember to place such ads on their own? Not many. And here, a reminder may not be enough. You may have to tell franchisees when and how to buy *Yellow Pages* space. The same holds true for insurance. Most new business owners would probably expect to invest in business liability coverage. But would they think to insure a $4000 plate glass window? Expensive tools and equipment? The owner's car that is often used for deliveries?

The list of preopening tasks expands when construction is involved. Here, franchisors must provide job scheduling plans that more resemble construction reports than franchise opening programs. For example, the plan may tell franchisees how many weeks before opening the site must be cleared and graded. It then may specify times for digging and pouring footers, erecting walls, framing the roof, installing equipment, paving the parking lot, painting and plastering dry wall, finishing landscaping, installing front-door locks, and any of a million other construction jobs.

And then there's preopening hiring and training to consider. Many of these issues should be handled in the company's operations manual. Still, the new franchisee faces special problems that require additional guidance and assistance. New businesspeople are constantly astounded by the difficulties in hiring reliable employees, especially for low to medium paying, unskilled jobs. And don't expect it to get any easier. The baby boom that provided franchises with huge pools of youthful employees during the 1960s and 1970s has turned bust. Today, many franchises openly compete for workers by offering higher wages, scholarships, and better benefits. Kwik Kopy, for instance, has instituted a retired workers' program that uses senior citizens to make sales calls on local businesses. Other franchises have resorted to busing workers from high unemployment areas to suburban locations.

Thus, new franchisees face plenty of competition in the employment market and often need the franchisor's complete support and cooperation in finding qualified personnel. You may have to send headquarters personnel to assist in recruiting or hiring, as well as provide names and addresses of recent applicants from other nearby franchises. To be prepared, you should structure the franchisee's opening schedule to allow plenty of lead time in finding those first important employees.

Closely related to recruiting is preopening training, which must be done fast and must be done right. Here, enthusiasm and energy are the keys. Franchisees should energize new employees to play active roles in the opening drama of the business. Like a coach readying his team for the big game, franchisees must instill a desire to perform beyond the range of regular duties. And franchisors can help.

For example, some franchisors require new franchisees to hold a preopening family night for employees to show their relatives the new business and how it works. Other companies throw similar shindigs for community leaders, inviting the mayor, city council, and local religious leaders. These dry runs allow employees to work out operational bugs before a more forgiving audience, but they also serve to reinforce how important each job is to a successful business send-off.

The grand opening remains a key factor to a successful business. No other event can as quickly win your business a place in the consumer's consciousness. First, you must decide when it should take place. Many franchises start low-key operations a week or two before their official openings to correct glaring errors, adjust inventories, and evaluate employees' initial performances. Others start with a clean slate, cutting the ribbon on the day the first pizza is flipped, sale is made, class is taught, or car is serviced.

NUGGET #15

A Sample Checklist for Opening a Unit

Days to Opening	Item
90 days before opening	Prepare site renovations or construction designs Obtain permits Incorporate business Contract construction or renovation
70 days before opening	Begin ground-breaking or renovations
60 days before opening	Check construction progress Contact suppliers and vendors Order signs, stationery, safe, equipment, and cash registers
45 days before opening	Determine manpower needs, including selection of managers and number and jobs of employees
40 days before opening	Attend 10-day, on-site training course
30 days before opening	Review final selection of and hire managers. Update managers on progress Order opening-day banners and advertising package. Place opening-day advertising in local newspapers or radio Contract for outside services (snow removal, landscaping, garbage collection, accountants, exterminators, snow removal, etc.) Purchase administrative supplies—pencils, pens, office furniture, closed/open sign. Establish MasterCard and Visa accounts Place *Yellow Pages* advertising Order telephones Place employment ads for personnel
21 days before opening	Hire opening crew. Establish personnel files. Obtain Workers' Compensation Receive equipment

NUGGET #15 (*Continued*)

14 days before opening	Begin training employees
	Order dry goods, paper supplies, and food items
	Send out opening day invitations
10 days before opening	Receive and inspect inventory
8 days before opening	Inspect equipment
7 days before opening	Complete final construction or renovation inspection
	Prepare opening week schedule
3 days before opening	Engage utilities
	Establish inventory control
2 days before opening	Run through complete opening checklist
	Receive all dry goods, paper supplies, and food
	Prepare food for opening
1 day before opening	Prepare for opening celebration
	Conduct final accounting of inventory
Opening Day	Open business
1 day after opening	Account for sales and inventory
	Report opening day results to company

Whatever your timing, the crucial element of grand opening success is public relations and advertising. As a franchisor, it is your duty to see that news of the opening spreads through the community. Some franchisors actually stipulate the amount a franchisee must invest in grand opening advertising in the franchise agreement. Others simply provide stock radio and newspaper ads, press releases, and advice and guidance.

To succeed, grand openings must attract people and the press. Giveaways, raffles, promotions, discounts, clowns, celebrities, and sports stars help lure the public. The press, however, proves a more jaundiced bunch. They usually require a local angle and/or special invitation to turn out. Once there, they also expect easy access to information, both written and verbal. Press packages should be made available so your franchisees can distribute them to reporters. But personal attention is the best ticket to winning a reporter's favor.

While working for a small-town newspaper, my co-author once covered the routine opening of a pizza franchise. He met the manager and gathered the usual quotes. Before leaving, however, the owner stopped him and asked whether he'd enjoy trying to spin pizza dough. He quickly obliged, donning an apron, and spending the next hour learning the fine art of pizza-making. Needless to say, the hour's worth of levity won the business a big mention in the next day's newspaper, and the shop still prospers, which may or may not reflect upon my co-author's contribution.

Franchisors should also encourage their franchisees to pursue more traditional promotion strategies. By joining the local chamber of commerce, franchisees can inform other local businesspeople of plans to open their businesses. By joining community groups, such as the Kiwanis or Rotary Clubs, franchisees can invite entire organizations to their grand openings. By personally visiting the business editor of the local newspaper or the news director of local radio stations, franchisees can increase their chances of getting reporters to show up for the big event.

All these techniques are relatively painless approaches to building local excitement, interest, and attention. But because few franchisees have prior business experience, it's doubtful whether any would take these initiatives on their own. Instead, their success depends upon the direction, forethought, and creativity you apply in developing grand opening guidelines and suggestions.

ONGOING SUPPORT AND SERVICE

"It's not over until it's over," goes Yogi Berra's famous line. But in franchising, it's not over even when it is over. Once you get your franchisees up and operating, your job hasn't ended. In fact, it's only just begun, because as a franchisor, you'll be expected to provide ongoing attention and care. You'll have to service your franchisees, offering continuing advice, guidance, marketing, advertising, and product and promotional development.

These ongoing obligations can concern most businesspeople. But in practice, new franchisors provide many of these services with little inconvenience simply by staying in contact with their franchisees, either over the telephone or, if distance allows, in person. In the beginning, your franchisees won't expect massive marketing or product development programs. Instead, they'll be grateful for simple advice, suggestions, and recommendations on effective business management. Much of this can be handled directly by you or by other experienced company personnel.

There are, however, some techniques even the smallest franchisors can apply to help speed up problem-solving. First, you should designate an answer man, someone through whom problems and inquiries can be channeled. If it's you, then give franchisees your direct telephone extension and be prepared to handle the onslaught. If that's impractical, designate a colleague to field the inquiries and relay them to other appropriate personnel.

Franchisees can be a demanding lot—they aren't about to let you forget that they pay for service. But often, anxieties are alleviated simply by talking to someone in the home office. Make that someone available! Have him or her respond immediately even if it is just to say, "We're working on it." And then put them to work solving the problem.

Next, consider establishing company newsletters, which go a long way in informing franchisees of innovative marketing and promotion techniques, and new products or services that affect their franchised business. Subway Sandwiches & Salads, for example, publishes two newsletters, one concerning management issues and the other focusing strictly on operational matters. "The operation's newsletter consists of three basic components," notes Kathryn White, the publication's editor. "First, it covers basic operational issues, including food presentation, training, motivation, inventory, and food waste management. Second, it features pretested promotions franchisees can use to increase sales volumes. Here, we outline costs, identify returns, and offer basic how-to suggestions on developing similar programs." Finally, the publication salutes heavy hitters—those franchisees with outstanding performance reports. "We find this adds human interest and gives other operators insight into success," she explains.

Initially, your newsletter can be a simple affair, consisting of two, four, or six typewritten pages of easy-to-read, lively information. The goal is to provide concise and accurate information on subjects of primary concern to franchisees. New marketing and advertising programs, simplified reporting methods, supplier information, training suggestions, inventory manage-

NUGGET #16

How to Increase Sales at Franchise Units

Searching for tried-and-true methods to increase sales at franchised units? Here is a sampling of promotion techniques used by major franchisors.

Problem	Solutions
Poor name recognition within the community	Offer special group rates to selected community groups on your product or service
	Donate a specific percentage of a week's sales to selected charities and then work with the charity to issue press releases regarding the program
	Sponsor community athletic teams, junior achievement clubs, bike-a-thons or other community events
	Undertake a direct-mail campaign
	Contract with a local celebrity to make an on-site appearance
Low return business	Check operational procedures and pricing
	Circulate a questionnaire to discover the root of the problem
	Develop a punch-card campaign, whereby repeat customers become entitled to some free product or service
	Establish a valued customer club, offering special service or prices to frequent customers
	Institute weekly specials; make Sundays family days, Tuesdays special-value days.
	Conduct a frequent-shopper raffle, whereby a customer's chances of winning increase with the number of repeat visits (the customer's name is entered once on the first visit, twice on the second, ten times on the tenth)

NUGGET #16 (*Continued*)

Low average sale	Remind salespeople to suggest add-ons or additional products to customers. "Would you like to see ties to match those trousers?" "Did you know we are running specials on laser discs this week?"
	Encourage family days or buy-one and-a-friend-gets-one-free campaigns
	Give away special products or services with high volume sales
New competition	Review operating procedures and pricing to assure competitiveness
	Conduct a customer appreciation campaign that reinforces the sales relationship
	Offer to meet or beat competitor's discounts

ment techniques, and other related issues are all fair game for your publication.

But don't forget the human interest angles. People love to read about other people, and you should use this fact to complement your newsletter. If your Southern California franchisee wins the Sacramento Marathon, write up a short congratulations, or better yet, interview the guy and tell your readers when he first started running, how many miles he runs a week, his athletic goals, and thoughts regarding competition. Sound like window-dressing? It is to an extent, but getting people to read your newsletter is half the battle in educating them to important issues within the company. Use human interest as a bait that lures franchisees into learning more about success.

Once you start to grow and expand, you may want to upgrade your newsletter, which is a relatively easy chore. Many printers offer layout and design services, and will insert graphics and photographs into the body of typeset pages. If you're really ambitious, investigate desktop computer publishing systems that turn secretaries and receptionists into design wizards who can set type styles; arrange columns; and draw charts, diagrams, and other graphics with the mere strike of a key.

But there is more—much more—to providing service than simply offering advice and guidance, and producing a newsletter. You'll also need to undertake in-field reviews and consultations. "The reviews have many purposes," according to consultant Jerry Cusack. "They facilitate communication between franchisees and company management and also serve as training tools." More importantly, however, the regular consultations measure franchisee compliance with the company's standards and operations program, as well as document the franchisee's performance and the company's commitment to improving that performance.

What are the important aspects of in-field reviews? First, you need to send competent operations specialists, who understand a broad range of business functions. "We have generalists in the field who meet with franchisees and evaluate the business in total," says William LeVine of Postal Instant Press. "It's not enough that the company man identify a revenue shortfall; he also must provide workable solutions to the problem."

Also, you want to present the reviews as problem identification opportunities, not fault-finding missions. To accomplish this, most franchise companies give franchisees ample notice of the impending visits, along with checklists of the things the review will include. "No one enjoys being graded, and franchisors can avoid adversarial situations by constantly reassuring franchisees that reviews are intended to achieve mutual goals of greater sales and lower costs," says Cusack.

After weeks, months, or years of operation, even the most conscientious franchisee can lapse into bad work habits. You need to design reviews and in-field consultations to correct these tendencies effectively and efficiently without alienating your franchise owners.

The last, but certainly not the least, service you'll need to provide franchisees is ongoing research and development, which sounds imposing but actually entails no more than developing methods to cut costs and increase sales. Profitability is the name of the game for your franchisees. As their businesses grow and develop, they'll want their incomes to increase accordingly. And there are only two methods of accomplishing this—by boosting efficiency (reducing costs) or adding cutomers (increasing sales). As a franchisor, it's your duty to develop new operating programs to cut expenses and add novel products or services to generate greater revenue.

How is this accomplished? Sometimes it comes by identifying unfilled needs or niches in the marketplace. "After analyzing certain sectors of the air-freight market," begins Richard Dingfelder, vice-president of sales and marketing for Pilot Air Freight, "we discovered that shippers in the one-hundred-to-five-hundred-pound freight category were experiencing service difficulties." The problem stemmed from the fact that the freight industry's rate structure is designed for full truckloads. "The result was that shippers were being penalized for cargo under certain weights."

Seeing an opportunity for their franchisees, Pilot developed a program, Time Definite Transportation Services, that scheduled and operated vehicles, regardless of whether the truck ran full or not, and then published a service guide and rate schedule for franchise customers. "The service provides an additional revenue source for our franchisees," Dingfelder explains.

Market testing and research is another means of discovering new market opportunities. "Every six months we review our menu with an eye to developing new, potentially profitable products," says Subway Sandwiches & Salads' Kathryn White. "We'll test a new product at selected units across the country to determine customer acceptance." Winners include a hot bacon and cheese sandwich added in late 1985. Soup, on the other hand, received a cold reception and failed to survive testing.

But perhaps your best source of new product or promotion techniques is your franchisees. "We focus on one major retail concept every year," says Docktor Pet Centers' Les Charm. "The great majority of these come from our franchisees. They have a million good ideas. It's often just a matter of listening and adapting their ideas to the system as a whole."

Franchisees can also tell you when new concepts won't work. "We experimented with radiator repair as an adjunct to our transmission business," says D'Arcy Williams of Speedy Transmission Centers. "But after listening to franchisees, I discovered they weren't interested in entering a new business. Instead, they wanted workable suggestions for increasing their present transmission business."

Franchisors live in a world of constant development and change. To meet new market conditions and needs, they must continually upgrade services and promotions. To appease growth-conscious franchisees, they must provide viable new products and programs regularly. And although the race for growth and profits is never an easy one, it's often made more complicated in franchising, where the demands of many often fall on the shoulders of few.

But if you enjoy new and exciting challenges, then offering novel products and innovative marketing programs often proves one of franchising's most exhilarating experiences.

SERVANT NOT SLAVE

So the services are many. As a franchisor, you'll be expected to employ your energies and imagination in ways you never before imagined. There'll be decisions to make and locations to choose, advice to offer and communications to develop. But all is not service. A franchisor is also a master, and Chapter 11 outlines the controls you must impose to guarantee an effective and profitable franchise system.

CHAPTER **11**

CONTROLLING YOUR FRANCHISE SYSTEM

Control—it's one of the most overrated issues in franchising. Don't misunderstand. As a franchisor, it's your right and responsibility to develop systems and procedures that provide adequate management, maintenance, and direction of your franchise system. But you should never allow control of franchisees to become such an obsession that it robs you of excessive time and resources and your franchisees of creative input into their businesses.

Yet it happens. In their eagerness to win total compliance, franchisors often develop sophisticated control mechanisms that do little more than generate costs and breed ill will. For example, I remember one major nationwide franchise that spent hundreds of thousands of dollars to develop and implement a massive program to assure that franchisees paid their fair share of royalties. The company, however, soon found that the costs of the program outweighed the revenue saved and abandoned it. Why? Because no control mechanism is foolproof. Franchisees and people in general employ a wealth of creative techniques to avoid paying money.

And the same situation exists in system protection and control. One of the first questions businesspeople ask when considering franchising is, "How can I prevent people from stealing my idea?" The answer is you can't, at least not completely. Courts have ruled time and time again that there's nothing new in flipping hamburgers or fixing mufflers. The fact that you developed a particular system for the preparation and presentation of a product or service doesn't give you exclusive ownership to that idea. Anyone operating a similar business can employ related methods. Certainly, copyrights, trademarks, and patents afford some security against others pilfering your *exact* words, symbols, or inventions. But these can often be sidestepped.

"One of the reasons I originally purchased Stained Glass Overlay was because the staining process was patented," begins owner Peter Shea. "Although this is often an important selling point to franchisees, I quickly learned that patents are made to get around. All anyone has to do is obtain your filing from the patent office, change a few points, and provide a basically identical product or service."

So protection is never guaranteed. The mere act of opening your doors to the public allows current and potential competitors to learn something about your business's system.

Perhaps the only security for a good idea is quick action. If you conceive of a novel product or service, embrace your brilliance and run with it. By the time a competitor studies and duplicates your innovation, you'll have gained a near-insurmountable lead.

The same holds true for internal control of franchisees. If your business can succeed under franchising, move to build a franchise. Don't be distracted by the measure of control you forfeit in the process. Remember, by its very nature, franchising decentralizes decision-making, allowing for independent behavior on the parts of franchisees. As a franchisor, you're more partner than boss, more consultant than employer. You will never wield absolute control over your franchisees. So abandon the thought now, before you invest an inordinate amount of time and money in a futile objective.

Nevertheless, there are legal, contractual, and managerial mechanisms that help control a franchised business. And although none work perfectly, together they provide the degree of mastery most franchisors require.

CONTROLLING SKIMMING

Ask a franchisor for his opinion on franchisee skimming, and he'll tell you the problem doesn't exist, at least in his franchise. "Our franchisees report every cent they earn," you'll be told. Off the record, however, you'll hear a different, more disturbing answer. "I'm convinced that many of my franchisees take something off the top before reporting gross sales to the home office," one successful franchisor confides. As evidence, the entrepreneur recalls a recent meeting held for the company's veteran franchisees. "During the meeting, some of them started to complain that the royalty was too high. I began thinking maybe they were right, so I offered them a deal. I agreed to cut the royalty by one-third if they signed a statement to the effect that if I ever discovered them cheating, I got their stores no questions asked. Not a single franchisee accepted the deal. They knew it was too big a risk."

Don't become paranoid, however. It's not just you that most franchisees are trying to cheat. Franchisees may also try to avoid local, state, or federal taxes, which can easily add up to more money than you receive.

But that's no excuse, and you must still work to lessen your losses. Consider a 25-store franchise. If the royalty is six percent and each owner grosses $250,000 a year but reports only $225,000, the franchisor stands to lose $37,500 a year, or $375,000 over the life of their 10-year franchise agreements.

How can you control such leakage? First, through your contract. In your franchise agreement, you must specify that failure to report or pay the proper amount of royalty is a major breach of contract, punishable by termination of the agreement. You'll also need to contractually stipulate your rights to receive and/or inspect reports, tax returns, records, and books.

Financial statements represent another accounting document to which you'll want access. Most franchisors require franchisees to submit a profit-and-loss statement and/or balance sheet within a few months of the end of each year. In addition, the franchisor may request quarterly or monthly updates on the financial performance of the franchised business.

Whatever their frequency, financial statements prove an important management tool for evaluation of compliance and the success of your franchisees. They also can supplement your sales efforts, providing figures on income potential that you can present to prospective franchisees.

But there's a strong warning here. Many franchisees delay or object to filing financial statements—particularly audited ones, which can cost thousands of dollars to prepare. Therefore, you may need to waive audit requirements for annual statements, unless the franchisee is in breach of an obligation. Moreover, if franchisees fail to submit any required documents in a timely, complete, accurate, and legible fashion, they should be obligated to pick up all costs associated with an audit of their books.

But contractual controls go only so far. In practice, you'll also need to employ managerial safeguards for reducing franchisee skimming. And here the methods range from counting cars in parking lots to installing sophisticated computer accounting systems that report sales, expenses, and inventory directly to the home office.

However, problems persist. "Someone can always build a better bread box," says one franchisor. "We use a relatively complex numbered invoicing sytem that makes franchisees account for every transaction. They still find ways to circumvent the rules." To illustrate, the franchisor recites a story that occurred during a routine inspection of a franchise. "While in the shop, I noticed that something seemed peculiar about the invoices hanging on the wall. So I grabbed one, took it back to the office, and discovered it was counterfeit."

The moral is clear: No system, no matter how elaborate, can assure that you will see a percentage of every sale. Invoices can be faked, cash register receipts forged, and cash transactions conveniently hidden. For every process you devise, a disreputable franchisee can develop a counterstrategy to dupe you out of your fair share.

Are there any ways to combat the problem? Yes, but they're more managerial than procedural. "The more profitable you can make your franchisees, the less likely they'll steal from you," a major franchisor explains. "If the franchisee feels you're robbing him, he'll just rob you right back. The more they make, the less they'll take."

And there are other ways to mitigate your losses. First, make the reporting and payment system as concise and simple as possible. Hours of tedious and unnecessary paperwork only motivate franchisees to miss payment schedules and compensate their unpaid efforts by dipping into your percentage.

Second, take a firm and clear stand when cheaters are caught. "We catch them," says the founder of a major franchise company. "Inevitably, they get sloppy and stumble, and when they do, they meet me in my office. I look them straight in the eyes and tell them I know there's more revenue than reported and that if it persists they're out of the franchise. I also demand compensation according to the extent of their skimming and how long I believe it's been going on. If they refuse to pay, I read the franchise agreement, which clearly identifies false royalty reporting as grounds for revocation. Most franchisees, however, act like guilty children, beg forgiveness, and clean up their act or at least become less flagrant."

How else do franchisors deal with skimming? If suspicions warrant, some threaten to place company employees on site to gain actual counts of customers and sales. Others pay confederates to make cash purchases to see if the transactions turn up on weekly or monthly sales reports.

Finally, a franchisor may be forced to make examples of particularly obvious skimming cases. "If you're in this game long enough, you're bound to find at least one owner who cheats so blatantly that termination is the only option," explains another franchisor. "When that happens, move quickly and assuredly, and let others in the franchise know the reason for your actions. Then, watch the repercussions surface in higher grosses reported by your franchisees in their next royalty reports."

So you now know the bitter truth about skimming. It exists and probably always will. As an honest businessperson, you have the duty to correct any wrongs and receive what is rightfully yours. But no matter how hard you work, chances are you'll have to tolerate a certain amount of dishonesty. There are three positions you can take.

First, you can simply ignore it, figuring this is a cost of doing business. Second, you can take positive stands against the practice, implement some of the suggestions outlined here, and boldly reiterate your opposition to the practice whenever possible. Finally, you can become a police officer, constantly running covert operations in attempts to uncover wrongdoings.

I warn you, however, if you choose the last of these options, if you allow skimming prevention to permeate your strategic decision-making, you'll only undermine the good that comes from a properly managed franchise company.

PROTECTING YOUR SYSTEM: THE NECESSARY STEPS

Even though you know your system can only be marginally protected, that doesn't mean you shouldn't safeguard it to the fullest extent possible. By employing a few preemptive techniques, you may not totally prevent the unauthorized use of your ideas, but you certainly can discourage it.

First, you'll want to file and obtain the legal registrations that identify your ownership of important parts of your franchise. And although copyrights, trademarks, and patents are no panacea, they do serve to inform others of your legal claim to precise words, symbols, phrases, and inventions.

Obtaining copyrights to manuals, advertisements, and policy statements is a relatively easy and inexpensive process. In fact, you can copyright any newly written material in your office upon its creation by appending the proper copyright notice. However, to provide legal evidence of your ownership you must obtain a formal copyright from the U.S. Copyright Office in Washington, D.C., and affix a copyright symbol to your document.

But remember, copyrights pertain only to the exact wording of your document. If a writer paraphrases your information, he or she does not infringe on your copyright. The value of copyrights rests solely in (1) deterring others from freely representing your written documents as their own and in (2) providing evidence that you, in fact, were the creator of the written document.

Trademarks are a bit more complicated and much more important. Technically speaking, a trademark is any name or symbol adopted and used by a manufacturer or seller to identify and distinguish its goods or service from those manufactured or sold by others.

More generally, trademarks serve as a company's name tag or I.D. bracelet. McDonald's Golden Arches, Coca-Cola's distinctive cursive signature, Jiffy Lube's red pointing *J* all allow the consumer to quickly identify the company's product, service, location, or advertisement.

Thus, trademarks are critical to any business, but particularly franchises where they provide the instant identification new franchisees need to win immediate customer followings.

How can you trademark a name, logo, or symbol? If you have adopted a name or symbol to identify your goods or services, and that designation is currently being used in interstate commerce in connection with those goods or services, then you can apply for federal trademark registration to the U.S. Patent and Trademark Office in Washington, D.C. But not all applications are accepted. For instance, if your name or symbol too closely resembles an already-existing trademark, your registration may be refused.

Moreover, the Patent and Trademark Office maintains a principal and supplemental register, which influence the nature of your right to a trademark. Registration on the principal register offers official government notice of your ownership of the trademark, its validity, and the registrant's exclusive right to use it. Registration on the secondary register provides no notice of ownership, and thus affords much less protection to the trademark.

For new franchisors, making the principal register involves submitting a name that avoids common surnames ("Jones' Laundry" probably won't make the principle list), simple description ("Quality Dry Cleaners" is similarly weak), and specific geographic locations ("Detroit Dry Cleaners" also misses the mark).

Regardless of register, both federal trademark registrations afford you the right to sue to prevent another party from improperly using your trademark, which is an extremely important consideration for franchisees. After buying the business, franchisees want tangible proof of their ongoing right to use your name in the business.

Patents represent a final method for legally claiming a part of your franchise business. But unlike copyrights and trademarks, patents apply to tangible, workable devices of original effort—inventions of one sort or another. Therefore, patents don't apply to ideas or processes. You can't patent your company's sales technique. You can, however, patent a device that automatically dials customers and leaves a prerecorded sales message.

Because of the body of law that surrounds patents, it's best to consult with a qualified attorney before filing a patent application.

CONTROLLING INFORMATION: CONFIDENTIALITY AND NONDISCLOSURE

Many businesspeople operate under the misconception that they possess a great secret that no one else knows. And although it's true that businesses differ, every idea builds on another. McDonald's borrowed from Howard Johnson's, Precision Tune-Up from AAMCO, Sylvan Learning Systems from Comprehensive Accounting, and so on. Most of us overestimate the scope of our own ingenuity and search for ways to keep the secrets all to ourselves.

That's where nondisclosure and confidentiality enter the scene. "We'll swear franchisees to secrecy. We'll make them agree not to divulge our trade secrets," a franchisor may decide. But we've already seen how difficult it is to wield absolute control over your franchisees. If they choose to photocopy your operating manual and send it to their out-of-state cousins, you're going to have a heck of a time stopping them. If they enjoy meeting friends after work and explaining the company's future marketing plans, there's little you can do to prevent them.

Yet information is knowledge, and knowledge is power. And to retain your power in the marketplace, you'll have to implement some tactics—regardless of their marginal effectiveness—to plug information leaks throughout your franchise system.

First, communicate the proprietary nature of your operating manual, technical and product information, bulletins, or other related documents by expressly retaining your ownership in the franchise agreement and prohibiting their removal from the franchised location. Some franchisors go so far as obtaining signed receipts from their franchisees for selected documents and charging hefty replacement prices if they should be lost ($350 to $500).

Also in your franchise agreement, you'll want to prohibit the duplication or distribution of any confidential information, trade secrets, methods, techniques, or other knowledge provided by you to the franchisee. And include family members in those to whom distribution is forbidden (unless employed by the franchise). It would be unfair for the relative of a franchisee to use your trade secrets to develop a similar, competitive business. But it happens.

Additionally, you may want key employees to adhere to similar restrictions to prevent them from disseminating inside information.

But, as I warned, none of these safeguards are surefire. At least, they serve to clearly express the importance you place on keeping vital aspects of your business confidential. At most, they severely discourage thoughtless or disreputable franchisees from freely dispensing the knowledge on which your success depends.

CONTROLLING OWNERSHIP: DECIDING WHERE THE BUCK STOPS

The person who signs the franchise agreement is the owner. This seems obvious. Right? Well, what happens if the one who signs is a corporation? Or what if he or she dies? Is disabled? Sells out? Then ownership is not so clear, and you may be stuck with a franchisee you neither bargained for nor even know. So it's best to work out the contingencies beforehand to reduce chaos later.

Allowing Franchisees to Incorporate: A Practical Approach

Developing policies on franchisee incorporation presents a quandary for the newly franchising company. On the one hand, you want franchisees to answer personally to you for their liabilities. If they mismanage the business or if they walk away from the deal, you need some recourse to their personal assets to fulfull any obligations or debts. And that means making them sign the franchise agreements as individuals.

On the other hand, franchisees gamble everything on your franchise opportunity. They quit their jobs, invest their entire savings, and incur tremendous personal debt to take part in your franchise. Expenses for rent, inventory, utilities, construction, and renovation all come under their name.

And on top of all the risks, you add one more. You tell these insecure people that incorporation is out of the question, that their only means of protection is off limits. Now if they fail, it's not just a lost opportunity, but rather a repossessed car, a forfeited home, that small savings account they've hidden for their child's college tuition. It's all on the line, and it's often too much for the individual investor.

The big, well-established franchising companies stand firm during such negotiation. "Take it or leave it," they tell prospective franchisees. "We don't sign corporations." And they can make bold assertions. Their track record affords them the power position in negotiations.

But new franchisors simply don't wield such clout. In the initial stages of your franchise offering, you'll have to make concessions to close deals—and some will be dear.

When franchisee incorporation falls in this category, make sure your franchisees form a new corporation, clearly separate from other business interests. You wouldn't want the success of your franchised unit to hinge upon the profit and loss of side businesses about which you know nothing.

Also, retain your right of approval over current and future stockholders. For obvious reasons, it's wise to know the qualifications of anybody holding interest in your franchised business.

Likewise, you'll need to reserve access to that person within your corporate franchise who has direct responsibility over the operation of the business. Whenever you're dealing with multiple owners, indecision and lapses in communication are inevitable. For effective operation of your business, you'll need to designate a corporate liaison officer and identify him or her in your franchise agreement as the individual responsible for efficiently handling problems and communication between yourself and appropriate people within the franchised organization.

Finally, if you simply can't live with corporate franchisees, ask your attorney for alternative methods of allowing franchisees to sign as corporations and still remain individually responsible to you.

Assignment of Ownership: Who Owns the Business?

Okay. So you think determining the ownership of your franchise represents a minor challenge? Then answer this. If you sell a franchise to an individual who takes on a partner, and they then incorporate and are bought out by a third shareholder, who dies shortly thereafter, who owns the franchise? No answers, please. The example is used only to illustrate the fact that simple business arrangements become very complicated, very quickly if you don't provide for a broad range of contingencies, such as:

1. What happens if a franchisee decides to sell? Do you possess the right of first refusal? Often franchisors retain the right to buy back franchises within a specified time after franchisees give notice of purchase offers. But forward-thinking franchisees may resent such contractual clauses, claiming they limit the resale value of their units.

Also, franchisors should reserve the right to approve new buyers and decide the franchise terms they'll be offered. For example, must new franchisees agree to pay the current royalty of six percent or can they assume the sellers' payments of only three percent? Are any operational upgrades or renovations a part of the agreement? Do new buyers play out the remaining years on the previous agreement, or can they sign for a full term?

2. What happens if a franchisee should die? It's a morbid question that, surprisingly, elicits particular interest in prospective franchisees, who often overlook more pressing issues to ask, "Will my widow and children get

the business if I die?" Meet their concerns by providing a mechanism to smoothly transfer the business to family members and train them if necessary.

3. What happens if the franchisee should be disabled? Even more common than franchisee death is franchisee illness or incapacitation. Will the family retain ownership? Will the franchisor help train and ready them?

4. What happens upon termination? No new franchisor cares to think about terminating its association with any of its franchisees. It's a difficult problem that often breeds bitter and costly disputes. For example, some states mandate lengthy cure periods that provide franchisees who are in breach of contract plenty of time to correct problems before franchisors can even begin action to terminate the agreement. Moreover, many courts side with franchisees when a seemingly powerful corporation attempts to strip individuals of their businesses and livelihoods. What constitutes a breach? Technically, a breach may result for any of a multitude of reasons, including:

Falsifying information

Failing to offer company service

Failing to pay money owed

Offering unauthorized services

Conducting a supplemental business in conjunction with the franchised business

Abandoning the business by the franchisee

Attempting to terminate the contract by the franchisee

Nonauthorized assignment of the agreement to a third party

Misusing trademarks

Sometimes, simple breaches don't prove enough to terminate a contract. To rid your system of a particularly dishonest or incompetent franchisee, you'll often need to show a record of contract violations.

Once a contract is terminated, you'll have to have policies in place to make a clean and total break. You'll want a do's and don'ts list that could include any of the following:

Do collect all monies owed to you.

Don't allow further use of your name, trademark, copyright, business system, or other information important to your franchise.

Do prohibit further advertising under your name or related to your name. (Don't allow a terminated franchisee to advertise his new business as formerly your franchise.)

Do make sure your terminated franchisee cancels fictitious name registrations.

Don't allow a terminated franchisee's new business to look like yours.

Do make sure your company stationery is destroyed, or else buy it back.

Do get back manuals and other items, and reclaim their telephone number.

Do provide for continued access to the franchisee's books for a year after termination.

Do provide for possible assumption of the franchisee's lease, so you can retain that location for your franchise.

Finally, you may want to control terminated franchisees' ability to compete directly with your company by including a not to compete covenant in your franchise agreement. But be careful. A few states prohibit these contractual clauses, and courts in many other jurisdictions frown on any provision that limits a person's ability to earn a living. Your hope of retaining their potency hinges upon reasonability. If the covenant limits competition for a reasonable time (say one or two years) in a reasonable geographical territory (perhaps a 10-mile radius of the former franchised unit), its likelihood of withstanding a legal challenge increases significantly.

Controlling the Management of Your Franchise

For the most part, the effective, on-site operation of your franchised unit is determined by the skill with which you train your franchisee and prepare your operating manual. If your manual tells franchisees how to greet and service customers, how to order and account for inventory, how to prepare and present the product, and covers all the other issues essential to the operation of your business, then properly trained franchisees should experience little difficulty in following your program.

To guarantee their compliance, however, you must bind them to your system and procedures using your franchise agreement. Here, you need general language that ties your franchisees to all policies, procedures, standards, and specifications now in effect or which could be implemented in the future. In addition, you'll want to stipulate their compliance to your advertising programs, promotion techniques, and accounting methods.

You also will want to include specific provisions for the daily operation of the business. For example, you can state the hours of operation, the size and placement of signage, the maintenance and cleanliness of the franchised unit, the products and services to be offered, as well as the equipment and supplies on hand.

And finally, you'll need to specify the precise management of the business. If your company allows only owners to manage the business, this needs to be stated in your agreement. If you allow nonowner managers, you'll want to retain some control over these essential employees, and here some important considerations include:

Who trains managers? To assure accurate operation of the franchised business, many franchisors retain the right to train managers in the same way they educate franchisees.

Do you have the right to approve managers? You approve franchisees. Shouldn't you reserve the same right to okay others intimately involved with the business.

Will you specify the duties of the manager? Detailed specification represents the heart of quality control in franchising. Shouldn't you specify the responsibilities of key personnel.

Who dismisses incompetent managers? Franchisees should hold a vested interest in ridding their businesses of ineffective employees. But many find it difficult to fire longtime employees, or even recognize their incompetence. Can you step in and do the necessary dirty work?

Should you make managers sign noncompetition, confidentiality, and operational agreements? Since managers oversee day-to-day operations, shouldn't they be bound to your operating procedures? Since they are privy to your confidential information, shouldn't they sign a covenant not to compete or an agreement not to divulge company secrets?

Aside from managers, who else should you control? The assistant manager? The account executive? The sales manager? The head chef? What types of control are necessary here?

YOU AS THE MASTER

So these represent a franchisor's primary control mechanisms. Some are simple, some are complicated, but none are guaranteed. For every strategy you develop, there's an equal and opposite tack your franchisees can take to avoid your desired goals.

The only solution is constant vigilance and frequent communication. If you know the average grosses of your franchisees, you'll discover who's skimming. If you speak and meet frequently with your franchisees, you'll learn about improper practices, operational divergences, and incompetent managers.

Control mechanisms serve only to make a statement. They can't replace your role in the effective management of the franchise system.

CHAPTER 12

SELLING YOUR FRANCHISE

Let's face it, no matter how well-conceived your franchise program and no matter how masterfully prepared your franchise legal paperwork, you're not a franchisor until you sell that first franchise. Everything else—operating manuals, marketing programs, legal compliance—is secondary to the most fundamental component of successful franchising—sales. "If you want to be a franchisor," says Tony Martino of MAACO, "Then go out and sell franchises." Martino may be overlooking the volume of work it takes to get to that point. But he's correct in designating sales as the heart of franchising.

Consider that every franchise in the country, every McDonald's, every Midas, every Just Pants, every Ben Franklin Store, was sold at one time or another. No matter how you cut it, your success depends on an ability to attract qualified prospects and then sell them on your business opportunity. You must sell to grow. You must sell to expand. That's what franchising is all about.

I keep coming back to Peter Shea's comment mentioned earlier: "Ours is a lead-generation business. The more leads we get, the more franchises we sell." In a nutshell, Shea articulates the way you need to think to sell franchises. To begin, you have to find that pool of people to call upon. You need prospects and leads. Yes, there will be some expense. And, yes, there will be some tough times. But success comes to those who persevere, to businesses and entrepreneurs who continue through difficult times. "There are three ways to make money in this country," according to Tom Fleisher, former chief operating officer of Rampart Industries. "You're either lucky or you outspend your competition or you work your duff off."

I imagine that most of you, for one reason or another, must adopt the third approach. But don't be dismayed, because in sales, the hard work approach is often the best path to success.

DEFINING YOUR FRANCHISE MARKET

As with any product, you can't sell a franchise without first determining who your customer is. Many new franchisors wrongly assume that the people inside their industry are the ones most likely to buy the franchise offering. For example, many restaurant owners believe that people with food and beverage experience will choose to purchase their franchised concept. However, that is not the case. Rarely do franchisees have experience in the business they buy. Why? Because most prospective franchisees search for new and exciting opportunities that will provide lucrative returns. They care little whether these opportunities fall within their professional expertise. So, a schoolteacher becomes a restauranteur. A corporate executive becomes a Jiffy Lube owner. A mother buys a Stained Glass Overlay franchise. A government employee purchases a franchised convenience store.

And there's another element to this job-shuffling phenomenon. Skilled workers simply don't need the support and services franchises offer. An experienced carpenter wouldn't appreciate the training Neil Balter's California Closets provides. A lifelong pizza maker would learn little from adopting the Domino's Pizza recipe. Those with substantial business experience, seeking to remain in their industry, want to strike out completely on their own. They aren't searching for someone else's business. They want to be the total entrepreneur, free from the shackles of big-brother franchisor constantly peering over their shoulders.

And franchisors know to stay clear of this kind. "Many franchisors aren't really searching for free-thinking entrepreneurs to become franchisees," says Barbara Kaban, co-owner of Dental Insurance Systems. "Instead, they need people who can follow orders and commands."

And franchisors have other reasons for not targeting experienced prospects. "We do not look for printers, because it's easier to teach new techniques than to break old ones," says William Levine of Postal Instant Press. In franchising, it *is* harder to teach old dogs new tricks.

But if franchisors aren't looking for seasoned veterans, what are they looking for? That's a difficult question that many franchisors can't answer. "If you could develop a profile of the successful franchisee, you would make a lot of money," says Bud Hadfield of Kwik Kopy. "All franchisors can do in choosing franchisees is avoid certain types of individuals. We stay away from people who run through jobs, jumping from one position to the next throughout their career. We also avoid undercapitalized individuals. After that, you have to use your gut instinct. But you can always be fooled."

George Gardner, director of franchise sales at MAACO and a lifelong salesman, seconds those sentiments. "I consider myself a pretty fair judge of character, but frankly, I can't tell what type of person will and won't be supersuccessful," Gardner confides. "I remember one young kid who got his father to finance the deal. The kid was very polite, but extremely shy. I thought he was simply too reserved to make the business work. Today, the young man is one of our most productive franchisees. And the success has completely changed his personality. He often speaks at company meetings and has all the interpersonal skills of a good businessperson."

And Peter Shea at Stained Glass Overlays tells similar stories. "You can never tell who is going to perform well until you get them out in the field to experience the realities of sales," he says. Shea believes that new franchisees often fail because they don't understand the rigors of personally selling a product. Then again, that sometimes works to your advantage. "I have seen housewives-turned-franchisees outperform businesspeople with a lifetime of sales experience. These women come to the training course and take volumes of notes. Once released into the real world, they follow the program to the letter, never questioning the purpose and never fearing rejection. They absolutely set the world on fire."

Which isn't to say you should sell exclusively to housewives. It is, however, intended to illustrate the difficulty franchisors face in selecting competent owners. Prospective franchisees, as well as people in general, are great actors. They know the answers you want to hear and can recite them accurately to win your approval. But some franchisors have developed tentative guidelines to help select their franchisees.

AAMCO, for instance, looks for middle-aged prospects with management experience, who because of layoffs and cutbacks, fear they may lose their jobs with major corporations. John Edwards, of Pilot Air Freight, believes that the critical skills for franchisees in his industry are a bit more specific. "If I had to identify characteristics of successful franchisees, I'd choose listening. To me, the ability to receive and use knowledge from other people is a telltale sign that the prospect will make a good franchisee. Next, a basic understanding of and respect for the customer is crucial in our company, which depends heavily on repeat business. Finally, organizational management skills are important. An owner who can garner the respect of his employees and lead them effectively will go far with Pilot." Edwards' company is also one of the few franchises that prefers past experience in the industry before qualifying as a franchisee.

As you can see, the qualities franchisors look for in franchisee prospects is as varied as the types of businesses franchised. But for the new franchisor, there are some basic attributes you should look for in each prospect you meet. First, the prospect must have the cash, or at least access to it. Meeting with under- or noncapitalized prospects only wastes your time and company resources. For efficiency, you have to concentrate on those individuals who have a realistic chance of financing your franchise opportunity.

But ability to pay shouldn't be your only consideration. "By all means, don't just grab the first guy with money that comes along," says Tidy Car's Goranson. "Sure, you'll have to make some concession in the quality of the individuals you accept to get your early program off the ground. But remember, you're going to live with these people for a long time."

So what other qualities should a franchisor expect in prospects? Consistency. A proven track record of quality performance increases the chances that your prospect can continue his or her professional accomplishments with your business. "You need someone who will stay in the hunt. If the prospect hasn't made it in other jobs, he or she probably won't make it in franchising," says PIPs LeVine.

Other success indicators include previous managerial and sales experience, an eagerness to learn and grow, and a healthy attitude. "We look for positive people who are willing to sell. These characteristics take franchisees through even difficult periods," says Stanley Bresler of Bresler's 33 Flavors.

Things to avoid include belligerence and know-it-all attitudes. "If the new franchisee starts with the outlook that he's going to show you, then it's best to say good-bye right away," says Kwik Kopy's Hadfield. "We've dismissed people from our training program for that very reason." Remember, franchising is like marriage; bad characteristics tend to worsen with familiarity. If the franchisee doesn't show interest and enthusiasm early in the relationship, don't expect things to change later on.

Rigid thinkers are another type of prospect many franchisors shy away from. "At one point, we gained success in recruiting retired military officers," says MAACO's Gardner. "But we found they didn't make the best operators, because they gave too many orders and expected them to be followed to the letter. The real world doesn't work that way. Ordering around employees like an officer does soldiers, risks losing your work force."

Surprisingly, technically trained people may also present problems. "I believe technical-oriented individuals look too much at numbers and not enough at the intangibles of human interaction," says John Amico of The Hair Performers. Consultant Tom Fleisher experienced similar problems at Rampart, the burglar alarm franchise. "Because the business required some knowledge of electronics, it tended to draw formally trained engineers. Although these people became masterful at wiring and installing alarm systems, they neglected the business and marketing aspects of the franchise. Some of the franchisees, either consciously or unconsciously, lost themselves in the nuts-and-bolts end of the business simply to avoid pounding the pavement, drumming up sales."

ATTRACTING PROSPECTS

At any given time, a significant percentage of the U.S. work force stands frustrated and unfulfilled. Their tiresome and mundane jobs hold little excitement or satisfaction. Their professional hopes, dreams, and aspirations sit squashed beneath uncaring bosses and corporate bureaucracy. These people grew up subscribing to the American ideal that hard work brings financial and personal rewards. Yet they have faithfully labored all their lives, dedicated their hours and efforts to boss and company, and the rewards are nowhere in sight. These are the discontented, searching for the chance to prove their worth. They also are the stuff of which great franchise companies are made.

NUGGET #17

What to Look For in a Prospective Franchisee:
Experts Give Their Impressions

Stanley Bresler, president of Bresler's 33 Flavors Ice Cream: "We look for positive people who will sell. It takes them through even the hardest times."

Les Charm, president of Docktor Pet Centers: "Our ideal franchisee is a person who has been with Sears or another major retailer for seven years and has some money through profit sharing or his or her family. Short of that, we search for the person who is really motivated to go out and do things. The natural salesperson. That sheer energy is hard to beat."

George Gardner, director of franchise sales, MAACO: "Our successful francisee has to know his customers and employees. In that respect, we look for the same qualities we would in an employee. We look for a good career track record, management experience, and perhaps some sales experience."

William LeVine, president of Postal Instant Press: "We want consistency. If a person held half a dozen jobs in five years, he won't be a good franchisee. Strong financing is also important. At PIP, we tell people they won't be able to take money out of the business for the first year. So they had better be able to live outside the business. We do not look for printers, because it's easier to teach new techniques than to break old ones."

Paul Modzelewski, director of franchise sales, The Athlete's Foot: "I look for someone who is hungry and not just looking for a job with a guaranteed return on their investment. I'm looking for a person who is vigorous, very involved, and wants to jump in with both feet."

Robert Snelling, president, Snelling and Snelling: "We want highly moral and ethical people, because our franchisees deal with a very important commodity—a person's career. Also, we find that repeat business is crucial in our success, so the franchisees must do their jobs well."

Robert Morgan, co-founder of AAMCO Transmissions: "The keys to franchisee success are motivation and involvement,"

NUGGET #17 *(Continued)*

> *Bud Hadfield, founder Kwik Kopy:* "The best franchisees are people who don't need your business to succeed. They can make it one way or the other."
>
> *Fred DeLuca, president and founder of Subway Sandwiches & Salads:* "Self-confidence and ability. Also, we look for people who want, almost need to go into business on their own."
>
> *John Amico, president of The Hair Performers:* "I never look for a franchisee. I look for a partner, someone I can go into business with for twenty, twenty-five years. To meet this requirement, I search for people skills—someone who relates well to others. Also, I place emphasis on an attitude of quality. Someone who won't compromise standards."

And there are plenty of this breed to go around. Just check the business opportunity section of any local newspaper, and you'll see scores of franchise companies competing to cash in on this lucrative market. But aren't those franchisors your competition? Yes and no. Certainly prospective franchisees compare opportunities to find businesses that best suit their interests. But after comparing, they concentrate their search on one or two desired industries. Thus, most franchisors consider their main competition other franchises in their industry. For instance, The Hair Performers looks at The Hair Crafters as their rival, not Subway Sandwiches & Salads. Likewise, Uniglobe, the travel agency franchise, considers International Tours more a threat than Sir Speedy Printing.

Where should new franchisors consider placing their ads for franchisees? Many major franchisors cite *The Wall Street Journal* as the premier newspaper for drawing qualified franchise leads. But *The Wall Street Journal* receives mixed reviews from new, small franchisors. Tom Fleisher, our business consultant, formerly with Rampart Industries, explains "The *Journal* attracts big investors. If your company has low name recognition or modest returns, it may not be the best place to advertise your opportunity."

George Gardner of MAACO gives another reason why small franchisors may do better without *The Wall Street Journal*. "You have to remember that *The Wall Street Journal* has tremendous coverage. Advertising in even the newspaper's regional editions will draw a bunch of leads in areas you're not

NUGGET #18

The Reasons for Franchisee Failure:
Expert Opinions

Fred DeLuca, founder and president, Subway Sandwiches & Salads: "In our business, franchisees fail for one of three reasons. First, they choose a bad location. Second, they choose a good location, but for some unforeseen reason its characteristics change. Third, management problems. Some franchisees display an unwillingness to change or try new promotion techniques. It's franchisee dogma, and it's deadly."

Tony Martino, founder and president, MAACO: "A lot of people believe that the American dream of owning their own business is the dream of not working hard. That simply is not the case. It's always easy to swim with the current, but many people don't want to swim against it. And that is what it usually takes to make a small business successful."

Peter Shea, owner, Stained Glass Overlay: "When franchisees fail, which is rare, it's usually because they don't grasp the reality of going out and making sales."

Paul Modzelewski, director of franchise sales, The Athlete's Foot: "Lack of attention by the franchisee. Absentee and many other owners find it very difficult to work when they don't have to answer to anyone. Also, insufficient capital causes problems."

Arthur Karp, co-founder, The Original Great American Chocolate Chip Cookie Company: "People sometimes buy franchises for the wrong reasons. They think that going into business doesn't require hard work. It does and a lot more."

Bud Hadfield, founder, Kwik Kopy: "A lot of people want to own a business but don't want all the work associated with it. I tell each franchisee up front that the first year won't be tough, it will be miserable."

targeting. We try to be careful that the media we use produce the leads in the area where we want to market."

National magazines present similar drawbacks, but often yield impressive results. "I found *Entrepreneur* magazine brought a good quality and quantity of leads," says Stained Glass Overlay's Peter Shea. In fact, Shea liked the magazine so much he purchased a major interest in it! Other good draws frequently cited by franchisors included *USA TODAY*; *Venture, Inc*; *Success*; *Money*; and *Franchising*.

In which of these should you advertise? Most franchisors attempt to link the demographic profile of a publication's readership to the cost of the franchise. For example, the average income of subscribers to *Income Opportunities* was a modest $20,000 to $30,000 in 1985. "The magazine addresses individuals interested in seeking to own and run their own businesses, either full- or part-time," says Jim Cappello, the publication's advertising director. "Our readership would be interested in franchise opportunities for $15,000 to $25,000, but more than that is out of our readers' ballpark," he confides.

On the other end of the spectrum, the average income of *Venture* magazine readers ranged well above $100,000 in 1985—fertile selling ground for expensive franchise opportunities.

And costs are another consideration when buying advertising space. Don't be fooled; seeming bargains often aren't. For instance, a one-eighth page ad in the business opportunities section of *Money* magazine cost about $4000 in 1987, nearly double the price of a similar ad in *Venture* (about $2000). Yet, *Money* boasts a circulation of 1.7 million readers while only one-fourth that number reads *Venture* (about 340,000). To compare costs, advertisers often divide ad prices by total circulation to determine cost per thousand. In the above example, *Venture* costs about $5.90 per thousand readers while *Money* costs less than half that amount—$2.35 per thousand.

Are there other strategies for saving money on advertising? Certainly. The most obvious is to establish an in-house advertising agency to save commissions on media purchases. This sounds like a formidable task, but it's not. To understand, remember that many newspapers and magazines give advertising agencies a 15-percent discount on time and space purchases. This discount is retained by the agency as commission. Franchise companies that place ads directly with these media are not afforded the same price breaks. To obtain the 15-percent discount, you need to establish an advertising agency, which could consist of choosing a name, getting stationery printed to that effect, and then submitting your checks with the agency's stationery. Is this illegal or unethical? No. Most major franchises support in-house agencies. You're entitled to the same competitive advantages.

Even with price breaks, however, advertising in national magazines and newspapers may be beyond the scope of new franchisors. To begin, small franchise entrepreneurs may have to concentrate their efforts on a specific geographical area and then branch out as the undertaking grows. Here, regional or metropolitan newspapers are the logical media for advertising your franchise offering. "Because national advertising tends to attract people interested in relocation, we use regional newspaper advertising to draw local prospects who want to remain in that area," says The Athlete's Foot's Paul Modzelewski. "Also, we find that people often don't respond until an ad appears in their local or regional newspaper."

What should you say in a franchise advertisement? Remember, franchise advertising is direct-response advertising. Your primary objective is to generate inquiries from serious prospects. "I started to receive responses the day I stopped advertising the hair-care industry and started to advertise income potential and return-on-investment," says John Amico of The Hair Performers." Amico believes that because most prospects look at franchises as income opportunities, they're motivated by personal finance appeals.

But Hadfield of Kwik Kopy sees things a bit differently. "Our ads try to appeal to the guy who wants to take control and own the keys to his own business. We emphasize the professional opportunity Kwik Kopy presents."

Whichever angle you choose, remember that franchise ads represent the first step in qualifying your leads. If your ad fails to mention the specifics of your franchise opportunity, you can expect a greater number of junk leads. "At Rampart," begins Tom Fleisher, "we rarely had bad prospects because our ads stated up-front that the business was a franchise opportunity in the burglar and fire alarm industry. We even mentioned the cost to screen out no-capital inquiries."

How else can you generate leads? Referrals from present franchisees and customers often provide a wealth of inquiries. "Many of our prospects come from shop owners who receive inquiries from their customers," says Fred DeLuca at Subway Sandwiches & Salads. "Customers, better than anyone else, know the value of the product and see the opportunity in selling it."

John Amico is even more specific regarding the importance of in-shop leads. "Seventy-five percent of our leads come from our stores, but not all are customers. Many of our own employees see the opportunity in owning a franchise and work to become franchisees."

Referrals also tend to generate a better quality lead than those gained through national or regional advertising. "It took Kwik Kopy fifty-two leads to make one sale from national advertising," Bud Hadfield states. "But it takes only twenty-one or twenty-two leads to sell a franchise through a referral from a franchise owner."

WINNING LEADS THROUGH PUBLIC RELATIONS

"I built the company on things I didn't have to pay for," says Neil Balter of California Closets. Balter alludes to the critical role public relations played in California Closets' rapid growth and development. "We never advertised for franchisees and may never have to." Instead the company has relied on leads generated by feature-length articles in a half-dozen major business magazines, as well as *The Wall Street Journal*. "There are two types of entrepreneurs: the inventor and the promoter. I'm the promoter who knows how to get his company a lot of free publicity."

Balter isn't alone. Joan Barnes at Gymboree employed the novelty of an infant exercise company to win media coverage. "When we want ink, we march down to the local newspaper, introduce ourselves, our company, and our concept. Inevitably an article results."

But Balter and Barnes are the exceptions. Both had interesting stories to tell. "I was fortunate in that the California Closets odyssey possesses all the elements of a great story," says Balter, "My parents threw me out of the house when I was seventeen. I started the company with only a thousand dollars and succeeded while I was young. The media eats that stuff up."

Balter's correct to an extent. He did have a good story to tell, but that wasn't the only reason for his public relations success. Balter, like Barnes, also promoted himself to the right people. He called editors and told them about his business. He wasn't shy about repeating his story to reporters, journalists, and anyone else who would lend an ear. As a result, the young entrepreneur won the type of credible media coverage that no advertising campaign, no matter how expensive or creative, could capture.

New franchisors can follow Balter's lead by first becoming cognizant of public relations' opportunities. It's amazing how many companies run right by such possibilities. While researching this book, my co-author and I contacted hundreds of franchisors for information, input, and anecdotes. Many never responded to the opportunity to win no pain, no strain exposure. Unbelievably, one president of a medium-sized employment franchise had his secretary respond, asking us to contact a larger competitor that was better staffed to handle such inquiries!

If you can't field a media inquiry, don't direct the questioner to your competition! The president's handling of the situation shows why his company is chasing a larger competitor and may always run second in the race.

On the other hand, it seems no coincidence that franchisors who responded quickly to our letters and telephone calls lead some of the nation's most successful franchises. Fred DeLuca, Gary Goranson, Peter Shea, Robert Morgan, Stanley Bresler, Tony Martino, Bud Hadfield, John Edwards, Neal Balter, William LeVine, Joan Barnes, D'Arcy Williams, Robert Snelling, Les Charm, Bernard Browning, and dozens of other highly successful franchisors made themselves readily available not only because they have an interest in our project, but because they understand the value of free media exposure and capitalize regularly on it.

And as a new franchisor, you can, too. Whether your business is big or small, rich or poor, you should seek media coverage of your operation and its plans for growth. "Public relations serves two functions for the franchise company," says John P. Hayes, president of Co-Writers & Associates, a public relations and editorial consulting firm based in Philadelphia. "First, it helps generate leads. Second, it adds credibility to your company by conferring legitimacy on your undertaking. The mere fact that a reputable publication deems you newsworthy suggests that you're a growing, viable business."

Hayes believes new franchising companies should take positive steps to secure favorable publicity. One method is through news releases. "News releases, sent to newspapers and television and radio stations, are vital to gaining media coverage. The rule is to keep them short—one to three pages—and make them concise, free from jargon and wordiness." Hayes explains that the better written the release, the more likely it will run. "Releases can either win stories or be used as filler," he says. In deciding which stories to develop, editors and writers look for local tie-ins. "Another doughnut franchise isn't news. But to the local newspaper, a hometown company that decides to compete with the big names in doughnuts is worthy of a news story."

Creativity is also important in developing news releases. "Writers constantly search for the offbeat and interesting. A company that cleans and waxes cars isn't exciting. But an automotive detailing outfit that uses toothbrushes on radiator grills and coco butter on vinyl roofs is the stuff that good reporters turn into interesting articles. The way you present your business in news releases often triggers media response."

But if you can't write well, Hayes cautions, you'll need a specialist to get your point across. "Newspaper editors and broadcast professionals are just like anyone else. They don't have time to deal with poorly communicated ideas or sloppy presentations. If you're not sure of yourself, look for a qualified public relations specialist who has a track record of using news releases to win media exposure. If cost is a concern, seek out skilled freelancers or strike a deal offering continued work in exchange for early price discounts."

SELLING FRANCHISES

Once advertising, public relations, or word-of-mouth start generating leads, you'll need a plan of action for dealing with inquiries. The first step is lead qualification. "When I am speaking to a prospect for the first time on the telephone, I try to gain some idea of how sincere and urgent his interest is," says Jim McGlinchey, a franchise salesman and consultant based in Rochester, New York. McGlinchey asks prospects whether they are actively employed and determines if they are ready to buy immediately. "If the person is between jobs, he or she is a much livelier lead than a person who has a job and is simply exploring career options."

McGlinchey also asks up-front whether prospects have the money to finance the deal. "I'm diplomatic, but I definitely inquire into their ability to pay. Without the money, you can't sell franchises."

From there, most salespeople try to get prospects to fill out questionnaires or applications requesting personal and financial information. "A lot of salespeople talk too much during the initial telephone contact," says consultant Tom Fleisher. "Sometimes you can pique curiosity by limiting the information and making the prospect either fill out an application or arrange a personal meeting."

Applications are sent along with franchise sales letters and brochures, the caliber of which vary according to the franchise. For example, H&R Block, the income tax franchise, sends prospects a simple one-page letter describing the company and its application process. Burger King, on the other hand, distributes four-color brochures that feature stories and photographs on the company's most successful franchisees.

In preparing brochures, new franchisors must remember that, in themselves, printed communications don't sell franchises. "People don't invest their entire savings and make complete career changes on the basis of a franchise brochure," says McGlinchey. "Most prospects are savvy to the risks involved with purchasing a business. A fancy brochure means little compared to the past success of the company."

Yet brochures are a customary part of franchise sales and do serve an important role in bridging the gap between a telephone call and a personal meeting. Thus, new franchisors should strive to develop simple and concise brochures that explain their franchise offerings in positive and accurate terms. And creativity is also important to separate yourself from the rest of the crowd.

What issues should be covered? Certainly, you should give a brief company history and introduce the individuals behind the business. "For whatever reasons, people enjoy reading and learning about other people," says Fleisher. "Human interest sells." While running Rampart, Fleisher designed brochures that were heavy on anecdotes and personality. "I wrote short vignettes on our top franchisees and included their stories and pictures in the text," he explains. "I chose franchisees that prospects could readily relate to. They illustrated how others could similarly succeed with the company."

Brochures also should include a brief description of your industry—its growth, prosperity, and future—as well as a specific discussion on your company—its unique market position and advantages. Here, you'll need some numbers and hard facts to portray the viability of your opportunity, along with a brief discussion of your business approach and philosophy.

Finally, you'll want to build credibility by including reprints or photocopies of newspaper or magazine articles written about your franchise. Reading what others say about your company proves potent persuasion for wary prospects who often doubt the honesty of company-produced communications.

But what if you're a brand-new franchisor? What should you say in promotional literature if you have yet to gain the facts, figures, and franchisees that impress prospects? The truth! Every franchisor began somewhere, and prospects that take that early leap often enjoy the greatest long-term appreciation of their investments. "A ground-floor opportunity" has a clichéd ring, but still attracts risk-takers seeking to latch onto up-and-coming franchise stars.

The rookie franchisor needs to artfully explain the potential rewards of joining a new and growing venture. It could be your strongest, if not your only, early selling point.

SALES PRESENTATIONS AND PERSONAL MEETINGS

Of all the brochures and applications you send, only a few will elicit responses. Yet these replies represent your liveliest, most valuable leads. Prospects that take the time to fill out and return applications are seriously investigating the purchase of a franchise—yours and probably your competition's. The majority of your sales resources should be employed to convince this small but fruitful group.

Critical to this process is the personal meeting. Like most high-ticket sales, franchise purchases depend on the human interplay of the buyer and seller. Some franchisors go to the prospects, traveling to Syracuse or Seattle, Springfield or Sarasota, or a hundred other locations where leads lie. Others invite serious prospects to visit the home office and pick up part or all of the costs if the prospects sign.

Whenever possible, it's best to meet prospects on your home turf, where you're better able to orchestrate the proceedings. Industrywide franchisors report much higher close ratios at home than on the road. It only makes sense. The more prospects learn about your company and its personnel, the more comfortable they become with buying into the franchise. If on-site visits aren't possible, many franchisors choose neutral grounds—traveling to meet five or six regional prospects at a local hotel or restaurant.

Whatever the venue, it's wise to invite everyone involved with the purchasing decision to the initial meeting. "Often, the wife plays as large a role in buying the franchise as the husband," says Jim McGlinchey. "We like to meet both, as well as any personal attorneys, consultants, or accountants reviewing the deal so they can see first-hand the legitimacy of the opportunity."

How is the sales meeting conducted? Tom Fleisher offers his insights. "You have to treat a franchise sale like any other, which starts by building rapport with the prospect. The decision to buy a franchise is always emotional. Even the most methodical prospect looks to his gut instinct before signing on the dotted line. So you have to create a friendly working relationship with the prospect; you have to make them like you. I always try to engage the prospect in conversation. I ask questions regarding their interests, families, hopes, and aspirations, as well as why they chose franchising and this particular business. If they're slow to respond, I'll tell anecdotes about current franchisees, and the problems, challenges, and accomplishments they face."

Once connected on a personal level, a good franchise salesperson will work from a set presentation. "I always have a game plan before meeting prospects," Fleisher says. "I use flip charts and presentation manuals that cover the general areas of franchising: training, income potential, service, the product, and sales."

But every prospect responds differently, and Fleisher plays to the contrasts. "You have to recognize the flashes that make people buy and tailor your presentation accordingly," he says. "Some people, for instance, are turned on by the completeness of the package. Others find reassurance in hearing about the training program or the ongoing service the company provides.

"You should avoid complicated discussions of the nuts-and-bolts aspects of the business, which intimidates many people. Often, prospects feel obliged to ask specific questions to prove they're doing their homework. I usually dismiss them by saying, 'We cover that fully in our training program and operating manual' or even less specifically with an assuring 'You'll see that's not a problem.'" Such statements are often enough to pacify even the most apprehensive prospect, according to Fleisher.

Franchise sales differ from typical business sales in two important respects. First, FTC rules require the franchisor to present the prospect with a disclosure statement no later than the first personal meeting. Second, the salesperson is prohibited from closing the deal until 10 business days after the meeting was conducted and the documents provided.

"This is a very dangerous period," McGlinchey notes. "During the ten days, prospects become bombarded by negative thoughts. Their lawyers start asking questions. Their bankers balk at lending money on a startup venture. Even their so-called friends tell them to forget the idea and settle for their station wagon and track home."

Fleisher witnesses the same phenomenon. "The first thing a prospect does during the 10-day cooling off period is test the concept on a neighbor by trying to sell the product. Of course, he fails because he isn't trained. But that never occurs to him and only serves to reinforce the negative thoughts."

How can franchisors keep the love alive over the 10-day wait? The first and most obvious method is frequent and soothing telephone calls. But even then, prospects have plenty of time to give in to skepticism. So franchisors employ a variety of psychological weaponry aimed at keeping the prospect's interest high. "I try to replace negative thinking with positive tasks," Fleisher explains. "Before leaving franchisees, I ask them to perform a few exercises designed to take their minds off the risks of buying a business."

For example, a franchisor may ask prospects to list every conceivable market for their product. Or the prospect may try to identify major competitors and see how their products compare with the franchisor's. "I make the chores easy but detailed so the prospect invests time in the company, which is a powerful motivator for him or her to sign," says Fleisher.

Finally, franchise sales differ from conventional sales in the information you can provide prospects regarding the income potential of your franchise opportunity. For obvious reasons, prospective franchisees will want, if not demand, some idea of how much money they can expect to make after quitting their jobs and investing in your business. But franchise law strictly regulates the manner in which you can present such information, as well as establishes liability for misrepresentation.

Consequently, many franchisors don't provide prospective franchisees with income projections or actual sales figures from operating units. And that can be a mistake, because a substantiated record of success is often your most convincing sales tool.

There are two ways of presenting sales figures. The short form provides specific numbers on the actual performance of franchises within your system. The figures can be presented as averages or as a detailed list. For example, a franchisor may state that for all reporting franchises in 1986 in operation more than six months, sales averaged $225,000. Or the franchise company may simply provide the figures for each unit in operation more than six months, and permit prospects to draw their own conclusions.

The long form offers a range of sales levels and estimates expenses and break-even at each level. They can be based on actual or projected performance. For instance, the disclosure may appear as follows:

Sales Levels	Fixed Costs	Salaries & Inventory	Break-even	Profit
$100,000	$40,000	$60,000	$100,000	$ 0
150,000	40,000	90,000	130,000	20,000
200,000	40,000	120,000	160,000	40,000
250,000	40,000	150,000	190,000	60,000
300,000	40,000	180,000	220,000	80,000
350,000	40,000	210,000	250,000	100,000
400,000	40,000	240,000	280,000	120,000

The advantage here is that prospects gain better ideas of expenses and profitabilities at various income ranges.

Whichever form you choose, franchise law requires you to:

1. employ a reasonable basis for making income statements and state the assumptions made in gathering the information.

2. prepare to substantiate your claims and state the franchisees included in your calculations.

3. assure geographical relevance (you can't represent sales figures from San Antonio as relevant to a Boston prospect for a taco franchise).

4. provide a disclaimer, the wording of which is outlined in the Uniform Franchise Offering Circular.

In addition, there may be other requirements that apply to the preparation of income figures. Your franchise attorney should be able to help you.

THE CLOSE

Once the meeting is over and the wait complete, pen must meet paper and the deal must be sealed. But hurdling that last obstacle is no small accomplishment. The fears and apprehensions each prospect experiences while evaluating your franchise opportunity are inexplicably magnified as the irrevocability of the decision nears in the form of a signed contract. What was once a certainty now becomes dubious. That hell-bent, self-assured prospect degenerates into a quivering mass of semisolid liquid, sloshing in a sea of fear and self-doubt. The time and effort you've invested in eloquent persuasion now hangs on befuddled vacillations. Stand silent and you risk losing prospects to confusion and uncertainty. Push too hard and you confirm their suspicions that your only intent is to gain another notch on your monthly performance report.

What to do? You need a focal point, an eye through which wavering prospects can pass to become signed franchisees. Scheduling of a training course often serves this purpose. "If you're going to move on this thing, we have to get you into that spring training course before it's filled," salespeople urge prospects. Selecting a territory can play a similar role. "Before we go any further, you should stake out your territory now so others don't claim it," a franchise salesperson may say.

Still, indecision is a powerful crippler, which is often only remedied by the negative sell. "We don't use undue pressure, but prospects are made to understand that our franchise is in demand, and if they don't act, they risk losing a territory to someone else," says MAACO's Gardner. Some franchise salespeople go a step further. "Let's face it, any prospect that stays with you through the ten-day waiting period is serious about your opportunity," begins one franchise salesperson. "Still, they may need a kick in the pants to act. So I often play the heavy, questioning their talents and ability as a means of making them act. For example, I might say, 'Well, maybe you shouldn't become a franchisee, because frankly, your indecisiveness may prove a real liability in the business world.' To prove otherwise, prospects often pull out their pens and sign the contracts."

And there are other, perhaps more compassionate, ways to sign stragglers. "Usually, when a prospect continues to balk, it's because he or she has one last apprehension that has yet to be articulated," says Fleisher. "That's when I try to get a present franchisee to contact the prospect. Often just hearing from someone inside the business is enough to convince the person to sign."

How many deals per inquiries should you expect to close? That's extremely hard to answer. Some companies structure their advertising to receive only serious inquiries. Others are less concerned with entertaining a manageable number of junk leads. Tidy Car, for example, needs 100 leads to sign a multiunit deal. Stained Glass Overlays has a similar close rate of about .7 percent, while The Athlete's Foot does less well, closing one sale for every 200 leads received.

Your rate will depend on the attractiveness and cost of your offering, the skill of your salesmanship, and the effort you make to entice interested parties. In general, closing ratios will run low (perhaps as low as one in 500 gross unqualified inquiries) as you first try to sell your untested business. However, once you open a number of units and prove your concept, closing ratios will increase as a higher number of serious prospects inquire into your opportunities. Finally, your marginal effectiveness may again slacken after your mature franchise exploits easy prospects and is forced to concentrate on selling franchises in less-desirable and accessible areas of the country.

THE FRANCHISOR AS SALESMAN

Explaining franchise sales in one short chapter is roughly akin to teaching the piano in one short lesson. Much information simply gets left out. I guess the only real way to learn is by doing. As a franchisor, you'll have to find those media that draw best for you, hone your presentation style to fit your personality, and develop a close that works for your business. It'll take time and patience. But if your product is good and you stick with it, there's little doubt that you *will* sell franchises.

CHAPTER 13

ONE LAST LOOK AT LEGALITIES

By now, you should have a pretty fair idea of whether your business can survive and prosper as a franchise. You've studied the personal and professional qualities required. You've learned the history behind some of today's biggest and best-managed franchises, as well as the policy, sales, marketing, and promotional considerations that go into building such companies. You've also considered some of the legal aspects of franchising and seen the impact they have on the marketing system.

Now it's time to delve deeper into franchise law to learn about the actual legal documents of franchising and see how they interrelate. It's a subject that tends to be technical and probably outside your past experience. But it's a critical component of your eventual success.

A properly prepared disclosure document provides a masterful blueprint or business plan on which your company can build. A skillfully written franchise agreement protects you from possible liability. Your legal franchise program should serve as both a saber and a shield, spearheading your franchise assault while safeguarding the spoils you acquire.

THE NEXUS: HOW POLICIES AND FRANCHISE DOCUMENTS INTERRELATE

Which came first, the chicken or the egg? No one knows for sure, and at first blush, franchise law appears to present the same quandary. Should your franchise agreement take its lead from your disclosure document or vice versa? The truth is, neither document represents the first stage in a franchise legal program. Instead, the process begins with your company's policies and procedures.

We're talked at length about defining your franchise program—about the very structure of your franchise opportunity. We've examined the critical policy decisions you need to make regarding everything from initial license fees to retail advertising programs to grand-opening celebrations. Your franchise legal program now must take all these issues and formalize and codify them first in the disclosure document and then in your franchise agreement. It's a flow-chart process that begins with general considerations and ends with specific, detailed obligations that franchisees must agree to and abide by.

For example, consider your royalty structure. Here, your primary policy concern is: What percentage should I charge as a royalty?

Once decided, you then disclose that percentage in your disclosure document. And that represents the primary function of this legal statement. It's a fact sheet or booklet for prospective franchisees—a quick reference for them to learn about your franchise opportunity. The disclosure tells prospects when, where, how, and how much they must pay in royalties. Along the way, it also relates whether all or some of the royalty is refundable and how the franchisor calculates the percentage.

From there, you incorporate your royalties into your franchise agreement. Here, all extraneous chitchat is stripped away and replaced with only those terms your franchisees must agree to live by, along with other legal mechanisms important for your protection.

For example, your franchise agreement will no doubt detail the exact percentage of your royalty, how it's calculated, when it's due, and what accompanies it (reports and statements of gross receipts). But it also may include conditions that provide for royalty payment during any disputes, arbitration, or litigation between you and your franchisees. With this last provision, you legally assure you won't get stuck providing services while franchisees hold payments pending the outcome of some legal problem.

So your legal groundwork is a three-step process that schematically appears as follows:

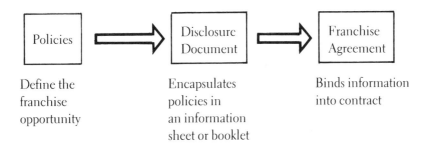

Policies	Disclosure Document	Franchise Agreement
Define the franchise opportunity	Encapsulates policies in an information sheet or booklet	Binds information into contract

Policies define your franchise, which are then enunciated in your disclosure document, and made contractually enforceable with a franchise agreement.

PREPARING YOUR DISCLOSURE DOCUMENT

Your disclosure can follow either the FTC's basic disclosure format or the Uniform Franchise Offering Circular (UFOC). Which one should you choose? The UFOC has an advantage in that it's accepted by more states than the FTC format. However, the FTC format asks fewer and less comprehensive questions, which some franchisors find attractive. For example, the FTC rule does not require you to disclose a franchisee's total initial investment or your obligations as a franchisor. The FTC rule also limits the information you must provide concerning prior litigation, bankruptcies, and status of trademarks. In addition, it offers new franchisors up to two additional years to obtain audited financial statements.

In general, however, unless your company possesses a compelling strategic reason for using the FTC format, the wider acceptance of the UFOC makes it preferable.

In preparing your UFOC, common sense and honesty represent the two principle guides. The document's 23 items ask specific questions regarding a wide variety of business-related issues—all requiring careful and accurate answers.

So avoid embellishment or extraneous detail. For example, if the item asks you to state any criminal or civil actions alleging or involving violation of any franchise law, fraud, embezzlement, fraudulent conversion, or other business-related allegations, you don't have to list your recent divorce proceeding.

However, the UFOC implicitly requires disclosure of any item that could materially affect a prospect's decision to buy into your business. Therefore, if you risk losing half your business as a result of the divorce, it must be stated.

The following discussion presents an item-by-item overview of the UFOC. It's intended to familiarize you with the document. It's not meant to provide all-inclusive advice on preparing a disclosure document. That chore is best left to your franchise attorney.

Item 1: The Franchisor and Any Predecessor

Here, you'll list the names and addresses of the franchisor and any predecessor, along with a description of the business. Basically, the item details your business's history and current components. It tells when the company began, whether it changed hands, and something about its market. Pretty easy, right? Well, what if your business operates two offices in different states? What's your address for disclosure? Can you choose the address of the state with the more lenient franchise laws? Your lawyer will have to help you decide.

In describing your business, you can opt for either the short form—the franchise business is a fast-food franchise, for example—or the long form —the business offers gourmet oversized hamburgers, secret-recipe french fries, and thick and frosty milk shakes at reasonable prices in clean, comfortable, and convenient settings for a family-oriented clientele.

The same holds true for disclosing markets. A jewelry franchise, for instance, could define its market as women's jewelry. But a better disclosure would read, "The business caters to women between the ages of 30 and 60, who possess high disposable incomes and can afford to purchase precious gems for personal use."

NUGGET #19

Acts that Violate the Franchise Rule

According to the Federal Trade Commission (FTC), it is an unfair or deceptive practice for any franchisor or franchise broker:

1. To fail to furnish prospective franchisees, within the time frames established by the Franchise Rule, with a disclosure document containing information on 20 different subjects relating to the franchisor, the franchise business, and the terms of the franchise agreement
2. To make any representation about the actual or potential sales, income, or profits of existing or prospective franchises except in the manner set forth in the Franchise Rule
3. To make any claim or representation (such as in advertising or oral statements by salespeople) that is inconsistent with the information required to be disclosed by the Franchise Rule
4. To fail to furnish prospective franchisees, within the time frames established by the Franchise Rule, with copies of the franchisor's standard forms of franchise agreements and copies of the final agreements to be signed by the parties
5. To fail to return to prospective franchisees any funds or deposits (such as down payments) identified as refundable in the disclosure document

Violators are subject to actions brought by the FTC, which can include fines up to $10,000 per violation.

Item 2: The Franchisor's Personnel

Relatively straightforward, Item 2 requires the names, titles, and business experience of key personnel in your organization, including directors, partners, officers, chief operating and financial executives, as well as other people with management input into your business. In general, prospective franchisees are impressed with quality personnel, so it's often best to list more rather than less under this item. You may want to disclose any member of your management team, even if they are just acting as consultants or advisors.

Items 3 and 4: Litigation and Bankruptcy

Everyone's closet houses a few skeletons they would rather forget. But franchise disclosure isn't so kind. You'll have to declare significant civil or criminal business-related litigation brought against your company or key personnel in your organization. You also must disclose any bankruptcies filed by you, your predecessor, officers or general partners in your business.

Many prospective franchisors view these requirements as larger impediments than they are. In actuality, franchisees rarely give substantial weight to your past legal battles when deciding to buy the franchise. If the opportunity appears attractive, they'll often take a chance, even if your past court history is less than clean.

Bankruptcies, however, prove a sorer point, especially recent ones. If your business history is pockmarked with failure, you'll need to consult your attorney on how to present the facts and circumstances in the most accurate yet positive and permissible terms.

Items 5 and 6: Initial and Other Fees

These items ask for a complete disclosure of all fees franchisees must pay you prior to and during operation of the franchised business, including initial license fees, recurring or isolated fees, grand opening, service, advertising, and training fees, as well as royalties.

Moreover, you must detail how the fees will be paid, and whether they are refundable. For example, your disclosure may state that a total initial fee of $10,000 is payable to you as follows:

1. $5000 upon signing the franchise agreement
2. $5000 a week before training commences

Additionally, if your initial license fee differs for certain franchisees, you must disclose this fact and provide the formula used to determine the differences.

Item 7: Initial Investment

Here, you are obliged to calculate total costs of opening the franchised unit, including the initial license fee, cost of equipment, opening inventory, signage, training, working capital, real estate, construction, renovation, and other miscellaneous expenses. Your estimations must be reasonable and accurate. You also must provide information on how the costs are paid, as well as when and to whom they are payable.

Items 8 and 9: Product Purchase Requirements

Your blueprint for quality control goes here. If you require your franchisee to buy products directly from you, that must be stated, along with any purchase or lease requirements from designated or approved suppliers. Also, if you provide specifications for product acquisition, that should be disclosed with the specification criteria.

Item 10: Financing of the Franchise

Will you provide financing for part or all of your franchisee's initial investment? If so, the terms and arrangements of such financing need to be disclosed, as well as any affiliation the franchisor may have with others providing financing for the franchisee.

Item 11: Obligations of the Franchisor

This is an important disclosure, because you must outline the services you intend to provide as a franchisor. If you plan to assist in franchisee grand openings, that should be stated. Will you aid in site selection, construction, remodeling, or hiring and training? If so, these items need to be disclosed. Will you provide regional advertising, marketing, new product or promotional development, continuing education, accounting assistance, an operating manual? All these services should be described under Item 11.

Item 12: Exclusive Areas or Territories

Under Item 12, you'll need to detail any exclusive areas or territories you choose to grant. And here the general rule is to retain as much flexibility as possible while still complying with the disclosure document. For example, you may wish to describe the general parameters used to decide territories —such as cities or population—and leave the specific territory to be defined in your franchise agreement. Also, if your franchise imposes minimum performance requirements, you'll need to explain them.

Items 13 and 14: Disclosure of Trademarks, Patents, or Copyrights

Prospective franchisees will want to know whether your company legally owns the rights to important aspects of the business. You'll inform them under items 13 and 14 by disclosing trademarks, patents, and copyrights.

For a trademark, you must state whether it's registered with the U.S. Patent and Trademark Office and, if so, whether it falls on the principal or supplemental list. You'll also want to clearly identify the franchisee's rights and obligations relating to the trademark.

Much of the same advice holds for patents and copyrights. But you may choose to disclose only those patents or copyrights integral to the operation of your franchise. That way, if you lose inconsequential patents or copyrights, your franchise opportunity won't appear to weaken.

Item 15: Owner/Operators

Who will operate your franchise? The owner? A manager? Item 15 articulates who you expect to direct the day-to-day operation of the franchised business, as well as any restrictions or controls you retain over a franchise's managers or other key employees.

Item 16: Restrictions on Goods and Services

Item 16 asks for a description of the limitations on the goods and services franchisees will be allowed to sell. In addition, any restrictions on customers or markets must be noted.

Item 17: Renewal, Termination, Repurchase, Assignment

How long will your franchise agreement run? What are the terms for renewal? Of termination? For the franchisee? For the franchisor? Are there any posttermination obligations? Are there any repurchase provisions? How is the business sold or transrferred?

Item 17 demands creative and comprehensive answers to all these questions.

Item 18: Arrangements with Public Figures

This item is a throwback to the 1960s when franchise companies used celebrity endorsements to entice prospective franchisees. Today, most endorsements are used mainly for retail advertising—such as O.J. Simpson for Hertz—but the requirement remains, and plays an infrequent role in new franchise disclosures.

Item 19: Income Projections

Don't listen to people who say income projections are illegal in franchising —they are not. If you should decide to disclose income figures, follow closely the rules set out by the Federal Trade Commission or in the UFOC. And be forthright. Don't write that franchisees can earn $30,000 and then tell these same people in personal meetings that they can earn $100,000. Here, the challenge is to show your business as valid and exciting while avoiding any possible legal liability that can arise from the disclosure.

Item 20: How Many Franchises You Have

The item asks how many franchises you presently have as well as how many you expect to open in the coming year. The first part is easy. Just count your franchises and disclose that number. The second part proves more problematic. Don't be tempted to overestimate. This is not a wish list; instead it's a situation where your testimony can be used against you. So show conservative optimism.

Item 21: Financial Statements

The UFOC requires you to present prospective franchisees with audited financial statements for your last three years of operation and unaudited statements current to within 90 days. If you presently don't prepare such formal accounting documents, you'll need to contact an independent certified public accountant who has some familiarity with franchising and can meet your needs in a timely fashion. The keys to your selection are experience and service. Your accountant must understand how a franchise generates income. He or she should also stand ready, willing, and able to prepare all necessary financial records.

Item 22: Attach all Other Contracts

Item 22 simply requests all related contracts—that is, franchise, advertising pools, or site selection agreements—to be attached to your disclosure.

Item 23: Acknowledgement of Receipt

This provides evidence that the prospect received your disclosure at least 10 days before signing your franchise agreement or paying any money. It's an important technicality, so make the acknowledgement easy to understand and keep it as part of your records.

But preparing a disclosure document is only half the legal battle, because you also must prepare a franchise agreement—a no less serious undertaking.

YOUR FRANCHISE AGREEMENT: THE ARTFUL APPROACH

There's a delicate trade-off in writing a franchise agreement. On the one hand, you need the contract to shield you from every contingency and offer maximum protection. On the other, you don't want the agreement to be slanted so obviously in your favor that it scares off prospective franchisees.

So you must ask yourself: How greedy can I be? How much is too much in my franchise power play? For instance, in case of a lawsuit, can the company collect attorney's fees if it wins and not extend franchisees a similar right? Can it terminate franchisees without providing a reasonable opportunity for them to cover problems?

Anyone can draft a contract that clearly creates a winner and a loser. But the true art of drafting a contract is in constructing an agreement that binds both parties to a mutually advantageous relationship. Therefore, you must write with an eye to franchisee objections, and stand ready to make reasonable adjustments should provisions prove particularly distasteful to prospective franchisees.

Many of the same principles extend to contract negotiations. It would be nice to present your agreement as ironclad—no changes allowed. But in the real world, you'll seldom sign a prospect by offering take-it-or-leave-it contracts. Prospective franchisees and their lawyers will always seek an adjustment, request an allowance, or ask for a compromise. So expect their objections and prepare for minor concessions.

But what's negotiable and what's not? Simply stated, anything that doesn't affect other franchisees could, under the right circumstances, be negotiated. For instance, your initial license fee has no direct bearing on other franchisees in your system. The amount you choose to charge a new franchisee won't make or break established franchisees. Therefore, if a prospect provides compelling reasons for a modest reduction in an initial license fee, feel free, where laws permit, to consider his or her argument. Likewise, if a prospect asks for reasonable concessions regarding security deposits, opening schedules or certain financing arrangements, allowances could be made.

Charity stops, however, when negotiations affect others within your franchise. If everyone pays an equal advertising fee, you can't cut sweetheart deals to bring new blood into the business. Similarly, if all your franchisees work to develop a single, easily identifiable image, you can't promise new prospects a novel trademark or business system. It's simply not fair. To preserve your integrity, you must provide consistency in any aspect of your business that could influence, upset, or affect another component.

A FEW BRIEF DRAFTING POINTERS

In many ways, a franchise agreement is like any other contract—it's meant to cement the relationship between two parties. And like all contracts, you should leave nothing to the imagination, by clearly identifying and defining all issues. For example, if you want your franchisees to be independent businesspeople (and all franchisors do!), you'll have to spell that out in an independent contractor clause. If you want the venue for possible litigation to be your state, you'll need to include that in the agreement. If you favor arbitration over litigation, that also must be spelled out beforehand to avoid problems later.

Many of these considerations are best left to your franchise attorney. And don't hesitate to use his or her experience. For every potential problem, a remedy exists. For every possible mistake, a provision has been developed to mitigate the effects. By employing this knowledge, you can prevent massive headaches and difficulties.

Your attorney will also need an intimate understanding of the actual operation of your franchised business. To understand the ultimate results of a specific clause, he or she must appreciate the intricacies of your operation. Remember, policies dictate your franchise legal program. Your lawyer must provide the legal mechanisms that bind the operation of your franchised business to these predetermined specifications. But to do so, your attorney must first understand the depth and breadth of your policies and how they function in a real-world business setting.

To become familiar with these policies is an all-encompassing task. Practically every item listed in your disclosure document must be dealt with again in the franchise agreement, and the issues include: opening requirements, contract term and renewal, trademarks, initial fees, royalties, advertising, promotion, security payments, training, reporting and accounting, operational specifications, franchisor services, incorporation, non-disclosure and system protection, assignment, termination, covenants not to compete, and a wealth of others.

When helping to draft the agreement, use plain, everyday language, keeping the provisions as short as possible and easily readable. If written effectively, your contract can be a sales tool as well as a legal document. Jargon only turns off prospects. Similarly, you'll want to present the most concise contract possible, so consider smaller print and/or typing on both sides of the paper to give the appearance of brevity.

Contract preparation, development, and negotiation represent your most serious responsibilities as a franchisor. Approach the issues cautiously, employ a degree of flexibility and a willingness to listen and learn from others, and you will weather the experience in a safe and effective manner.

THE LEGALITIES OUT OF THE WAY

In a nutshell, that summarizes many of the legal issues you need to consider before and while franchising your business. But remember, your actual legal franchise program depends on the composition, needs, and requirements of your business, as well as the advice of your attorney. So it's impossible to outline here every contingency or recommend specific provisions for your franchise agreement. What is possible, however, is for you to learn the basic legal requirements of franchising and then work with your attorney to use them to your best advantage.

CHAPTER 14

SELECTED MANAGEMENT ISSUES

En route to establishing your franchise, you'll no doubt encounter and overcome a wide variety of problems and obstacles. It should be expected. No business is perfect. Changing markets, consumer whimsy, innovative products and services, updated technology, and aggressive competition will provide you more than enough fires to fight.

But that's part of the beauty of business. It's organic, constantly evolving and growing. What's new today is old tomorrow. As a franchisor, you'll run on a treadmill of change requiring speed, endurance, and skill. Knowledge, forethought, and planning will play equally important roles in securing your franchise success. To avoid adversity, you'll have to plan for problems beforehand and manage them efficiently at the appropriate time in the appropriate manner.

What is management? It's the effective planning, organizing, directing, and controlling of resources critical to the operation of your business. It's the decision-making that drives an organization forward—the engine of that great machine you call your company. And it places you at the helm with a crew of capable and committed lieutenants at your side.

DEVELOPING A MANAGEMENT TEAM: STAFFING YOUR EARLY FRANCHISE

"How did you know when it was time to add early personnel?" I once asked Kwik Kopy's Bud Hadfield. "When my eyeballs turned yellow from exhaustion, I knew it was time to add staff," was his answer. Not a very analytical approach. But it serves to dramatize the intense personal control many franchisors retain over their company, particularly during the initial stages of development, when many simply can't afford to invest in a fully-staffed home office.

But there's a second, less obvious reason why franchisors stay so close to their systems: Franchising demands it. This highly interactive business system requires continual monitoring, updating, adjusting, and communication. Remember, franchising works best as a marriage between the franchisor and its franchisees. To service the relationship, most franchisors find it valuable to retain as much personal contact as possible with franchisees.

No one can do everything, however. And when and if your eyeballs turn yellow, you'll need to hire home office personnel. But who should you employ first? What jobs are critical to your success? What positions must you fill? That depends on where your needs lie. "I took a very pragmatic approach to early staffing decisions." says Fred DeLuca of Subway Sandwiches & Salads. "The jobs I could perform, I left to myself. Those skills I lacked, I bought on the job market." You should employ a similar approach. And to help make those decisions, consider some basic staff positions of other franchise companies.

Vice-President of Franchise Sales and Marketing

Sales is the heart of any franchise company. If you don't understand franchise sales or marketing, you may have to hire someone who does. What should you look for in a salesperson? A professional with experience in all aspects of franchise sales, from advertising the opportunity to screening leads to making telephone contact to closing deals. You need a salesperson with a track record of success—someone who can handle rejection and relate well to prospects. And you'll want your salespeople to work on commission. The real pros in franchise sales don't stand for anything else. They know they can make more by getting a percentage of each deal closed. So be leery of a salesperson seeking salary only.

What about francisee brokers or outside sales agencies? Be careful! Horror stories abound regarding brokers who care more about gaining commissions than signing qualified candidates. "Would you allow someone else to raise your children?" one franchisor said about franchise brokers. "Then why would you let someone else sell your business?" It's food for thought, and just one of the many reasons franchisors use brokers sparingly.

Chief Financial Officer

"Unless you're an accounting whiz, you'll want a numbers person to keep tabs on the money you're making," says Peter Shea of Stained Glass Overlay. From the time you open your first franchise, you'll receive an ongoing revenue stream from royalties and advertising and other fees. In your initial stages, outside accountants may be able to account for the money. But as you grow and add franchises, you'll want someone on the inside to develop spreadsheets, make projections, calculate break-evens, analyze investments, and comply with state and federal regulations as well as perform other financial services.

Training Director

The better you train, the less the strain—on resources once your franchisees begin operation. Also, poor training exposes you to possible legal liability in case a franchisee should fail.

Who should train your franchisees? Obviously, no one knows your business better than you, and if you have the time, energy, and temperament, it might be wise for you to handle the training of early franchisees.

But in the crush of roles you'll have to perform as a franchisor, training may simply become too much. If and when that happens, you'll need to hire a trainer to develop competent and effective franchisees. There are two options. First, you can recruit a professional trainer, someone who understands the learning process and knows how to convey information to others. Second, you can hire an operational expert from within your industry—a person who understands your business and its essential components. Which option is best for you depends on the needs of your business and the candidates available.

Vice-President of Operations

Who will deal with your franchisees on a regular basis in the retail and service aspects of your business? Who will develop new products for your franchisees? Who will conduct innovative retail marketing and promotional campaigns? Chances are, you eventually will need someone to monitor the day-to-day operation of your company, identifying new product and market opportunities and taking care of operational concerns, such as inventory management, quality control, franchisee compliance, and so on. An operations expert should be acutely aware of efficiency, productivity, and waste management. Cutting costs and increasing sales are the only ways your franchisees can grow and prosper—and these are the primary responsibilities of an operations professional.

A Final Word on Staffing

You're only as good as the people around you. In building a franchise, you need to choose both your franchisees and your employees wisely. Certainly, a new franchisor can't expect to fill all of the posts listed above. But you undoubtedly will have to complement your staff with appropriate personnel. But what if you don't have the money? "If I were just starting out in franchising," says Hadfield, "I would search for someone who had past experience with a reputable franchisor and offer him an equity interest in the company to come on board." It's a route worth pursuing if you desperately need a skill and know a franchise professional who can provide it.

CONTROLLING GROWTH

"If I could offer prospective franchisors one piece of advice," begins Robert Morgan, co-founder of AAMCO, "I would tell them to build one unit at a time, learning as much as possible from each new franchise, and then picking up speed as they grow. In its early stages, AAMCO ran into trouble simply because it grew so quickly that it lost contact with some of its franchisees, and the company suffered. Splinter groups formed among franchisees. Discontent built. Lawyers entered the scene. My strongest advice is to pick a speed at which you're comfortable and learn about franchising before hitting the rapid growth mode."

That advice is echoed by William Cherkasky, president of the International Franchise Association. "Controlling growth is a major responsibility that many franchisors overlook. One of the biggest mistakes in franchising is growing too big too fast. The next thing you know, the franchisor can't support the franchisees it has out there. Consequently, franchisees rebel, stop paying royalties, and the franchisor goes broke—or at least experiences severe financial difficulties."

How do you balance a desire to grow with a need for caution? By concentrating on developing successful franchisees and not simply on selling franchises. Too often, franchisors dream of expanding their business solely off the income earned on sales. Although your sales effort may prove profitable, the heart of franchising economics and the real indicator of franchise health is the royalty stream that flows from successful franchisees.

As a responsible franchisor, it's your duty to provide all reasonable services franchisees need to succeed. But first you must identify their requirements and determine critical services. And that takes time. Before establishing a service center, you must live with early franchisees and learn what support they need, which is impossible if explosive growth consumes your time and resources. Franchisors that concentrate solely on sales often neglect this vital initial step and live to regret it later.

DEVELOPING A CORPORATE CULTURE: YOUR MANAGEMENT PHILOSOPHY

Every company develops an internal atmosphere that guides decision-making on both conscious and subconscious levels. For example, DuPont, the chemical giant, displays an intense sensitivity to industrial safety that dates back to its roots as a gun powder manufacturer. Today, it's one of the safest companies in all of industry. Similarly, IBM's acute awareness of the needs, wants, and desires of its customers distinguishes Big Blue as one of the premier marketers in the world.

Smaller companies can develop similar operating atmospheres. "One factor in Kwik Kopy's success," says Bud Hadfield, "is our corporate culture. We consider our franchisees to be owner/partners. If they don't make it, we don't. To foster the relationship, the company built a six-million-dollar headquarters on a one-hundred-fifty-acre tract with a lake, tennis courts, and log cabins. It's a place for new franchisees to learn about the company and a place for veteran owners to return and enjoy."

But there are other, less costly ways to achieve the same results. "We came into franchising with little knowledge of the marketing system, which was good because we also possessed few preconceived notions," says Arthur Karp of the Original Great American Chocolate Chip Cookie Company. "We made a conscious attempt to investigate other franchisors and see what they did well and not so well. From that we developed four corporate values on which our company is based. They are: (1) Fairness. Fairness in the way we treat franchisees, in the way they handle employees, and in way employees deal with customers. (2) Pride. We want to be proud of our franchisees and, conversely, we want them to be proud of our system, trademark, and image. (3) Responsiveness/responsibility. The company takes telephone calls at any time from troubled franchisees. Solving their problems is our most important job. No matter what, franchisee inquiries are returned within four hours of when they're received. It's a measure of our care and interest. Likewise, we expect franchisees to respond when we show concern regarding a particular issue. (4) Profitability. We want both the company and our franchisees to receive a reasonable profit on efforts and investments."

Do such statements really work to create internal cohesiveness? Not if they're unsupported by behavior. But when words match actions, a corporate philosophy proves powerful guidance in the day-to-day operation of your franchise. As proof, consider that the Original Great American Chocolate Chip Cookie Company is routinely referred to as one of the best-managed franchises by trade journals and government officials alike.

Your corporate philosophy, the culture you care to cultivate, depends upon the essential components of your business. If service is paramount, then it should rank as an important plank in your philosophical platform. If integrity tops the list, then this must be articulated. "Honesty is an integral part of the transmission business, because the customer can't see the repair and always wonders whether the work was necessary," says D'Arcy Williams of Speedy Transmission Centers. "Consequently, we emphasize integrity in all aspects of the business."

Build your business on the values important to you, deal with others according to those values, and you'll have taken an important step forward in effective management.

GOING PUBLIC: THE FRANCHISE AS A PUBLIC COMPANY

Sooner or later, every successful business considers going public. Public stock offerings often provide a company with hard-to-come-by capital for further growth and expansion, marketing, product development, investment, or liquidity for the founder's stock. But franchisors may face special problems in turning their privately owned enterprises into public companies.

Brian Thomas of Thomas James Associates, based in Rochester, New York, sheds some light on this seemingly mystical process in a series of questions and answers designed to clarify some of the issues involved and how they apply to franchising companies:

Interviewer: What track record does a company need to go public?

Thomas: It varies according to the underwriter and its clients. For example, very large underwriters, such as Goldman Sachs, look for well-established, well-capitalized, mature companies that may interest their institutional clientele or large retail clients. Smaller underwriters, however, are less numbers sensitive. They choose to work within various market niches. Some might specialize in medical companies while others might concentrate on small offerings or even large junk bond financings. Thomas James specializes in underwriting public offerings of small to medium-size businesses—those companies with between $5 million and $100 million in annual sales, looking to raise $3 million to $10 million through a stock offering. We feel these companies offer the general public a better opportunity for significant long-term capital appreciation, and we are not afraid of taking a calculated risk in an effort to find tomorrow's success story, today.

Interviewer: What problems do these smaller companies have in going public?

Thomas: Frankly many of these businesses overvalue themselves during their startup phase, which means they offer too much stock at too high a price, with the end result being the value of the outstanding stock exceeds the company's real worth. For example, I have seen many startup companies with low annual sales with 2,500,000 shares outstanding at $4 a share—a total capitalization of $10 million. In some cases that situation is out of line with other publicly traded companies and is actually a detriment to the company because overvalued companies have little hope of attracting underwriters to handle stock offerings. In the case of a startup, a total capitalization of $4 million to $6 million on a postoffering valuation is usually fair both to the company and its public shareholders. If the company has earnings we will take them into account in addition to other financial criteria that might affect our valuation, such as goodwill and their rate of expected growth, and again try to assign a reasonable share price. The key to success here is to develop a win-win situation. The company may never again be in a position to take on several thousand shareholders at once and it's important to leave a little something on the table in an effort to have the stock trade up to keep the initial investors happy.

Interviewer: Is there a minimum sales level a company should attain before going public?

Thomas: Our clients seem to like companies that have at least $5 million to $15 million in annual sales, not including franchisee sales. This seems to represent a critical mass necessary for strong future growth. However, we do not turn down entrepreneurs in startup situations who possess super ideas that fill specific market niches when the near term profit potential is excellent.

Interviewer: How do you value a company?

Thomas: We first research what other companies are trading for in the industry. We then consider the uniqueness of the company we are valuing and work out a capitalization by assigning a multiple that represents how many times a company's earnings an investor would pay to buy the business outright. For example, if the company we are valuing is in the restaurant industry and other comparable companies are trading at a multiple of 18 times their net earnings, we would then value, say, $325,000 of earnings at $5 million. Assuming for this case the company had very little stockholders equity or other assets of any value, we may offer 40 percent of the company to the public for $2-½ to $3 million. There are obviously exceptions to this rule; in particular the case of a rapidly expanding company with a high price-to-earnings ratio.

Interviewer: What role does franchising play in valuing a company?

Thomas: It plays a major, often positive, role because highly visible companies often trade at higher multiples and higher volumes, which spell higher profits for the underwriter and shareholders.

Also, the ability to successfully replicate a business often evidences a sound concept and competent management, two critical elements in appraising a company's worth.

Interviewer: How do you evaluate the future potential of a franchise company?

Thomas: We look at the franchise plan and determine whether it makes sense. We also make sure the franchisees have been successful, which is the best indicator of a franchisor's future success.

Interviewer: When should a franchise company begin to think about going public?

Thomas: The day the company incorporates is when it should start thinking about future financing needs.

Interviewer: When is the best time to go public?

Thomas: The old school teaches that a company should stay private until earnings are very high and the Wall Street community is certain to take notice. The new school advises going public earlier so when earnings start to take off the company can come back and perform secondary offerings or take advantage of higher stock prices.

So the real question is not when to go public, but when does the deal make sense? When can it be valued fairly? An exciting developmental company with a high likelihood of success may want to go public right away. On the other hand, a company in a mature industry might be better off waiting until it can show a history of earnings.

Interviewer: Is there anything special in marketing the stocks of a franchise company?

Thomas: Selling franchise stock often requires teaching the public about basic franchising economics. It is amazing how many investors do not realize that franchise companies make their money off royalties and fees and not directly from franchisee retail sales.

Interviewer: Is it easier to sell franchise stocks?

Thomas: In established franchises, it is easier to sell franchise stock because of the company's visibility and because of Wall Street's sensitivity to past franchise successes, including McDonald's.

For startups, however, franchise stock is sold much like regular stock. The early buyers are usually investors with some association to the business. Here again, visibility helps. Even the smallest franchise has thousands of patrons. If these customers like the product, they may buy the stock and once they buy the stock they may become more loyal customers of the company; in other words, own GM stock and then buy a Chevrolet.

Interviewer: How are the proceeds of an offering used?

Thomas: For the purchase of equipment, retirement of debt, research and development, and—particularly in franchising—marketing. There are literally thousands of franchise business opportunities competing with one another, and the successful franchisor may need a unique marketing plan that is national in scope. This varies from one situation to another, although marketing is usually an area where money is typically used in a franchise company.

Interviewer: What percentage of my company do I surrender to the outside investors?

Thomas: It varies according to the enthusiasm the underwriter shows for the issue, the demand for the offering, and the negotiation skills of the business owner. Thomas James usually takes 25 to 50 percent of a company in return for major financing. Less than that usually doesn't make sense. More than that and the company's management fears it has lost effective control of the business. The key to giving up very little of your business is to convince the underwriter, and eventually his clients, that the company's management is extremely skilled at building a large, profitable company from a smaller one.

INTERNATIONAL FRANCHISING: THE LURE OF FOREIGN MARKETS

It seems ridiculous for new franchisors to consider the prospect of foreign expansion. Domestic markets pose more than enough challenges to overcome, at least for now. But in today's global community, foreign markets may prove more accessible than you think. For example, Gymboree, the infant exercise franchise, began franchising in 1981, but already is considering expanding into Japanese, French, and Australian markets. National Health Enhancement Systems, a health franchise based in Arizona, opened its first franchise in 1983, but has already been approached by investors in West Germany and Australia.

If your concept works, if it makes money for franchisees, you can bet that prospects from around the block and around the world will inquire into its availability. And as a franchisor you can apply one of two strategies to tap overseas markets. First, you can take an early plunge, hoping to beat your competitors to foreign shores, or you can wait until domestic markets are fully exploited, expanding at a more cautious and calculated rate.

"Quite frankly, we're holding off on foreign expansion until we have more domestic units operating and as many operational problems as possible ironed out," says Gregory Petras, president and chief operating officer of National Health Enhancement Systems. Jiffy Lube subscribes to the more ambitious approach. "We want to get into Europe now, making it more difficult for our competitors to gain a foothold later," says Neil F. O'Shea, the company's vice president of franchising.

But each method represents a risk. Cultural, legal, taxation, and commercial differences make foreign expansion an extremely complex undertaking. "You must realize that the way Americans conduct business in this country may not be appropriate in other nations," says Lauren Buchanan, a cultural liaison for businesses conducting overseas commerce. "Simple translation errors as well as differences in protocol, tradition, and etiquette can breed unintended misunderstandings. Buchanan tells how a one-page telex once ruined a multimillion dollar deal on which she was working. "We issued a simple statement on inventory control, and the overseas buyer took the message as an insult. It just shows that international business brings with it a wealth of unforeseen problems."

And those problems aren't simply cultural. To succeed overseas, you'll also need to understand the foreign country's legal and regulatory climates. In the Philippines, for example, the government severely discourages foreign business investment unless the investment provides some needed technology. Similarly, Taiwan classifies all investment as either worthy or unworthy. Those that receive the government's stamp of approval enjoy tremendous tax and legislative advantages. Those that don't can be brutalized.

Moreover, some countries control a company's ability to repatriate money, leaving you with no way to gain royalties from overseas units. Others may forbid franchising practices that are common here in this country, such as exclusive territories or cooperative advertising.

Are there any ways to overcome such problems? Sure. The most obvious is to work with consultants or attorneys who understand international markets and law and can prevent critical errors. These same professionals should know about any tax treaties that could limit a foreign country's ability to tax your income from their shores. Operationally, you may want to sign master franchisees to oversee the development of foreign franchises. "Our goal is to develop five thousand franchises by 1994," says Fred DeLuca. "Total saturation for this country is projected between three thousand and four thousand. Overseas expansion is the logical way out. And we're working with local master franchisees who know the cultural differences in specific markets and can adapt our concept to local needs and tastes."

Jiffy Lube follows a similar philosophy. "We feel master franchisees have a better handle on the local markets," says O'Shea. "For instance, West Germany seems an ideal market for automotive aftermarket franchisors. The country's love of cars should make it ripe for a quick lube and oil change service. But West German motorists are extremely loyal to the deal-

NUGGET #20

The Ins and Outs of International Franchising

What should you consider before franchising internationally? Leonard Swartz, executive vice-president of business development for Postal Instant Press and a seasoned veteran of the overseas market, suggests six components to foreign franchising success:

1. Fully evaluate whether international franchising will add to or detract from your base business. Many people mistakenly go into international franchising to gain prestige or soothe egos. Your decision should be based solely on business considerations.
2. Stand ready to invest both financial and personnel resources. Foreign franchising requires money and people.
3. Prepare to wait for your returns. Paybacks in international franchising can be deferred for as long as five years.
4. Closely monitor your foreign entreprise, especially the quality of your overseas product. Many domestic franchisors get into trouble overseas because they can't replicate the level of product or service quality that customers demand.
5. Employ foreign nationals with vested interests in your enterprise. You can't place an American in a foreign market and expect the same results as a local businessperson who understands the particular market and culture. Use this fact by recruiting foreign master franchisees or other native businesspeople who could help your endeavor.
6. Make a full commitment or none at all!

And what are the major problems associated with foreign franchising? Again, Swartz offers his insights:

1. *Quality control.* The physical distance between you and your foreign franchisees often makes operational control and monitoring difficult.
2. *Language.* Even in countries that speak English, words hold different meanings from American connotations.

NUGGET #20 *(Continued)*

---

3. *Cultural differences.* The traditions, beliefs, and customs of a foreign country will have an impact on the receptivity and marketing of your product or service.

4. *Legal differences.* Business practices that are commonly accepted in the United States may be prohibited, restricted, or time consuming under foreign laws or business practices. For instance, obtaining a lease often takes six months in Great Britain.

---

ers that sold them their car. They're not familiar with outside automotive services. In fact, most of their gas stations are self-serve. They don't know what a two-bay garage looks like. Consequently, we have to educate them to the concept. And that may be best left to a master franchisee who knows the market and culture."

International franchising by domestic companies will continue to increase as foreign markets grow and their understanding of U.S. products and services increases. But it's a complicated undertaking often rife with cultural and operational problems. Be careful. Study your foreign market well and learn its idiosyncrasies before setting up shop on foreign soil.

JOINING THE INTERNATIONAL FRANCHISE ASSOCIATION

So far, I have stated many of the problems you'll face as a franchisor and have offered steps to avoid each. But if you're serious about franchising, perhaps the best action you can take is joining the International Franchise Association (IFA). Founded in 1960 by a small group of franchise executives, the IFA has grown into the world's premier organization of franchisors. Its code of ethics provides a model of integrity by which every franchisor should abide. The organization also offers a variety of services that simply are not available anywhere else, including trade shows, educational programs, im-

---

NUGGET #21

International Franchisor Associations

1. The Association of Canadian Franchisors, Ste. 1050, 595 Bay St., Toronto, ON, M5G 2C2. (416) 595-8000.
2. The British Franchise Association, Franchise Chambers, 75a Bell St., Henley-on-Thames, Oxon, RG9 2BD, England. (0491) 57849 or 578050.
3. European Franchise Federation, 16 bis rue Dufrenoy, 75116, Paris, France. (504) 0183.
4. Franchisors Association of Australia Ltd., Ste. 7, Ground Floor, Corporation Centre, 123 Clarence St., Sydney, New South Wales, Australia, 2000. (02) 29 7941.

---

portant publications, and a staff of franchise professionals that stands ready to serve its members, as well as the general public, on issues regarding franchising. In addition, the IFA is an effective lobbier, making sure federal and state franchise regulations are kept reasonable and compliance costs low.

But most important, the IFA serves as a meeting ground where new franchisors can learn from veterans, where beginners can gain vital franchising information. "If I could give your readers one piece of advice," says Neil Balter at California Closets, "it would be to join the IFA. They should become a member for the same reason people buy franchises—people learn from other people. And a lot of what I learned came from the people at the IFA."

How can you join the IFA? The association offers two memberships that you can learn about by writing:

The International Franchise Association
1350 New York Avenue, N.W.
Suite 900
Washington, D.C. 20005

NUGGET #22

The International Franchise Association's Code of Ethics

1. In the advertising and granting of franchises or dealerships a member shall comply with all applicable laws and regulations and the member's offering circular shall be complete, accurate, and not misleading with respect to the franchisee's or dealer's investment, the obligations of the member and the franchisee or dealer under the franchise or dealership, and all material facts relating to the franchise or dealership.

2. All matters material to the member's franchise or dealership shall be contained in one or more written agreements, which shall clearly set forth the terms of the relationship and the respective rights and obligations of the parties.

3. A member shall select and accept only those franchisees or dealers who, upon reasonable investigation, appear to possess the basic skills, education, experience, personal characteristics, and financial resources required to conduct the franchised business or dealership and meet the obligations of the franchisee or dealer under the franchise and other agreements. There shall be no discrimination in the granting of franchises based solely on race, color, religion, national origin, or sex. However, this in no way prohibits a franchisor from granting franchises to prospective franchisees as part of a program to make franchises available to persons lacking the capital, training, business experience, or other qualifications ordinarily required of franchisees or any other affirmative action program adopted by the franchisor.

4. A member shall provide reasonable guidance to its franchisees or dealers in a manner consistent with its franchise agreement.

5. Fairness shall characterize all dealings between a member and its franchisees or dealers. A member shall make every good faith effort to resolve complaints by and disputes with its franchisees or dealers through direct communication and negotiation. To the extent reasonably appropriate in the circumstances, a member shall give notice of and a reasonable opportunity to cure a breach of their contractual relationship.

6. No member should engage in the pyramid system of distribution. A pyramid is a system wherein a buyer's future compensation is expected to be based primarily upon recruitment of new participants rather than upon the sale of products or services.

YOUR FUTURE AS A FRANCHISOR

The facts have been laid out. Your decision is near. I urge you to seriously consider your future as a franchisor, because franchising is a system that's growing, and I'd like you to be a part of this prosperity.

Certainly, you won't want to jump in ill-prepared. You'll need to invest time in serious planning and deliberation. But don't miss the boat. Over the past 30 years, franchising has proved a legitimate means for business growth and that trend will continue, according to current franchisors, franchisees, outside economists, and even the U.S. government. So opportunity exists and it's an exciting challenge. As a franchisor you'll become intimately linked with the talents and enthusiasm of other independent businesspeople. You'll be a part of their lives, experiencing their struggles and accomplishments.

And growth will come, too. The success stories related in this book illustrate that claim. Franchising offers a fast track to business expansion—a valuable head start in winning regional or national markets. And it all could be yours if you're willing to invest the time, energy, and hard work that any worthwhile endeavor requires. So start now to map your strategy, and who knows, maybe someday you'll be another Ray Kroc or Robert Morgan. But then again, you don't have to become a business superstar to franchise your business. Hundreds of small to medium-size franchisors have discovered that smaller franchises yield many rewarding personal and financial gains. These franchisors have realized their goal—they're entrepreneurs, people who have started businesses and watched them grow and prosper.

Think back to the first page of this book. If there were a Hall of Fame for American entrepreneurs, it would be peppered with the names and accomplishments of today's biggest and brightest franchisors. If you should assume the challenge of franchising your business, maybe someday you, too, could be inducted.

INDEX